Department of the Environment   Welsh Office

DRINKING WATER 1995

June 1996

London : H M S O

recycled
paper

Designed by DDP Services. B5468. June 1996.

Contents

Chapter 3   **Technical Audit of Individual Water Companies:**

DRINKING WATER INSPECTORATE

Room B150
Romney House
43 Marsham Street
London SW1P 3PY
Direct Line: 0171-276 8199
Enquiries: 0171-276 8808/8666
Facsimile: 0171-276 8405

10 June 1996

To

the Rt Hon John Gummer MP
Secretary of State for the Environment

and

the Rt Hon William Hague MP
Secretary of State for Wales

I am pleased to submit the Inspectorate's sixth Annual Report covering the year ending 31 December 1995. It provides an account of the checks made by the Inspectorate and the conclusions it has reached upon the quality of the water supplied by the 31 water companies of England and Wales.

I am able to report further significant improvements to the very high quality of drinking water with 99.5% of tests showing compliance with the standards. This compares with 99.3% in 1994 and 98.9% in 1993 and reflects the success of the improvement programmes that have been carried out since 1989. The number of tests failing to meet the standards in 1995 was about one third of that in 1992.

The Inspectorate continues to take a tough line in the operation of the enforcement process. Most of the improvement programmes were completed on time but on those occasions when there has been slippage, for reasons within the control of a company, a Notice of the intention to make an Enforcement Order was actioned immediately. However, in all cases the companies completed the work within the period of the Notices and it was not necessary to issue the enforcement orders.

In line with its Code for Enforcement the Inspectorate works closely with the water companies towards improving the efficiency of regulation without compromising the effectiveness of the enforcement processes. The priority always is the protection of public health in the best interests of the water consumers. I appreciate the cooperation given by the companies in our day to day operations and in our painstaking investigation of incidents.

During the year there has been a valuable exchange of information with those responsible for drinking water quality regulation within the European Union. An informal network has been established and I hope that, in time, the greater understanding being achieved will result in comparable information on drinking water quality being available from each member State.

The Inspectorate will continue to pursue improvements in carrying out its regulatory functions.

Michael Rouse

Michael Rouse
Chief Inspector

Department of the Environment

Welsh Office

Chief Inspector's Statement

Introduction

1. This, the Inspectorate's sixth report, provides a comprehensive account of the Inspectorate's activities for 1995. In particular, it records the outcome of checks made by the Inspectorate on the quality of water supplied by the water companies of England and Wales.

2. This report is necessarily technical and fairly detailed and, as such, is not easily digested by the lay reader. As in the last two years I have produced a companion to this report, a leaflet which is written for a wider audience. 65,000 copies of last year's leaflet were distributed. The leaflet describes how the Inspectorate, in its role as the guardian of drinking water quality, operates as part of the structure that has been established to control drinking water quality in England and Wales. It gives a summary of the compliance results for 1995, particularly for some substances which are known to be of concern to consumers.

3. It is important that the facts about drinking water quality are widely available. Naturally consumers are most interested in the quality of water supplied in their area. All of the compliance data is available on the Public Records kept by water companies but these are fairly detailed. Last year I introduced inserts to the leaflet which covered the areas of supply of each of the water companies. In some areas these leaflets were distributed widely providing those water consumers with a brief independent summary of the results of the inspection carried out in that year together with the main elements in any ongoing improvement programmes. From feedback received I have attempted to improve the information provided in this year's inserts to the leaflet. I am seeking ways of improving the awareness of water consumers of drinking water quality and how it is maintained. Our open approach to communication seeks to provide an accurate picture on drinking water quality and the steps being taken to deal with any deficiencies. The information contained in the leaflets, together with other drinking water quality data, is now accessible on the Internet (http://www.open.gov.uk/doe).

Very high overall water quality - 99.5% of tests complied with standards

4. The overall quality of water in England and Wales remains very high with further improvements on the situation reported on 1994. During 1995 the 31 companies carried out a total of 3,154,249 tests at treatment works and service reservoirs and in water supply zones. About 80% of this total number of tests were made on samples taken from consumers' taps. 99.5% of tests demonstrated compliance with the standards. This is a good result which, when compared with previous years, reflects the ongoing impact of improvement programmes.

5. Each of the 17,341 tests (0.5% of the total) which contravened the standard has been assessed by the Inspectorate. There is no evidence that any of these contraventions was of such a magnitude or duration as to endanger the health of consumers. Only some of the parameters are of health significance and their standards are set with a wide margin of safety. The other parameters are of aesthetic significance and contraventions of these standards do not necessarily imply that the water is unfit to drink.

6. Many of the contraventions which were detected arose in circumstances which were already the subject of legally binding undertakings, given by the water companies, to carry out improvement works in order to achieve compliance, but which at the time were not yet due for completion. These undertakings are designed

to meet the required standard in the shortest possible time. Of the remainder of the contraventions, most were considered to be trivial or unlikely to recur; however, some indicated the need for further action and the Inspectorate has initiated enforcement action to require the companies involved to prepare and implement additional improvement programmes. This is part of the Inspectorate's continuing process of monitoring and enforcement action.

7. During 1995, 209 improvement programmes, as specified in legally binding undertakings or as conditions of authorised relaxations, were due either for full completion or for completion of intermediate steps. I am pleased to report that 174 (83%) of these were completed by their due dates. In nearly every case where a delay occurred it was of short duration and due to reasons beyond the control of the company concerned. However in four cases, in which failure to complete improvement programmes by the due date of 31 December 1995 was considered to be wholly the responsibility of the companies, further enforcement action was taken immediately. Notices of the Intention to make an Enforcement Order were issued. In three cases the companies completed the work within the 28 day period of the Notices and it was not necessary to proceed with the enforcement orders. In the fourth case, the company objected to the notice. The objection was not accepted but the company completed the work whilst the objection was being considered and it was not necessary to proceed with the enforcement order. In one further case the company sought to demonstrate that some of the works required by the undertaking had not been carried out as they were not necessary. Having considered the evidence presented, and making additional investigations, the Inspectorate concluded that the works were necessary and issued a Notice of Intention to make an Enforcement Order. An Order will be issued after the necessary period for representations or objections has passed. This is a further demonstration of the strong enforcement process in operation, with undertakings having been accepted after formal notification had been given to water companies that enforcement orders were being considered, and with such orders remaining an option at all times. The Inspectorate keeps all improvement programmes under close scrutiny to ensure that final completion of the necessary work is achieved as soon as possible.

8. Chapter 4 gives an overview of drinking water quality and the achievements of improvement programmes. The key points are:

- the number of treatment works with coliforms detected reduced from 445 in 1991 to 355 in 1995, a reduction of 20%;

- the number of service reservoirs with coliforms detected in more than 5% of samples was slightly higher than in 1994, 56 compared with 43 but still a reduction of 66% compared with the figure of 164 in 1991;

- 2,455 (99.4%) of water supply zones, as checked largely on samples taken from consumers' taps, complied with the coliform standard in 1995 compared with 2,442 (94.8%) in 1991; and

    NOTE: The definition of coliforms was changed in 1995 with the effect that the 1995 results show higher failure rates than that would have occurred with the old definition. See Chapter 4, paragraph 4.19 for a discussion of the differences.

- more zones, as checked largely on samples taken from consumers' taps, complied with the standards for 15 of the other 16 key parameters in 1995 than in 1991 - the odd one out being PAH. See Chapter 4, paragraph 4.27 for commentary on this parameter.

Enforcement action in respect of contraventions of water quality standards

9. The enforcement process is ongoing. For a small number of contraventions of water quality standards in 1995, enforcement action against the companies concerned has been or is under consideration. The mechanism and significance of enforcement action is discussed in more detail in Chapters 1 and 5 of this Report. In some cases water companies will take remedial action immediately. In others, where a longer timescale is needed for practical reasons, they, following notification that an enforcement order is being considered, will enter into a legally enforceable undertaking to take appropriate action. These undertakings, which form an integral part of the system of enforcement, are kept under review by the Inspectorate to ensure that the work is carried out as quickly as possible. Should any water company fail to meet the specified completion dates, without being able to demonstrate that there were circumstances outside its control, as in the five cases mentioned above in paragraph 7, further enforcement action will be taken immediately.

10. Chapter 5 of this Report shows that enforcement action has been taken or is under consideration in respect of contraventions of the microbiological standards at 0.6% of the treatment works and at 0.4% of the service reservoirs, and in respect of contraventions of standards in water supply zones in no more than 2.2% of the zones for any one parameter.

Measuring compliance

11. The level of compliance can be shown in two ways. The best, because it takes into account all the results in a whole year, is the total of all tests that meet the standards. As stated above that figure for 1995 is 99.5%. However we also check water quality in supply zones. We classify a zone as not complying if just one sample has not met the required standard, even though the standard was met for almost all of the time. This is because in those cases, in which the failure is non-trivial and likely to recur, enforcement action is taken and we require water companies to carry out improvement programmes for those zones. So although zone compliance figures can give a misleadingly poor picture of water quality they do give a measure of how much water quality has improved as a result of improvement work. It is for this reason that I report both measures of compliance.

A long-term target of 100%

12. The legal requirement on water companies is, of course, to achieve 100% compliance with the standards in the Regulations, for every treatment works, every service reservoir and in every water supply zone. How near to 100% is it practically possible to get? The improvement programmes are in place to deal with existing areas of non-compliance but there will always be unforeseen events such as an unexpected deterioration of raw water quality or main bursts.

13. Nevertheless, the legal requirement remains. The 'target' diagram was introduced first in Drinking Water 1993. The diagram below represents the compliance picture in 1995, using zone compliance figures, which are lower than the overall test figures, as explained in paragraph 11 above. It shows that water supplies are close to the 100% target in most respects with less scatter than for 1994 which itself was an improvement over 1993. I expect this trend to continue. The diagram is repeated and discussed more fully in Chapter 4.

Water supply zones complying with standards

PERCENTAGES IN 1995 (see paragraph 4.40)

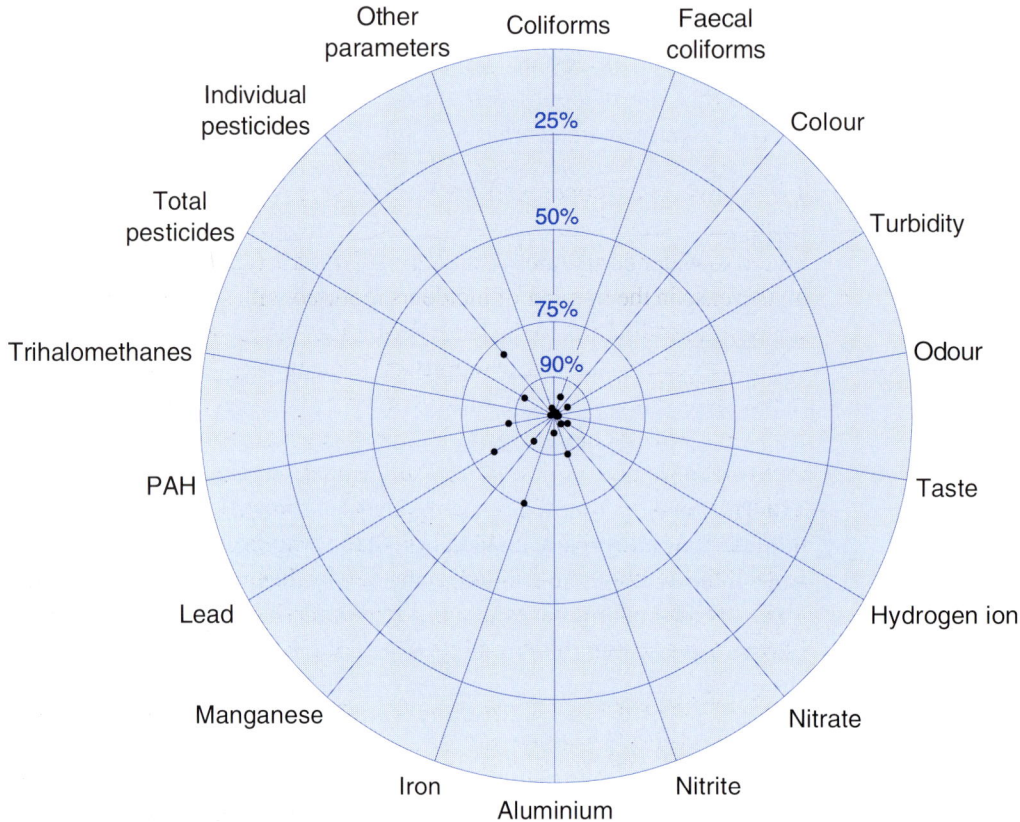

Water Quality Monitoring and Reporting

14. The legal monitoring requirements are fundamental to checking that drinking water quality is meeting the standards set in the Regulations. They are much more extensive than required by the European Directive. I am pleased to report that the companies conform to these monitoring requirements although one is facing enforcement action as a result of minor sampling shortfalls. Analysis is equally important and I am pleased to report that companies generally complied with the requirements of regulation 21 in 1995. Enforcement action was considered as a result of various contraventions in four companies, but the extent of these contraventions was rather less than has been noted amongst companies in general in previous years.

15. Making the water quality data readily available to the public is a key requirement of the regulatory regime. It is part of the complete openness in reporting, of which this Report is another component, adopted in England and Wales. Apart from one or two relatively minor deficiencies on the part of a small number of companies, which were rectified quickly, in respect of their Public Records on drinking water quality, each company met the requirements of the Regulations. Currently very little use is made of the public record and I would like to see water companies giving greater attention to making intelligible information more readily accessible.

16. In previous reports I have been critical of some water companies in respect to the quality of their data handling in providing the Inspectorate with easily assimilable compliance data. I reported an overall improvement last year but with some remaining deficiencies. With continuing difficulties, requiring unnecessary extra work by Inspectorate staff, I find it necessary to publish lists of companies according to the effectiveness of their data provision. These lists are given in Chapter 4. I should stress that this is not related to the water quality itself. Also, due to the efforts of the Inspectors I have every confidence in the validity of the results given in this report. These lists will be issued in each report in the future so that there is a published record of the water companies actions to improve their performance in this respect.

Incidents

17. I have been concerned about consistency in the notification of incidents. Comprehensive advice on notification and reporting of events and incidents was issued to water companies in January 1994. Last year I reported that there had been an increase in the number of incidents reported with some companies following the advice on notification to the letter. I am pleased to report a further improvement in the degree of consistency of reporting. The number of incidents reported has again risen, 83 in 1995 compared with 78 in 1994 and 52 in 1993. In addition companies notified the Inspectorate of a further 74 events, which might have resulted in incidents requiring investigation, but on analysis did not warrant classification as incidents. This openness in notifying events that might have developed into something more serious is a good demonstration of the progress made in this reporting area. In spite of the additional workload, generated by the higher level of reported incidents, I welcome the additional safeguards that the action brings in protecting consumers. Further general comments on incidents are given in Chapter 6.

18. Most incidents are relatively minor happenings. The Inspectorate's investigations of these are fairly routine and often result in recommendations to the company concerned on actions to minimise the chances of any future failures. Where there are lessons to be learnt which are applicable to other companies, then the Inspectorate will prepare a report to all companies. Should there be an incident involving the supply of water unfit for human consumption then the Inspectorate will consider the possibility of prosecution proceedings.

Prosecution policy towards incidents

19. The Inspectorate will recommend to the relevant Secretary of State that a prosecution be brought for an alleged offence under section 70 of the Water Industry Act 1991 of supplying water which was unfit for human consumption when:

    (a) it has evidence to demonstrate that:

        (i)   illness or other health effect was experienced by normally at least two consumers which was associated with the quality of the water supplied; <u>or</u>

        (ii)   the quality of the water supplied was such that normally at least two consumers rejected it for drinking or cooking or food production on aesthetic grounds; <u>or</u>

        (iii) the concentration of a substance in, or the value of a property of, the water supplied was at a level at which illness or other health effect may be expected in the long term even though none was manifest in the community at the time; <u>and</u>

    (b) the Inspectorate considers that the water company does not have a defence that it took all reasonable steps and exercised all due diligence for securing that the water was fit on leaving its pipes <u>or</u> was not used for human consumption; <u>and</u>

    (c) such a prosecution is regarded as being in the public interest.

20. For those incidents that do not justify full Court proceedings the Inspectorate may issue a caution which the Court could take into account in any future offences.

21. At the time of writing, the Inspectorate is investigating a number of incidents in which a prosecution might be recommended to the Secretary of State. Some of these involve complex technical and operational issues, requiring both Inspectors' involvement and that of experts contracted to advise on specific aspects of the cases. Inevitably, in these cases it takes a considerable amount of time before the information is available and recommendations can be made to the Secretary of State. Currently there is one case before the Courts, an incident that occurred in October 1994.

Regulation 25

22. This regulation aims to ensure that the legitimate use by companies of chemicals and materials coming into contact with drinking water during treatment and distribution does not compromise drinking water quality. Regulation 25(1)(a) provides for approval of new chemicals and materials by the Secretary of State. The work of the Committee on Chemicals and Materials, which advises the Secretaries of State on approval issues, is reported in Chapter 2. I am pleased to report that, on an experimental basis, the handling of applications for Regulation 25 approval is being integrated with applications for water byelaw approval so that applicants are able to approach a 'one-stop' shop. The experimental scheme which is being supported by UK Water Industry Research Ltd is being managed by the Water Research Centre under the overall supervision of the Inspectorate.

23. In November 1995 Wessex Water admitted an offence, under regulation 28 of the Water Supply (Water Quality) Regulations 1989, of failing to meet the conditions of approval under regulation 25(1)(a) in the application of epoxy linings in renovating water mains. There is no evidence that water unfit for consumption had been supplied and, as it was a minor technical offence, the Inspectorate issued a caution.

Our Code for Enforcement

24. 1995 was the second year of the operation of our Code for Enforcement. It sets down how the Inspectorate should operate and contains target completion times for various activities. The details of the Inspectorate's performance against the Code are given in Chapter 2. I was aware, when the Code was published, that the targets were highly demanding of the Inspectors with their heavy work loads but even so, following the experience of the first year, some have been tightened. However, it is important to have set highly demanding targets, although knowing that it will take some time to meet them. Our priority always is to safeguard water consumers. I am pleased that we have performed well in some areas, particularly in the speed in taking enforcement action and in handling requests for information from consumers. Equally, I recognise that our performance in meeting reporting targets, although significantly better than previous years, is still well below our target levels. Every effort, through continuously seeking more efficient ways of working, employing total quality principles, is being made to improve our performance.

25. An example of the improvement in performance is shown in the following diagram. The target for completing the investigation of an incident is three months from the receipt of the company's final report. The three month reporting target was established for, and is only feasible for, those incidents that can be classified early on as not likely to involve prosecution proceedings, so there are always likely to be a few that require a much longer period of investigation. The pie charts show the number of incident investigations outstanding at the end of each of the last three reporting years. The amount of investigation outstanding is illustrated by a combination of the size of the circles and the degree of shading of the segments. It should be borne in mind that the significant reduction in the backlog has been

achieved even though there have been a further 83 incidents during 1995. The Inspectorate will continue to work at eliminating the backlog and I expect to be able to report further progress next year.

Reduction in backlog on investigation of incidents

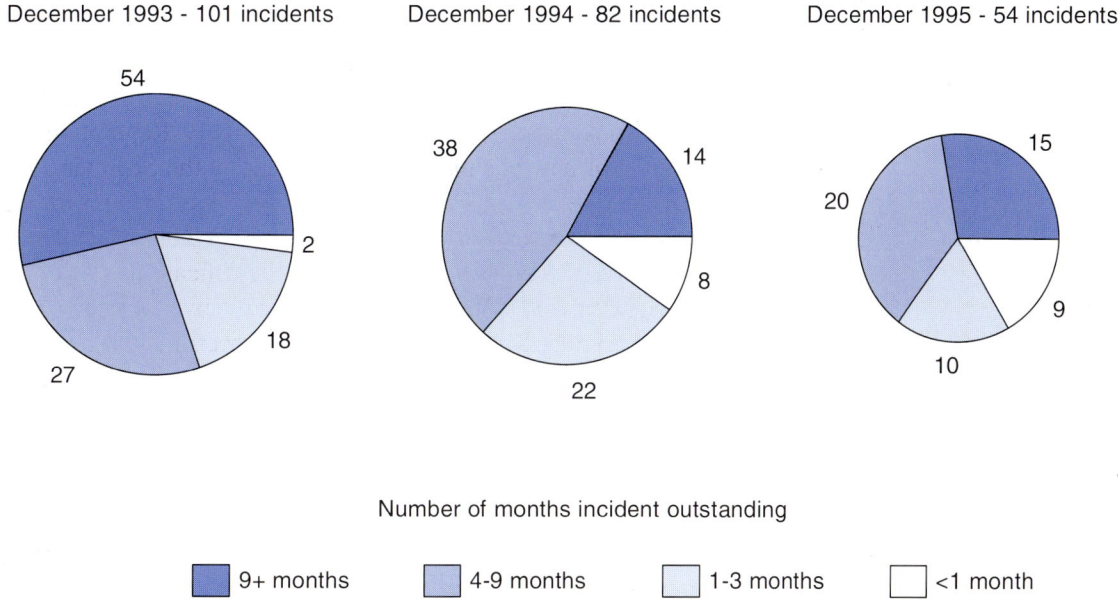

December 1993 - 101 incidents   December 1994 - 82 incidents   December 1995 - 54 incidents

Number of months incident outstanding

■ 9+ months   ■ 4-9 months   □ 1-3 months   □ <1 month

26. In the second year of operation the Code has been reviewed with the water companies and they provided valuable feedback by means of questionnaire returns. The companies consider the Code to be a valuable discipline for the Inspectorate and that no adjustments are required at this time.

Inspection of water companies

27. I mentioned last year that, from the knowledge and experience gained from the inspections over the first five years, the Inspectorate was in a position to tailor future inspections to reflect the individual situations in each company. Tailored inspections were introduced in 1995, based on a number of factors, including the size of the company, the extent to which accredited quality systems were in place, and most importantly, what had been discovered in previous inspections and how fully the company had responded to recommendations made by the Inspectors.

28. Some companies will have noticed a much reduced level of inspection during 1995, with little more than the essential audit trails, whereas some others will have experienced more searching visits with Inspectors following up specific concerns. The other change, particularly for the larger companies, was that visits were spread more evenly over the year to avoid the concentration of effort in the autumn. On some occasions an Inspector investigating an incident or a consumer complaint took the opportunity to carry out the formal inspection of the relevant facilities at the same time. The aim was to focus resources so that Inspectors were able to

concentrate their efforts in areas of greatest potential benefit to consumers. I believe that much more was achieved by this approach and inspections will continue to be tailored in future years.

29. The audit trails, which are an essential part of ensuring that the compliance data is reliable and a valid measure of compliance with the standards, necessarily involve checking of laboratories' data, even for those that have NAMAS (now UKAS) DWTS accreditation. This checking is not to duplicate the work of the UKAS assessors but is part of the work needed to audit compliance data from the taking of samples from sampling points, through analysis, to the public record. Some companies see this as unnecessary duplication in respect of the laboratory and the Inspectorate is considering, in consultation with UKAS, how we might minimise the effort involved by both sets of assessors, without compromising the thoroughness of the audit, and thus reduce the demands on the time of the laboratory staff. The Inspectorate will issue an Information Letter setting out how its Inspectors and UKAS assessors will cooperate for the 1996 inspections.

Distribution system undertakings

30. The investment in water supply over the next 10 years will be dominated by the requirement to solve the mainly aesthetic quality problems associated with the poor condition of some distribution systems. It is important that the approach taken will concentrate money and effort in the areas with greatest problems, and that companies are able to demonstrate that these refurbishment programmes have achieved the necessary improvements in drinking water quality. Accordingly the Inspectorate, to support the distribution system undertakings, is agreeing, with each water company, methods of pre and post renovation measures of water quality that reflect the conditions pertaining in each area. The companies are required to provide annual returns on the work carried out, together with the output performance results in those zones in which the work is due for completion. Some companies need to refurbish substantial lengths of main; consequently, the Inspectorate recognises that the timescales to achieve significant improvements in quality are longer than for those parameters which require only improvements to treatment plant.

Cryptosporidium in Water Supplies

31. The Expert Committee on Cryptosporidium in Water Supplies, which was chaired by the eminent physician, the late Sir John Badenoch, produced its second full report in October 1995. The conclusions of the Expert Group are reassuring. Although the absence of _Cryptosporidium_ from water supplies cannot be guaranteed, catchment control policies and optimisation of conventional treatment processes can ensure that any risk of infection is maintained at an acceptably low level. While reinforcing the advice given in its first report, the Expert Group has made new recommendations which should further enhance consistency in management of incidents involving _Cryptosporidium_ in water supplies. These recommendations include endorsement of the importance of quality assurance in monitoring for the organism, provision of specific advice aimed at protecting the immuno-suppressed population and the establishment of protocols for issuing and withdrawing advice to boil water.

32. There was a major outbreak of cryptosporidiosis in South Devon in July 1995. An outbreak control team was formed to manage the incident and reported in January 1996. The Inspectorate is carrying out a full and detailed investigation of this incident to assess whether or not the outbreak was associated with water supply and, if so, whether there is a case for recommending to the Secretary of State that a prosecution be brought against the water company under Section 70 of the Water Industry Act 1991 for allegedly supplying water unfit for human consumption.

Nitrate, Pesticides and Lead report

33. The analyses of the 1994 returns are nearly complete and a report covering 1991, 1992, 1993 and 1994 data will be published later this year.

34. The report of the Working Party on the Incidence of Pesticides in Water was published by HMSO in June 1996 (ISBN 0-11-753193-6). The Report gives a comprehensive account of monitoring results for pesticides in drinking water and in the water environment. The lead for this work, which began with the Inspectorate, has now been taken over by the Environment Agency.

35. A free leaflet giving consumers advice about lead in drinking water prepared by the Inspectorate has been in high demand, requiring a second print run. It describes how consumers can find out whether or not their service pipe is made of lead and whether the water supplied is likely to take lead into solution. It advises how consumers can minimise the levels present in the water consumed if lead is of concern.

Private Water Supplies

36. In 1995 the Inspectorate decided that it should obtain wider information on the laboratories used by local authorities to enable it to consider how many further inspections of laboratories analysing samples from private water supplies were necessary in order to discharge the Secretary of State's duty in regulation 19(2)(e) of the Private Water Supplies Regulations 1991 to ensure that any laboratory at which samples are analysed has a system of analytical quality control that is subject from time to time to checking by a person who is not under the control of the laboratory or authority. To this end a short questionnaire was sent to all local authorities in England and Wales in May 1995 requesting information on their arrangements for the analysis of samples from private water supplies. 18 laboratories were selected for inspection, based either on the number of local authorities submitting samples or the total number of samples analysed. With very few exceptions, Inspectors were able to conclude that the laboratories were carrying out analysis of samples from private water supplies competently. The majority of the laboratories met most of the very strict criteria necessary for the local authorities using them to meet the requirements of regulation 19(2)(d). However, in many cases, local authorities would not be able to demonstrate this compliance because of a lack of contractual obligations, and deficiencies in the laboratories' arrangements for reporting analytical results. Further details are given in Chapter 7.

Forward Look

37. In November 1995 the Inspectorate hosted the first meeting of an informal network of those responsible for drinking water quality regulation within the European Union. There was an exchange of information on how the Drinking Water Directive (EC 80/778) has been implemented in each Member State and how drinking water quality is monitored against the required standards. It was a valuable meeting in achieving a better understanding of each other's methods of regulation. It is intended that the network should meet from time to time to consider common issues. I hope that ultimately it might lead to comparable information on drinking water quality being available from each Member State.

38. I believe that the Inspectorate, in addition to monitoring compliance with the Regulations, has a responsibility to try to ensure that water consumers receive accurate information on drinking water quality. Most of our information is good news, with drinking water being very carefully monitored, of high quality and getting better. Sadly good news does not appear to be of much interest to some parts of the media which seem to prefer to seek out something that can be produced as a scare story. I am considering how best we can continue to improve the level and quality of communication so that consumers might get behind the sensational headlines.

39. The Inspectorate has been experimenting in the use of the Internet in making information on water quality more widely available. The information contained in the leaflet, giving the summary of the results in Drinking Water 1994, is accessible through the Department of the Environment pages, as is the leaflet 'Have you got lead pipes'. Preparations are underway to provide further pages that give some of the data contained in this report.

40. I and my colleagues seek continuously to improve our own performance towards using our resources more efficiently and more effectively as guardians of drinking water quality. We apply total quality thinking in our own internal improvement projects and work with quality systems, where appropriate, documented to ISO 9000 accreditation standard.

About this Report

1. This Report continues the style set by its predecessors. It has to convey the extent to which water companies comply with the legal requirements concerning drinking water quality and its monitoring and reporting. To do that, it has to provide some detail of the situations in which those requirements are not met. Given that regulations have been breached, it is inevitable that, particularly in the individual company sections in Chapter 3, a significant proportion of the text is given over to describing those situations and the actions taken as a result by companies and the Inspectorate. That in no way detracts from the facts that **all companies are complying with all the Regulations except where noted**, and that they are generally committed to improvement programmes to deal with those relatively few instances where regulations are breached.

2. **It is vital, for a correct understanding of the sections on individual companies, to read the Report as a whole.** Those sections, taken with the other chapters, contain a wealth of information which demonstrate companies' individual and collective achievements in providing very high quality water to consumers. The Inspectorate confides that each company will use the factual information expressed in its section to present its individual achievements to the public in its area.

3. **Chapter 1** sets out the regulatory framework in which water companies and local authorities operate, against which the Inspectorate assesses compliance and through which any necessary improvements are enforced. **Chapter 2** describes the activities of the Inspectorate and developments in 1995, including details of the Inspectorate's performance against the targets it set itself in its "Code for Enforcement" which was published at the end of 1993 and revised and re-issued in 1995.

4. **Chapter 3** contains sections on each of the 31 water companies in England and Wales. The introduction to the Chapter is essential to the correct understanding of those sections. **Chapter 4**, Overview of Water Quality in England and Wales, aggregates the compliance data of all companies and comments on the overall findings.

5. Both the individual company sections and the overview tabulate and discuss comparisons with 1994 and 1993. The Inspectorate considers that a "rolling" three-year comparison provides an appropriate means of illuminating general trends. However, some information comparing the past five years is tabulated in Chapter 4 and is also depicted in the Figures which appear at that Chapter's end.

6. **Chapter 5**, Improvement Programmes and Enforcement Action, summarises the position in 1995 and shows the extent of new enforcement action in comparison with previous years. **Chapter 6**, Drinking Water Quality Incidents, summarises the Inspectorate's continuing and developing activities in dealing with situations where drinking water quality has demonstrably deteriorated.

7. **Chapter 7** contains a brief guide to the aims and requirements of the Private Water Supplies Regulations 1991 and details of advice given in response to individual local authority enquiries. **Chapter 8**, Drinking Water Research, summarises the Department of the Environment research programme on water

quality and health which is steered by the Inspectorate. It outlines research completed during 1995, current research contracts, and research contracts let during 1995/96. Research is targeted on the main issues currently concerning drinking water quality. Finally, the **Glossary** provides short explanation of terms and abbreviations which may be unfamiliar to some readers. The Inspectorate will be pleased to provide further explanation of these terms or of any other matters contained in this Report.

8. As mentioned in the Chief Inspector's Statement, this Report has a companion leaflet, summarising the overall drinking water quality position in 1995. The leaflet - "How Good is Your Drinking Water?" is available free of charge from: The Department of the Environment, PO Box 151, London E15 2HF (fax 0181 533 1618).

Chapter 1 **The Regulatory Framework**

Public water supplies

1.1 The Water Industry Act 1991 ("the Act") is part of the consolidation of water legislation which followed the Water Act 1989 and requires water companies, when supplying water for domestic or food production purposes, to supply only water which is wholesome at the time of supply. The time of supply is the moment when water passes from the company pipe into a consumer's pipe. Companies are not held responsible for a deterioration of drinking water quality which occurs within a consumer's premises, except in respect of copper, lead or zinc. If there is a risk of the standards for these metals being exceeded after the water leaves a company's pipes, the company is required, with certain exceptions, to consider introducing or modifying water treatment in order to reduce the extent to which they are dissolved within plumbing systems. This is a measure designed primarily to reduce the exposure of consumers to lead.

1.2 A duty is placed upon the Secretary of State by the Act to take enforcement action against a water company which fails to supply wholesome water or which has failed and is likely to fail to do so again. However, the Secretary of State is not required to enforce if the breach is trivial or if the water company has given an undertaking to take steps acceptable to the Secretary of State to secure or facilitate compliance with the statutory requirements in a timescale acceptable to the Secretary of State. If a water company were to fail to give such an undertaking or to fail to comply with one it had given, the Secretary of State would issue an enforcement order enforceable through the Courts.

1.3 The Act makes it a criminal offence for a water undertaker to supply water that is unfit for human consumption. In any proceedings against a water undertaker for such an offence, the Act provides a defence for the undertaker to show that it:

(a) had no reasonable grounds for suspecting that the water would be used for human consumption; or

(b) took all reasonable steps and exercised all due diligence for securing that the water was fit for human consumption on leaving its pipes or was not used for human consumption.

1.4 Under the Act "wholesomeness" is defined by reference to standards and other requirements set out in the Water Supply (Water Quality) Regulations 1989[1], which have been amended slightly by the Water Supply (Water Quality) (Amendment) Regulations 1989[2] and 1991[3]. Water supplied for the domestic purposes of drinking, washing and cooking or for the purpose of food production, will be regarded as wholesome provided:

(a) it meets the standards prescribed in the Regulations for the particular properties, elements, organisms or substances;

(b) the hardness or alkalinity of water which has been softened or desalinated is not below the prescribed standards; and

(c) it does not contain any element, organism or substance whether alone or in combination, at a concentration or value which would be detrimental to public health.

This last requirement is a catch-all provision which reflects the concept of wholesomeness as developed over the years.

1.5 The Regulations incorporate all the standards (maximum admissible concentrations and minimum required concentrations) set out in the EC "Drinking Water Directive"[4] (80/778/EEC) and they also include 11 national standards. In total, numerical standards are set for 55 parameters and descriptive standards for a further two. The national standards are interpreted as either three or 12 monthly averages. In addition to these standards applying to water at the time of supply, a number of standards apply to water issuing from treatment works and to water held in service reservoirs within the distribution system. The Secretary of State may authorise the relaxation of a standard, but only in particular circumstances and not to the extent that public health could be endangered.

1.6 Statutory responsibility for monitoring the quality of water supplies is placed upon the water companies by the requirements of the Regulations. This "self-monitoring" rôle for water companies is subject to checks by local authorities and by the Drinking Water Inspectorate as described below.

1.7 The basic unit for monitoring is the water supply zone. This is an area designated by a water company, usually by reference to a source of supply, in which not more than 50,000 people reside. A discrete area served by a single source will always be delineated as a single water supply zone unless it normally has within it a population greater than 50,000, in which case the area must be sub-divided into two or more supply zones. A discrete area, whether supplied by one or more sources, will be divided into separate zones if there are, or could be, significant differences in water quality within the area.

1.8 Water companies are required to take a specified minimum standard number of samples for each parameter within each water supply zone according to the population served by the zone. Consumers' taps within the zones are used as sampling points. For monitoring copper, lead and zinc, the taps (in practice the properties in which they are located) must be chosen at random. For the microbiological parameters, at least 50% of the taps must be chosen at random. For the remainder of the parameters, the company has a discretion to choose fixed or random sampling points or a combination of the two. In all cases the number and location of sampling points must be such as to be representative of water quality in the supply zone.

1.9 The Secretary of State may authorise sampling for some parameters from strategic points rather than from consumers' taps, the particular parameters being those which do not change in concentration or value within the distribution system. If water quality can be shown consistently to be well within the standards, sampling may be at a reduced level. Conversely, if monitoring reveals a breach of a standard, an enhanced level of sampling is then required. The frequency of sampling, whatever the circumstances, is at least the minimum required by the EC Directive, and in most cases substantially more.

1.10 Monitoring information must be made publicly available. Registers of results must be open for inspection. A copy of information on the register must be provided to consumers on demand. Annual reports must be made to local authorities in a prescribed form. Water companies must also publish an annual report upon the water they have supplied, including a commentary upon its quality. These provisions of the Regulations are enforceable.

1.11 In the performance of their duty to supply wholesome water, companies are checked at two levels: by local authorities and by the Drinking Water Inspectorate. Local authorities receive information regularly from water companies upon drinking water in their areas. They also have powers to take samples and have them analysed in order to supplement this information. If a local authority is not satisfied that drinking water is of a satisfactory quality, either on the basis of information supplied by a company, or through samples it has taken itself, it is under a duty to notify the water company. Equally, if it receives complaints from members of the public, it will refer them to the water company. If the local authority does not obtain satisfaction from these references, it then has a duty to notify the Secretary of State who, in considering whether enforcement action is necessary, will seek advice from the Inspectorate.

Enforcement of standards

1.12 Under section 18 of the Act, the Secretary of State is required to take enforcement action to secure compliance when he is satisfied that an appointed company is contravening, or has contravened and is likely to contravene again, any statutory requirement enforceable under that section. Under section 19 of the Act, he is not required to take enforcement action if he is satisfied that the contravention is trivial, or that the company has already given an undertaking to take appropriate steps to secure or facilitate compliance with the requirements.

1.13 The Secretary of State is able to take enforcement action under section 18 for contraventions of the wholesomeness, monitoring and treatment requirements of the Regulations, and also for contraventions of the Regulations' records and information requirements. He may also institute prosecution proceedings under section 70 of the Act for the offence of supplying water unfit for human consumption.

1.14 Most enforcement action begins with a 'notice of intention to enforce' being served on the company. This usually results in the company giving an undertaking to carry out a programme of work to secure or facilitate compliance with the required standards for drinking water quality within a given timescale. If it subsequently appears that compliance can be achieved on a shorter timescale, replacement undertakings containing the shorter timescales are put in place.

1.15 In accepting undertakings, the Secretary of State has to take account of the duty to remedy contraventions of the standards in respect of parameters covered by the "Drinking Water Directive"[4] as soon as possible. In some circumstances, it may be appropriate to make a provisional or a final order for the purposes of securing compliance.

1.16 The Inspectorate is responsible for initiating enforcement action, on behalf of the Secretary of State for the Environment - or, for contraventions arising in Wales, on behalf of the Secretary of State for Wales - in the following circumstances:

    (a)   when a water quality standard set by regulation 3 is breached and the breach is not trivial or is likely to recur;

    (b)   when a breach of one of the other enforceable regulations, such as those covering sampling, analysis, water treatment or information requirements, is identified; or

    (c)   when existing undertakings or time limited relaxations, authorised under regulation 4, expire before the required improvements have been completed.

1.17 The Inspectorate will not initiate enforcement action when a company, after becoming aware of a breach of a regulatory requirement, takes immediate remedial action and demonstrates that compliance has been achieved and is likely to be maintained.

Private water supplies

1.18 Private supplies are defined in the Act as any supplies of water provided otherwise than by a statutorily appointed water undertaker. The Act preserves the long standing duty on local authorities to keep themselves informed about the wholesomeness and sufficiency of water supplies in their respective areas, including private water supplies.

1.19 Under the Act, local authorities are given powers to secure the improvement of private water supplies or connection to a mains supply. They are able to serve a notice on the owner and occupier of the premises receiving water from a private supply and the owner and occupier of the land where the source is situated which, in relation to that source, specifies the improvement steps to be taken, who is responsible, and the timescale. The person on whom the notice is served may object to the local authority. The notice must then be submitted to the relevant Secretary of State for confirmation with or without modification. In certain circumstances, the Secretary of State may order a public local inquiry or hearing.

1.20 The definition of wholesomeness in the Water Supply (Water Quality) Regulations 1989[1], as amended slightly by the Water Supply (Water Quality) (Amendment) Regulations 1989[2] and 1991[3], applies equally to public and private supplies and is incorporated in the Private Water Supplies Regulations 1991[5]. Those Regulations also:

(a) specify how local authorities are required to classify private supplies in their areas;

(b) specify the parameters for which local authorities are required to monitor private supplies, together with the frequency of monitoring which is determined by the classification of each supply;

(c) allow local authorities, subject to certain conditions, to enter into arrangements with prescribed persons for the taking and analysing of samples;

(d) prescribe requirements that local authorities must ensure are met when samples are taken and analysed; and

(e) prescribe the maximum charges that local authorities may make for sampling and analysis.

1.21 The Inspectorate is responsible for providing technical and scientific advice to the Secretary of State for the Environment and the Secretary of State for Wales under the Act for the purposes of their functions in relation to private water supplies. This includes advice, where appropriate, on improvement notices served by local authorities which are referred to the Secretary of State. The Inspectorate is also responsible for checking or arranging to check that local authorities in England and Wales are complying with the requirements of the Regulations.

1.22 Further information about the laws controlling private water supplies can be found in The Water Industry Act 1991 (sections 67, 77-85, 93 and schedule 6 paragraphs 6 and 7), The Private Water Supplies Regulations 1991[5] and the Department of the Environment Circular 24/91 (Welsh Office Circular 68/91) and a free Department of the Environment and Welsh Office leaflet "Private Water Supplies - A guide to the Laws controlling Private Water Supplies".

References

1. Statutory Instruments 1989 No. 1147.

2. Statutory Instruments 1989 No. 1384.

3. Statutory Instruments 1991 No. 1837.

4. Council Directive of 15 July 1980 relating to the quality of water intended for human consumption (80/778/EEC) OJ No. L229, 30.8.80, p11.

5. Statutory Instruments 1991 No. 2790.

Chapter 2   **Inspectorate Activities**

Main Tasks of the Inspectorate

2.1 The main tasks of the Inspectorate are to:

(a)   carry out the technical audit of water companies;

(b)   advise the Secretary of State on the steps required to enforce obligations under the relevant legislation;

(c)   investigate incidents which affect drinking water quality adversely;

(d)   advise the Secretary of State on the prosecution of water companies if water has been supplied which is unfit for human consumption;

(e)   provide technical and scientific advice to Ministers and officials of the Department of the Environment and Welsh Office on drinking water policy issues;

(f)   identify and assess new issues or hazards relating to drinking water quality and initiate research as required;

(g)   assess and respond to consumer complaints when local procedures have been exhausted;

(h)   assess chemicals and materials used in the provision of water supplies; and

(i)   provide authoritative guidance on analytical methods used in the monitoring of drinking water.

These tasks and their output are described in this and the other chapters of this Report.

Technical audit

2.2 The process of technical audit has been devised by the Inspectorate primarily for checking that water companies are complying with their statutory obligations. It consists of three elements:

(a)   an annual assessment based on information provided by water companies of the quality of water in each water supply zone, compliance with sampling and other requirements, and the progress made on improvement programmes;

(b)   inspection of individual companies, covering not only a general check at the time of the inspection on the matters covered above but also an assessment of the quality of the information collected by the company; and

(c)   interim checks made on aspects of compliance based on information provided periodically by companies.

2.3 A description of the processes involved in these three elements was given in "Drinking Water 1990" and, as they have since remained substantially the same, the reader is referred to that Report for further details.

2.4 During 1995 all 31 companies were inspected by small teams from the Inspectorate itself and also in the case of 22 companies, for certain inspection topics, by teams of consultants working under the general direction of the relevant Principal Inspector. The inspection programme generally ran smoothly and the Inspectorate continues to be grateful to companies for providing full facilities to its staff and consultants.

2.5 The 1995 inspection was based on the topics listed in table 2.1 below. It developed the tailored approach to inspections outlined in Drinking Water 1994. A number of core tasks were carried out for every company but many tasks were only included at the discretion of the Principal Inspector, based on the extent to which previous inspections had shown individual companies to have satisfactory procedures and practices in place. The Inspectorate sought to reduce the burden of inspection on companies by not inspecting procedures and practices which had already been found satisfactory in earlier years and had not changed. The practice in previous years of carrying out the whole of the year's inspection during a single visit had proved burdensome to both companies and the Inspectorate, and in 1995 Inspectors followed up specific tasks with individual companies at various mutually convenient

Table 2.1   1995 INSPECTION TOPICS

Action following 1994 recommendations

Sampling arrangements	-	Sampling points
	-	Sampling round (except where companies methods are accredited to NAMAS/DWTS)
	-	Delineation of water supply zones
Analysis arrangements	-	Performance characteristics and Analytical Quality Control
	-	Detailed audit of selected analytical systems (except where companies methods are accredited to UKAS/DWTS)
	-	Arrangements for microbiological parameters
	-	Sub-contracting of analysis
	-	Competence of laboratory staff
Reporting arrangements	-	Audit trails
	-	Public Record
Compliance programmes	-	General progress
	-	Detailed audit of selected completed schemes
	-	Detailed audit of selected schemes in progress
	-	Assessment of lead undertakings
Water treatment	-	Inspections at water treatment works [a]
	-	Audit of telemetry charts/data logger print outs and associated records [b]
Water distribution	-	Service reservoirs [a]
	-	Policy on operation of service reservoirs [b]
	-	Large scale transfer of water within companies [b]
	-	Mains rehabilitation
Incident and emergency procedures	-	Radioactivity monitoring. Company approach to its role in the DoE Green Book [b][c]
	-	Review of incidents and lessons learnt [b]
Communications with local authorities	-	Audit through discussion with some local authorities within the company's supply area
Quality assurance	-	Progress with the implementation of QA procedures
	-	Assessment of internal company QA audits [a]

[a] Task allocated to consultants for most companies.
[b] New or substantially new task for 1995.
[c] "Civil Emergencies involving Radioactive Substances: The Department's Role and Arrangements" Dept. of the Environment, June 1995.

times during the year. In tailoring the inspection to the perceived strengths and weaknesses of the individual companies, Inspectors were expected to address as necessary any matter within the Inspectorate's general remit whether or not it was included in the main list of inspection topics.

2.6 As for previous years, inspectors and consultants prepared reports to the Chief Inspector on the outcome of each company's inspection. Because inspections often involved a number of visits throughout the year, each inspection visit was the subject of a separate preliminary report which was made available to the company. At the end of 1995 the various reports made during the year were consolidated into a single report in which the preliminary reports were updated to take account of actions taken during the year in response to recommendations in the preliminary reports. Maintaining the development made in 1993, a clear distinction is now made between recommendations and suggestions. The distinction is that **recommendations** are now made only where, in the Inspectorate's opinion, action is required in order to avoid a foreseeable risk that the Regulations will be contravened. **Suggestions** are made in relation to matters which do not present such a risk, but which concern general good practice. As before, companies are requested to make a formal written response to recommendations. No such response is invited for suggestions, but in practice companies have in some cases commented on them all the same.

2.7 There are no simple means of attaching a value or weighting to individual recommendations. Simple comparison between companies of the number of recommendations is therefore not a valid indicator of an individual company's performance. Nor is the total number of recommendations an indicator of the depth or zeal of the inspection. However, it is of some interest to note that, within the 1995 inspection reports on the 31 companies, there was a total of 385 individual recommendations. The number of recommendations made to each company ranged from 0 to 43 and bore little relation to the size of the company. Suggestions totalled 829 amongst the companies.

2.8 The main conclusions drawn from the 1995 inspections are set out for each company in Chapter 3 of this Report, together with information on any contraventions of regulations and consequent consideration of enforcement action.

Relations with the National Measurement Accreditation Service

2.9 As reported in "Drinking Water 1993", the Chief Inspector and the Head of the NAMAS Executive signed in August 1993 a Memorandum of Understanding covering an Agreement on the accreditation of laboratories by NAMAS and demonstration of compliance with regulation 21 of the Water Supply (Water Quality) Regulations 1989 and regulation 19 of the Private Water Supplies Regulations 1991. During 1995 NAMAS became the United Kingdom Accreditation Service (UKAS) but the agreement was not affected by the change and accreditation continues to be given to the NAMAS standard.

2.10 Accreditation to the Drinking Water Testing Specification (DWTS) is optional. In its absence, companies' sampling and analysis arrangements are included in the Inspectorate's periodic inspections as before. NAMAS procedures and guidance to establish the specification were published in July 1994, in NAMAS Document NIS 70, entitled "Accreditation Requirements for Sampling and Testing in Accordance with the Drinking Water Testing Specification (DWTS)". The Inspectorate is currently reviewing with UKAS the implementation of the agreement with a view to determining whether there is any unnecessary overlap between the work of the NAMAS assessors and Inspectors. Two members of the Inspectorate's professional staff have received training to serve as NAMAS assessors if the need for their services should arise.

2.11 By the end of May 1996, 19 laboratories had achieved accreditation to DWTS for some or all of the parameters featuring in the Regulations. Applications for such accreditation had been received by UKAS from a further five laboratories.

Consumer complaints

2.12 In 1995, the Inspectorate received 67 written and 122 telephoned complaints about drinking water quality. These were mostly dealt with either by the Inspectorate asking the relevant company to look into the matter and comment or, where appropriate, by the Inspectorate advising the complainant to take this first step. In cases where consumers were dissatisfied with the response of the company, the Inspectorate either advised them to ask the environmental health officer of their local authority to investigate or, where there appeared to be some cause for concern, itself investigated. The Inspectorate also liaised with the Office of Water Services on consumer complaints in cases of mutual interest and received information about relevant complaints forwarded by the Office of Water Services from the Customer Service Committees.

Chemicals and materials

2.13 On behalf of the Secretary of State for the Environment and the Secretary of State for Wales, the Inspectorate operates a scheme for the statutory approval of chemicals used in water treatment and materials which come into contact with drinking water. The purpose of the scheme is to ensure that use of such products does not cause any adverse effect on water quality. The Inspectorate also operates a voluntary approval scheme for products which are used for the treatment of swimming pool water or for the production of potable water from seawater or brackish water. Advice on submissions which are presented by manufacturers for approval of their products under either scheme, is provided by the Committee on Chemicals and Materials of Construction for Use in Public Water Supply and Swimming Pools.

2.14 The Committee met on five occasions (six days) during 1995 and the Secretaries of State approved 119 products for use in water supply. A notice of refusal of approval was issued in respect of three products; no notices of prohibition of use were issued in 1995. In addition, 14 products were approved by the Committee under the voluntary scheme. On an experimental basis from 1 April 1996 the handling of applications for Regulation 25 approval is being integrated with applications for water byelaw approval to provide applicants with a "one stop shop". The experimental scheme is being managed by the Water Research Centre under the overall supervision of the Inspectorate.

2.15 A cumulative list of products approved under the statutory scheme was published in December 1995. A copy of the list and the 1995 revision of the guidance note on the approval system can be obtained from the Drinking Water Inspectorate, Room B155, Romney House, 43 Marsham Street, London SW1P 3PY. (tel: 0171 276 8808/8666, fax: 0171 276 8405) This list is included also in the Water Fittings and Materials Directory, which is published every six months by the WRc Evaluation and Testing Centre, Fern Close, Pen-y-Fan Industrial Estate, Oakdale, Gwent NP1 4EH. (tel: 01495-248454, fax: 01495 249234).

2.16 A list of substances and products approved for use in swimming pools is published annually by the Institute for Sport and Recreational Management in the magazine "Recreation". Details of publication dates can be obtained from the Institute (tel: 01664 65531).

- review of approvals

2.17 During 1993 and 1994 the Drinking Water Inspectorate appointed employees of WRc Medmenham as temporary technical assessors to carry out a review of the conditions of approval of each substance or product approved under regulation 25(1)a and the former voluntary scheme, including traditional chemicals. The objective of the review was to identify whether conditions of approval were consistent with latest toxicological and scientific knowledge and current operating practice.

2.18 The review has now been completed and the Inspectorate is in the process of issuing revised approval letters, which will include a condition that products must be used in accordance with manufacturers' or suppliers' written instructions. Copies of all instructions for use will be held by the Inspectorate. Water undertakers must ensure that their suppliers provide copies of the instructions which are referred to in letters of approval.

- variation of Conditions of Approval for Granular Activated Carbon (GAC)

2.19 The Inspectorate has received several reports of incidents involving the detection of odour or high chlorine demand on the filtrate from regenerated GAC filter beds. In 1995, an incident involving a high concentration of phosphate in the filtrate of a new GAC filter bed was reported. Details of investigations into the causes of these incidents were given to the Committee. The Committee also sought the latest information from manufacturers of GAC about production and regeneration processes.

2.20 These investigations revealed that odour or chlorine demand arise from the reduction of sulphate ions to sulphite or bisulphite species during regeneration. These soluble species give rise to chlorine demand during filtration and, depending on filtrate water composition, can be further reduced to sulphides which cause an unpleasant odour. It appears that significant reduction of sulphate to sulphite/bisulphite occurs infrequently during regeneration but it is most likely to cause a problem when the regenerated GAC is used to treat high mineral content surface waters which also contain a significant concentration of organic substances.

2.21 Leaching of phosphate ions from GAC was found to be associated with the use of phosphoric acid as an activating agent for virgin wood-based GAC. The Committee was informed that a number of chemicals are used in the production of GAC. Furthermore, depending on the raw material use and the composition of the water undergoing filtration, metals may leach from the carbon during the early stages of use of a virgin GAC filter bed.

2.22 The Committee concluded that the original condition of approval for GAC which required backwashing the bed until fine particles were absent, may not always ensure that the use of GAC does not cause an adverse effect on water quality. Therefore the Committee recommended a variation to the condition of approval, which requires water undertakers to conduct tests for chlorine demand and other parameters to ensure that the use of GAC does not cause a contravention of any standard prescribed in the Regulations.

- impact of European standardisation

2.23 The removal of technical barriers to trade is a major objective of the European Union's single market programme. Harmonised standards are being developed by the European Standards Institution (CEN) under European Union legislation. The purpose of these standards, among other things, is to remove technical barriers to trade resulting from national testing and checking requirements.

2.24 Very little progress has been made in the development of a European approval system for products used in contact with drinking water. In the meantime, Member States will continue to maintain national approval criteria which relate to the protection of public health. Nevertheless, the Committee will continue to consider the results of any relevant testing carried out in other Member States. The Committee will seek to minimise demands for re-testing, provided that the testing has clearly established the absence of any adverse effect on water quality.

2.25 Information on the approval systems in EC and EFTA countries is available in a report commissioned by the Drinking Water Inspectorate. The report, entitled "European Approval Systems", has been published by WRc Medmenham (tel: 01491 571531).

- enforcement of regulation 25

2.26 As part of its technical audit function the Inspectorate assesses water company arrangements for use of substances and products in contact with water supplies. Regulation 28 provides for criminal sanctions in the event of contravention of regulation 25. During 1995 a formal caution was issued to Wessex Water Services in respect of a contravention, which took place in 1994, of the conditions of approval for *in-situ* application of epoxy resin linings to water mains.

Water Byelaws

2.27 Water company byelaws, based on model water byelaws which were authorised by the Secretaries of State for the Environment and for Wales in 1987, have been made and are enforced by all water companies to prevent waste, misuse, undue consumption and contamination of water supplied.

2.28 The Inspectorate provides technical advice on byelaws issues to the policy divisions of the Department of the Environment and Welsh Office and to other governmental organisations. This involves input to water industry committees and liaison with water companies, manufacturers, trade and installer groups, and the Water Byelaws Scheme. Future enforcement of Byelaw provisions for waste, undue consumption, and contamination will utilise British standards transposing European standards.

2.29 The current water byelaws expire in 1997 and the options for their replacement were reviewed in the Department of the Environment and Welsh Office consultation paper "Replacing the Water Byelaws", which was issued in 1995.

2.30 Byelaw related issues form a substantial portion of the research programme managed by the Inspectorate. Further details appear under 'European Standardisation' in Chapter 8 of this Report.

European standards for water supply systems

2.31 The Inspectorate contributes to the development of European standards, on behalf of Department of the Environment, through representation on committees and working groups in the European Committee for Standardisation (CEN) and the British Standards Institution (BSI). The Inspectorate is currently represented on the following groups:

BSI - B/-/8	Coordination Panel for the water cycle
BSI - B504	Water supply
BSI - B504/2	Water supply, internal systems
BSI - B504/4	Water supply, backflow prevention
BSI - EH3/7	Effects of materials on water quality
BSI - CII/59	Chemicals for drinking water treatment
CEN - TC 164	Water supply
CEN - TC 164/WG2	Water supply, internal systems
CEN - TC 164/WG3	Materials vs water quality
CEN - TC 164/WG4	Water supply, backflow protection
CEN - TC 164/WG9	Drinking water treatment

2.32 In addition, the Inspectorate ensures that the Department's interests are represented via consultancy arrangements on the following groups:

CEN - TC 164/WG 3/AHG 2	Inventory of positive lists
CEN - TC 164/WG 3/AHG 4	Migration, surface/volume ratios, test waters
BSI - B504/13	Domestic water treatment

2.33 The Department's principal rôles in European standards work are to promote Government policy on the Single Market and to ensure that standards reflect UK traditions, practices and   regulatory requirements. While maintenance of the competitive position of the UK is an important consideration, the Department also provides technical input, represents the interests of users and attempts to secure effective management of work programmes.

Analytical methodology 2.34 Until 1 April 1996 the Inspectorate oversaw the work of the Standing Committee of Analysts (SCA), the post of Secretary being held by a Principal Inspector of the Drinking Water Inspectorate. SCA provides authoritative guidance on methods of sampling and analysis of drinking water, groundwater, river and seawater, waste waters and effluents, as well as sewage sludges, sediments and biota.

2.35 From 1 April 1996 SCA has been re-located within the Environment Agency under the responsibility of the Chief Scientist and Director of Environmental Strategy. This move reflects the response of Ministers to the 1992 review of the management and organisation of SCA. Ministers considered that there was merit in transferring SCA to the Environment Agency where air and soil analysis would be included in its remit. The Inspectorate has relinquished the post of Chairman. The post of Secretary, which is currently held by Dr David Westwood, has been transferred to the Environment Agency.

2.36 Preparation of the following publications was completed in 1995:

(a)   The second edition of "The Instrumental Determination of Total Organic Carbon and Related Determinands 1995";

(b)   "Methods for the Isolation and Identification of Human Enteric Viruses from Waters and Associated Materials 1995";

(c)   The second edition of "General Principles of Sampling Waters and Associated Materials 1996; Estimation of Flow and Load";

(d)   "Determination of Long Alkyl Chain Quaternary Ammonium Compounds in Environmental Matrices by High Performance Liquid Chromatography 1996"; and

(e)   "Inductively Coupled Plasma Spectrometry 1996".

These publications, which are part of the series "Methods for the Examination of Waters and Associated Materials", are available through HMSO.

2.37 The Main Committee of SCA met on two occasions in 1995 to monitor the activities of Working Groups and Panels. The Committee has also offered constructive comments on future work programmes which should ensure a continuing high standard of publications which reflect the priorities of the users of SCA services. The 1995 annual report on SCA activities has been published and copies may be obtained from the Drinking Water Inspectorate, Room B155, Romney House, 43 Marsham Street, London SW1P 3PY.

2.38 The Inspectorate has continued to support and participate in the work of BSI (the British Standards Institution), CEN (the European Committee for Standardisation), and ISO (the International Organisation for Standardisation). The Drinking Water Inspectorate was represented on the following committees in 1995, and provided the chairman, secretary or convenor for those marked with an asterisk:

BSI/EH3	Water quality
BSI/EH3-/1	Water quality/Accuracy and precision*
BSI/EH3/2	Water quality/Physical and chemical methods of analysis
BSI/EH3/3	Water quality/Radiochemical methods of analysis*
BSI/EH3/6	Water quality/Sampling
BSI/EH4	Soil quality
BSI/EH4-/2	Soil quality/Panel of UK working group experts in ISO/TC 190
CEN/TC230	Water analysis
CEN/TC230/WG1	Water analysis/Physical and chemical methods of analysis
CEN/TC230/WG1/TG3[a]	Water analysis/Nitrogen compounds*
ISO/TC 147/SC7	Water quality/Accuracy and precision*
ISO/TC 147/SC2/WG1[a]	Water quality/Nitrogen compounds*

[a] Joint committee

2.39 SCA has continued to support research into new or improved methods of analysis. Details of current and future research projects are given in Chapter 8 of this Report.

Code for Enforcement

2.40 Early in 1995 the Inspectorate carried out a review of its "Code for Enforcement" which was first published at the end of 1993. This Code summarises the regulatory functions of the Inspectorate and the way in which those functions and related activities are carried out. It also establishes quite exacting target times within which the Inspectorate will perform the tasks.

2.41 As a result of the review, a revised edition of the Code was published in July 1995. Changes made to the targets set in the Code mostly concerned the technical audit of water companies and reflected changes made in the pattern of inspections. Because of these changes, the Inspectorate's performance against the Code's targets in 1995 cannot be directly compared with that in 1994. The 1995 performance will form the baseline for future comparison.

2.42 For 1995, the Inspectorate's performance against the targets set in the Code has been as follows:

- seven of the 10 **letters notifying the consideration of enforcement action as a result of inspection in 1995** were sent to the companies concerned within four weeks (target previously 12 weeks) of the end of the inspection;

- 50 of the 87 **draft inspection reports** prepared by, or under the supervision of, the Inspectorate were sent for comment to companies within 4 weeks of the end of the inspection;

- in one of the five cases where single inspections were made of water companies, a **final inspection report** was sent to the company within four weeks of receipt of its comments;

- in six of the 26 cases where reports on more than one inspection were incorporated into a final **consolidated report,** this report was sent to the company by the target date of 1 March 1996.

- **preliminary assessment of 1995 compliance data** was sent within four weeks of receipt of the completed data set to 14 of the companies. (All 31 companies submitted data electronically, though in one case some revised data was received in hard copy form);

- of 13 **letters sent notifying companies of the consideration of enforcement action as a result of the 1995 compliance assessment,** nine were sent within the target of four weeks from the company's response to the preliminary assessment or within eight weeks of issue of the preliminary assessment, whichever was the sooner. In one further case, at 21 May 1996, notification of enforcement was still being considered within the target time;

- 60 draft **undertakings**, an application for one **relaxation** and three applications for **supply point authorisations** from three companies were dealt with and 56 of these were processed within the four week response time;

- of the 83 **drinking water quality incidents** notified to the Inspectorate in 1995, 48 had been assessed by 1 May 1996. In 19 of these cases the outcome was notified to the company within three months of the receipt of all the requested reports (or, as from 1 July 1995, within the more stringent target of three months from receipt of the company's final report). The 35 incidents remaining unassessed by 1 May 1996 required further information to be supplied or awaited completion of DWI assessment;

- 70 new applications for **approval of chemicals and materials** were received in 1995 and meetings to discuss these were arranged within four weeks whenever this was required. In all cases the Inspectorate provided information on progress made at committee meetings within the two week target;

- of 6108 **requests for information** received from all sources, 6095 (99.8%) were met within the three week response time;

- of 189 **water quality complaints** received, 188 (99.5%) were dealt with within the four week response time; and

- one **complaint about DWI** was received. Such complaints are required by the Code to be investigated by the Chief or Deputy Chief Inspector. In this case an enquiry was conducted by both which found that the Inspectorate had investigated properly the complainant's complaint about the quality of his water supply. The Inspectorate had been at fault only in not providing in its response to the complainant more advice upon what action to take, including the retention of a sample, should the problem be repeated.

Contacts

2.43 The Inspectorate provides scientific support to the Water Services Division of the Department of the Environment (now the Water Services and Regulation Division) and the Environment Division of the Welsh Office. It liaises with the Department of Health, the Ministry of Agriculture, Fisheries and Food, the Scottish Office Agriculture, Environment and Fisheries Department and the Department of the Environment for Northern Ireland. Contact with the European Commission, Member States of the European Union and other organisations elsewhere in the world is made from time to time.

2.44 Regular meetings are held with the Office of Water Services, the latter being concerned to link the substantial investment programmes of water companies to improvement of water quality. Inspectorate staff also attend meetings of the

Customer Service Committees of the Office of Water Services by invitation of their respective chairmen from time to time. Meetings are held with the National Rivers Authority at national and regional level. Medical advice is obtained from the Government's Chief Medical Officer and the Chief Medical Officer (Welsh Office) and their medical staff who may draw upon expertise from a variety of agencies including the Public Health Laboratory Service. Frequent contacts are made with Environmental Health Officers either directly or through the Institution of Environmental Health Officers. Contacts with the water industry other than those through water companies are made according to circumstance through The Chartered Institution of Water and Environmental Management, the Institution of Civil Engineers, the Royal Society of Chemistry and its Water Chemistry Forum, the Institution of Water Officers, the Water Services Association, the Water Companies' Association, and British Water. On research, the Inspectorate deals with WRc and other contractors.

Staffing

2.45   Throughout 1995 the Inspectorate had a complement of 31 posts of which 21 were for professionally qualified staff, eight for administrative support staff and two for technical support in information handling systems. Approximately two thirds of staff effort is devoted to Inspectorate duties with the remainder providing support to others within DoE. A list of all staff appears at the end of this Chapter.

Use of consultants

2.46   As described in paragraph 2.4, the Inspectorate engaged consultants to carry out inspections of water treatment works and service reservoirs in a number of water companies. The Inspectorate invited four firms of consultants to submit tenders for this activity and after consideration of the tenders, Rofe, Kennard and Lapworth were appointed. The outcome of the consultants' work is summarised in the reports on individual companies given in Chapter 3. The Inspectorate is again very grateful to its appointed consultants for their efforts and achievements against a tight timetable.

Publications, presentations and lectures

2.47   During 1995, the staff of the Inspectorate delivered lectures or presented papers on 34 occasions to learned societies, public bodies and teaching establishments. A press conference was held in July 1995 when the Chief Inspector's fifth Annual Report was published.

2.48   Since its establishment in January 1990, the Inspectorate has produced 28 publications, not including those produced under the auspices of the Standing Committee of Analysts. These publications are listed below.

Title and details	Date published
"Drinking Water 1990 - a report by the Chief Inspector." HMSO (ISBN 0-11-752483-2)	July 1991
"Report On A Drinking Water Quality Incident At Iver Water Treatment Works On 20 July 1991."	February 1992
"Your drinking water - who looks after it?" (leaflet explaining the role of the Inspectorate - DoE leaflet EP 0121)	April 1992
"List Of Substances And Products Approved For Use In The Production Of Potable Water From Seawater Or Brackish Water And For The Treatment Of Swimming Pool Water."	May 1992
"Nitrate, Pesticides And Lead 1989 and 1990."	July 1992
"Cryptosporidium In Water Supplies - Progress With the National Research Programme - Report of The Cryptosporidium Research Steering Committee."	July 1992
"Drinking Water 1991 - a report by the Chief Inspector." HMSO (ISBN 0-11-752676-2)	July 1992

Title and details	Date published
"Technical Audit Review." (By Prof P F Stott CBE FEng - a review of the Inspectorate's procedures for the technical audit of water companies.)	February 1993
"An Outbreak Of Cryptosporidiosis In North Humberside, December 1989/January 1990: Lessons For Water Supply."	February 1993
"Manual On The Treatment Of Private Water Supplies." HMSO (ISBN 0-11-752775-0)	April 1993
"Drinking Water 1992 - a report by the Chief Inspector." HMSO (ISBN 0-11-752853-6)	July 1993
"DWI/NAMAS Drinking Water Testing Specification."	July 1993
"Guidance Note On The Approval Of Substances And Products Used In The Provision Of Public Water Supplies, Revised October 1993."	December 1993
"Drinking Water Inspectorate Code for Enforcement." (Booklet setting out the Inspectorate's response to DTI's guidance "Working with Business") DoE and Welsh Office, PLAN 302	December 1993
"The Drinking Water Inspectorate's Response to the Technical Audit Review Report."	March 1994
"Drinking Water 1993 - a report by the Chief Inspector." HMSO (ISBN 0-11-752948-6)	July 1994
"How good is Our Drinking Water?" - a summary of the Inspectorate's 1993 report and information about the Inspectorate's work.	July 1994
"Proceedings of Workshop on Cryptosporidium in water supplies." HMSO (ISBN 0-11-753003-4)	August 1994
"International review of the composition of cement pastes, mortars, concretes and aggregates likely to be used in water retaining structures." HMSO (ISBN 0-11-753002-6)	October 1994
"Drinking Water 1994 - a report by the Chief Inspector." HMSO (ISBN 0-11-753131-6)	July 1995
"How good is your drinking water?" (A summary of the Inspectorate's 1994 Report and information about its work)	July 1995
"About your Water Company" (A single page insert to accompany "How good is your drinking water" giving brief information about the quality of drinking water supplied by each water company)	July 1995
"Lead in drinking water" Advice to consumers about lead in drinking water (DOE 95 EP 011)	July 1995
"Drinking Water Inspectorate Code for Enforcement" First revision.	July 1995
"Cryptosporidium in Water Supplies - Second Report of the Group of Experts" HMSO (ISBN 0-11-753136-7)	October 1995
"Proceedings of a Workshop on Treatment Optimisation for the Removal of Cryptosporidium from Water Supplies" HMSO (ISBN 0-11-753179-0)	October 1995
"Guidance Note On The Approval Of Substances And Products Used In The Provision Of Public Water Supplies, 1995 Revision."	December 1995 (latest edition)
"List Of Substances, Products And Processes Approved Under Regulations 25 and 26 For Use In Connection With The Supply Of Water For Drinking, Washing, Cooking or Food Production Purposes."	December 1995 (latest edition)

LIST OF INSPECTORATE STAFF
(1 July 1995 to 30 June 1996)

Chief Inspector Mr M J Rouse BSc CEng EurIng FIMech.E FCIWEM FIWO

Deputy Chief Inspector Mr O D Hydes BSc CChem MRSC

Superintending Inspector Mr A Lloyd BSc MPhil CChem FRSC

Principal Inspectors
Mr D F Drury CBiol MIBiol MCIWEM
Dr M J Gray PhD CChem FRSC CBiol MIBiol FCIWEM[a]
Mr A Hallas BSc MSc CBiol MIBiol
Mr M J Purcell BE MSc DIC CEng MICE MCIWEM
Mr R J Vincent MSc CChem FRSC MCIWEM[a][b]
Mr W M Waite BSc CBiol MIBiol MCIWEM
Dr D Westwood BSc PhD CChem FRSC MChemA[c]
Mr P R White BSc CEng MICE MCIWEM

Inspectors
Mr B S Bell LRSC MCIWEM
Miss C Y Hill BSc MSc MIBiol
Miss C R Jackson CChem MRSC FCIWEM
Mr P L Jiggins CBiol MIBiol MCIWEM
Dr P K Marsden MA(Oxon) DPhil
Mr R Millar BSc
Mr M Morgan CChem MRSC
Mr M S Smith BSc CChem MRSC[a]
Dr K J White BSc MSc PhD CChem MRSC

Administrative support (General)
Mr C H Parsons
Mr T Parsons
Mr C Newman
Mr N Jheeta

Administrative support (Technical)
Mr P Harry[d]
Ms M B McNally BA
Mr G Rees BA[d]

Secretarial support
Ms R Bartram
Ms Y K Chapman

Technical support
Mr M Raikundalia BSc
Ms J E Ramsdale

Secondee Ms L Taylor BSc[e]

[a] Registered Professional Water Chemist
[b] Transferred to Water Supply and Regulation Division, 1 January 1996
[c] Transferred to Environment Agency, 1 April 1996
[d] Transferred from Marine, Land and Liability Division, 25 March 1996
[e] On secondment from WRc

Chapter 3 Technical Audit of Individual Water Companies

KEY POINTS:

- **contents of individual company sections described;**
- **except where noted, all companies complied with the Regulations;**
- **how compliance with water quality standards is assessed;**
- **significance of contraventions of PCVs;**
- **what the tables mean;**
- **comparison of water quality between companies is not straightforward;**
- **limitations of 'percentage of determinations complying';**
- **comparison of zones complying a better measure of progress; and**
- **impact of change of coliform definition.**

Introduction

3.1 This chapter contains a separate section on each of the 31 water companies summarising the extent of compliance during 1995 with the requirements of the Water Supply (Water Quality) Regulations 1989, (the "Regulations") as amended (see paragraph 1.4 of this Report). Each section contains:

(a) an introduction which gives a summary of the company's water supply arrangements;

(b) a general statement about overall water quality which shows the extent to which the company's water treatment works, service reservoirs and water supply zones complied with the Regulations in 1995;

(c) more detailed information on compliance with sampling frequencies and the extent to which the company met the relevant water quality standards in 1995 itself and in comparison with 1994 and 1993 (but see paragraphs 3.29 onwards);

(d) conclusions from inspections of the company;

(e) a summary of progress with improvement programmes associated with undertakings given by the company or with conditions of relaxations authorised under regulation 4;

(f) where appropriate, details of the outcome of any review due during 1995 of relaxations authorised under regulation 4(1)(c);

(g) a summary of any events regarded by the Inspectorate as constituting incidents in which drinking water quality demonstrably deteriorated;

(h) where considered appropriate, details of any other notable events concerning water quality which came to the Inspectorate's attention in 1995; and

(i) a summary of the enforcement action (if any) considered for the company as a result of the Inspectorate's work in, or pertaining to, the calendar year 1995.

Except where stated to the contrary, the assessment of drinking water quality data for 1995, the findings of inspection in 1995 and the assessment in 1995 of any drinking water quality incidents showed that each company complied fully with the Regulations.

Assessment of compliance (general points)

3.2 Schedule 3 of the Regulations refers to the number of samples required to be taken for each parameter. In practice, water companies test each sample for several parameters so the text and the tables in the company sections relate to the number of determinations made of each individual parameter rather than to the number of samples taken.

3.3 The number of samples per annum specified in Schedule 3 is the minimum which a company is required to take in the various situations to which the Schedule refers. For 1995, the Inspectorate has looked for full compliance with the required sampling frequencies. Only where the annual requirement is for 50 samples or more has any shortfall been considered trivial, and then only to the extent of 2% of the requirement. Enforcement action is being considered in all other cases where shortfalls have been detected and the company has not taken steps to prevent a recurrence.

3.4 The term "total coliforms" refers to the parameter listed in Table C of Schedule 2 of the Regulations. It includes all coliform organisms whether faecal in origin or not (but see paragraph 3.35 below). In the following sections, the term "coliforms" has been used for the total coliform parameter to simplify the text. The detection of coliforms in a sample does not mean necessarily that the water supply will cause disease but is indicative of potential contamination which must be investigated immediately. The presence of faecal coliforms in the same sample would very probably mean that the contamination was of faecal origin and that, although disease would not necessarily result, urgent action must be taken to identify and eradicate the source of the contamination.

3.5 Water leaving treatment works and in service reservoirs and water supply zones is sampled for faecal streptococci and sulphite-reducing clostridia for investigative purposes only; there is no regulatory requirement to sample for these parameters. However, when a water company has carried out determinations for these parameters and supplied the information as part of its compliance information, the number of determinations and any breaches of the standards have been included in the assessment of water quality.

3.6 A few parameters specified in the Regulations have no prescribed concentration or value (PCV) assigned to them. These are: total organic carbon, colony counts, residual disinfectant, taste (qualitative) and odour (qualitative). Although all have an assigned sampling frequency, the absence of a PCV means that it is not appropriate to include the number of their determinations in the overall total of compliance determinations carried out by a company. However, any instances of failure to comply with the required sampling frequency have been included in the assessment of each company and, where not regarded as trivial, enforcement action is under consideration.

3.7 The parameters alkalinity and total hardness have a PCV assigned to them only for water which is artificially softened. The PCV in this case is a minimum value which must be exceeded. All determinations for these parameters made on samples taken to determine compliance have been included in the overall total of compliance determinations whether or not the supply has been artificially softened. The number and percentage of all individual determinations below the minimum value have been shown in the table on water quality in supply zones. However only those zones (if any) which received artificially softened water are included in the part of the table listing non-compliant zones.

Assessment of water quality at treatment works

3.8 Regulation 3(7) requires 100% compliance with water quality standards for coliforms and faecal coliforms at water treatment works. For 1995, the Inspectorate has generally regarded the detection of coliforms and faecal coliforms on a single occasion at most treatment works as a trivial breach of the standards unless there was a similar breach at that works in 1994. For works supplying more than 12,000 m^3/d and thus sampled daily for these parameters, a breach on a single occasion in 1995 has been regarded as trivial without reference to 1994 results. In the case of all other breaches, the Inspectorate is considering enforcement action unless the company has taken remedial action to prevent a recurrence.

Assessment of water quality at service reservoirs

3.9 Regulation 3(7), as amended by the Water Supply (Water Quality) (Amendment) Regulations 1991 allows that, if no more than 5% of samples taken in the preceding 12 months from a service reservoir contain coliforms, compliance in respect of coliforms is achieved. Compliance in 1995 has been assessed on the basis of results on samples taken from each service reservoir in the 12 months of the calendar year.

3.10 The detection of one or two faecal coliforms in 100 ml of sample on a single occasion has been regarded as a trivial breach of the faecal coliform standard. All other breaches of this standard and all cases of non-compliance with the coliforms standard in 1995 may result in enforcement action unless the company has taken remedial action to prevent recurrence.

Assessment of water quality in water supply zones - 'wholesomeness'

3.11 Regulation 3 prescribes concentrations or values for 55 of the 57 parameters as listed in Tables A to E of Schedule 2 to the Regulations. In general, to be wholesome, water must not contain a parameter in excess of a PCV; total hardness and alkalinity must not be below prescribed values if the water is treated by softening or desalination, and in the case of hydrogen ion the pH value must lie in a range defined by a maximum and minimum prescribed value.

- authorised relaxations

3.12 In particular cases, the Secretary of State may authorise, under regulation 4, the relaxation of a PCV. Relaxations may be authorised in emergencies, as a result of exceptional meteorological conditions or by reason of the nature and structure of the ground in the area from which the supply emanates. Regulation 5 places certain restrictions on the authorisation of relaxations - in particular, that public health shall not be jeopardised - and also requires the specification of the extent to which the PCV of any parameter is authorised to be contravened. Therefore, the granting of an authorisation for a relaxation does not change the PCV - it merely specifies the concentration or value of a parameter that can be allowed during the period of authorisation. In most remaining cases, authorisation is subject to the completion of improvement works to achieve compliance with the PCV from the date that the relaxation expires.

3.13 In assessing water quality in water supply zones, the Inspectorate takes into account the existence of authorised relaxations. Thus, throughout the text and tables of this Chapter and Chapter 4, reference to contravention of a PCV means that, where a relaxation is in place, a concentration or value greater than that authorised has occurred. Concentrations or values up to the authorised concentration or value are not included in the number or percentage of PCV contraventions.

- significance of contraventions of PCVs

3.14 Although the text and tables in the individual company sections and in Chapter 4 make extensive reference to contraventions of PCVs, there is no evidence that any of the contraventions were of such a magnitude or duration as to endanger the health of consumers. Only some of the parameters are of health significance and their standards are generally set with a wide margin of safety. The other parameters are of aesthetic significance, with standards set generally well below the level at which water would become unacceptable to consumers, and contravention of their standards is not necessarily indicative that the water is unfit to drink.

3.15 Contravention of a PCV, even for only one parameter and in only one sample out of the large number taken from each water supply zone in the course of the year, is of significance because the water supplied at the time the sample was taken cannot be regarded as wholesome. That does not mean that the water was harmful to health or otherwise unfit for drinking, but it may mean, when considered in the light of other results of monitoring, that the water quality needs improvement in order to meet the high standards which the Regulations specify.

- parameters with average or percentile PCVs

3.16 The general rule that any contravention of a PCV - even if revealed by only one sample - constitutes a breach of the Regulations and thus causes the water to be regarded as unwholesome, does not apply to a few parameters specified in regulation 3. Thus, zones have been regarded as non-compliant only if:

(a)   for trihalomethanes, the average concentration in any three-month period has exceeded 100 µg/l, the concentration prescribed in regulation 3(3)(e) ('trihalomethanes' refers to the sum of the concentrations of trichloromethane, dichlorobromomethane, dibromochloromethane and tribromomethane);

(b)   for sodium, 20% or more of the determinations carried out in the 36 months to the end of December 1995 exceed the prescribed concentration of 150 mg/l specified in Table A and regulation 3(5);

(c)   coliforms were detected in 5% or more of the samples taken in the 12 months of the calendar year or, where fewer than 50 samples were taken in 1995, in three or more of the last 50 samples; or

(d)   for Table D parameters, the average concentrations or values during the calendar year 1995 exceed the prescribed concentrations or values.

3.17 In all four cases, the number and percentage of individual determinations in excess of the relevant numerical PCV is shown for each company in the table on water quality in supply zones. This is in keeping with the practice adopted in previous Reports. However, only those zones (if any) which were non-compliant for those parameters on the basis described in the previous paragraph are included in the part of the table listing non-compliant zones.

- consideration of enforcement action

3.18 For 1995, the Inspectorate has generally regarded a breach of a standard for an individual non-microbiological parameter on a single occasion in a water supply zone as trivial, provided that ten or more samples have been taken in that zone or, if a smaller number has been taken, provided that there was not a corresponding breach in 1994. In other cases, the Inspectorate has taken into account the number of determinations carried out and the number and the extent of the breaches in deciding whether the breaches were trivial or not. The Inspectorate is considering enforcement in all cases where the breaches are not regarded as trivial, unless the company has already taken remedial action to prevent a breach recurring or the Inspectorate judges that the breach is in any case unlikely to recur.

3.19 A single breach of the faecal coliforms standard in a water supply zone has generally been regarded as trivial. Where more than 100 samples have been taken in a zone, two breaches of the standard have been regarded as trivial, provided that neither sample contained more than two faecal coliforms in 100 ml and there was no breach of the standard in 1994. No breach of the coliforms standard (see paragraph 3.16) has been regarded as trivial. The Inspectorate is considering enforcement in all cases where breaches of the standard for a microbiological parameter are not regarded as trivial, unless the company has taken remedial action to prevent a breach recurring or it can demonstrate beyond reasonable doubt that the breach arose solely as a result of the condition of the consumer's plumbing or tap from which samples were taken.

- parameters with no specified sampling frequency

3.20 Sampling frequencies are not specified in the Regulations for a few parameters which have prescribed concentrations or values (Kjeldahl nitrogen, dissolved and emulsified hydrocarbons, phenols, faecal streptococci, sulphite-reducing clostridia and substances extractable in chloroform). When a water company has carried out determinations for any of these parameters and supplied the information as part of its compliance monitoring, the numbers of determinations and any breaches of the standards have been included in the assessment of water quality.

- monitoring at supply points

3.21 Samples for certain specified parameters may be taken from supply points authorised by the Secretary of State instead of from sampling points (consumers' taps) provided that the concentration of the parameters is unlikely to change in the water during its passage from the supply point to consumers' taps. Sampling frequencies for the various parameters at supply points are specified in Table 5 of Schedule 3 of the Regulations. The number of determinations for the parameters are included in the information on compliance for all the supply zones to which the authorisation relates. Thus, for some parameters, the number of determinations recorded can greatly exceed the actual number of determinations made because one supply point can feed a number of supply zones.

- pesticide monitoring

3.22 The number of individual pesticides monitored by each company varies according to the monitoring strategy adopted by the company. Companies establish those pesticides used within catchment areas and which could reach water sources. Atrazine and simazine have been widely used in non-agricultural situations and all companies have been advised to monitor for them.

3.23 Individual pesticides are only included in the water quality tables in the section on each water company if the prescribed concentration was exceeded in any of the three years 1995, 1994 and 1993. "Other pesticides" refers to all other pesticides which were sought but found not to exceed the prescribed concentration.

3.24 The total pesticides parameter is defined in the Regulations as the sum of the detected concentrations of individual substances. In practice, the detected concentrations of whatever pesticides were determined in a particular sample are summed and compared against the prescribed concentration for total pesticides of 0.5 µg/l.

- explanation of table

3.25 The third table included in the section on each water company gives a summary of the water quality in water supply zones for the following 17 key parameters:

Coliforms	Aluminium
Faecal coliforms	Iron
Colour	Manganese
Turbidity	Lead
Odour (quantitative)	Polycyclic aromatic
Taste (quantitative)	hydrocarbons (PAH)
Hydrogen ion	Trihalomethanes
Nitrate	Total pesticides
Nitrite	Individual pesticides.

It can be assumed that for all other parameters the company complied in 1995 with the PCV, except where a parameter is additionally included in the table. However, any other parameters for which a breach of the PCV was recorded in 1994 or 1993 are also included in the table, even though there was no breach in 1995, so as to facilitate comparison between the three years.

3.26 The table shows, reading from left to right, the following information for each of the parameters listed:

(a) the total number of determinations reported for compliance purposes in the calendar year 1995;

(b) the number of determinations and the percentage of the total number of determinations which showed the numerical PCV (or the concentration or value authorised in a relaxation under regulation 4 - see paragraphs 3.12 and 3.13) for the parameter to have been contravened;

(c) the number of those determinations which contravened the PCV but which were made on samples from zones which were covered, for the whole or part of 1995, by an undertaking in respect of that parameter;

(d) the total number of zones which were covered by an undertaking in respect of that parameter for the whole or part of 1995, irrespective of whether there were contraventions in those zones;

(e) the number of zones for which new enforcement action is under consideration as a result of contraventions of the PCV for that parameter in 1995; and

(f) the number of zones which did not comply with the Regulations because of contraventions (including trivial contraventions) of the PCV for that parameter in each of the three years, 1995, 1994 and 1993.

3.27 The table row described 'Other pesticides' shows the number of determinations of those pesticides which, although included in the company's monitoring programme for the reasons given in paragraph 3.22, have not caused any contravention of the prescribed concentration for individual pesticides in 1995, 1994 or 1993. Where a company has supply point authorisation, this number may be considerably higher than the actual number carried out, for the reason given in paragraph 3.21.

3.28 The penultimate row of the table, described 'All others', shows the total number of determinations carried out for all parameters having a PCV but not otherwise appearing in the table. Paragraph 3.6 has already pointed out that parameters for which there is no PCV are necessarily excluded from compliance assessment and therefore from inclusion in the total number of determinations carried out for that purpose. The bottom row shows the grand total of all determinations and the total number of determinations showing contravention of a PCV (as explained in paragraph 3.13). The total number of determinations showing contravention is also shown as a percentage of the total number of determinations. The limitations of this statistic as a means of comparison between years or between companies are discussed in the following paragraphs.

Comparison of water quality

3.29 The information given in the sections about water quality in each company's area indicates the extent to which the company has or has not complied with the requirements of the Water Quality Regulations. It cannot be used to make comparisons of the overall quality of drinking water between different company areas. Nor does it necessarily provide an indication of the relative efficiency of different companies. The quality of drinking water varies within and between company areas, and depends not only on the treatment processes employed and the condition of the distribution system, but also on the nature of the source from which the water is obtained. For example, water from a borehole in a chalk aquifer would normally be of better microbiological quality than water from many other types of source. In addition, it should be noted that for many parameters, the greater the number of samples taken, the more likely it is that breaches of the standards will be detected.

3.30 Provided that monitoring frequencies at individual treatment works and service reservoirs have not differed significantly in each of the three years, the tabulated data for each company on the detection of coliforms and faecal coliforms in 1995, 1994 and 1993 can be statistically compared to identify any significant changes in water quality. The commentary in each section makes reference to such changes as appropriate. However, the change to the definition of the coliform parameter adopted for 1995 increased the range of organisms included in the parameter (see 3.35 below). To facilitate comparisons over the three years, the individual company sections also report contraventions of the standard based on the definition which applied prior to 1995, where companies have provided the necessary information. It must be recognised however that compliance with the coliform standard in 1995 is judged against the new definition only.

3.31 For water supply zones, differences between the number or percentage of determinations exceeding the PCV in each of the three calendar years are not necessarily of any significance. From a purely statistical viewpoint, comparison of the data for any two years must be based on the hypothesis that any differences are attributable solely to changes in the overall quality of water supplied by the company and that no other factors have varied which may have influenced the detection of breaches of the water quality standards. However, other factors which may account wholly or in part for a particular difference must be considered before drawing any conclusion about possible differences in water quality. These factors include:

(a) the adoption of an increased sampling frequency in accordance with regulation 13(7) as a result of breaches of a PCV for a particular parameter, which is likely to change the percentage of the total determinations of that parameter exceeding the PCV until remedial work is completed;

(b) the adoption of a reduced sampling frequency in accordance with regulation 13(3) for a particular parameter in appropriate zones, which may have the effect of increasing the percentage of the total determinations of that parameter exceeding the PCV in the company's area as a whole if other zones continue to be non-compliant with the standard for that parameter;

(c) in respect of individual pesticides, modifications to the monitoring strategy for pesticides in the light of reassessment of pesticide usage within a company's catchment area;

(d) improvements in analytical systems which may have reduced or eliminated the possible contribution to earlier data of erroneous results; and

(e) changes to the definition of the coliform parameter widening the range of organisms included in the parameter (see 3.35 below).

Any or all of these factors may result in an observed difference in the number or percentage of determinations showing contravention of the PCV for a particular parameter being largely a consequence of the changed sampling programme, rather than indicative of any underlying difference in water quality.

3.32 However, comparison between the three years of the number of zones showing non-compliance with the PCV for a particular parameter is rather less affected by the factors set out in the previous paragraph. Although the first of the factors may result in an increased number of determinations showing contravention of the PCV, the increased sampling frequency will only have been adopted because of an initial contravention and the zone will be non-compliant regardless of the number of contraventions. The second factor should apply only to those zones in which contravention is unlikely. The third factor may significantly influence a comparison - but only in respect of pesticides. The importance of the fourth factor is difficult to assess, but it is considered unlikely to have a significant effect on the comparison of zone compliance over the three years. Where the fifth factor is significant and companies have provided the necessary data, the extent of its impact is quantified in the individual company sections.

3.33 In the light of this consideration, this Report shows for each company the number of zones non-compliant for each of the tabulated parameters in each of the three years, 1995, 1994 and 1993, on the basis that this provides a reasonable illustration of any changes in water quality over those three years. However, it must still be borne in mind that zones in which only a single, trivial contravention of a PCV occurred will be included in the total number of non-compliant zones together with zones in which the contraventions were more extensive.

3.34 In order to focus attention on the extent to which water supply zones are compliant with the standards for water quality, this Report includes for each company, under the heading 'Overall water quality', a statement of:

(a)   the number of water supply zones which complied fully with the relevant water quality standards, had only trivial breaches of the standards, or had breaches which, while not trivial, were covered by an undertaking given by the company to the Secretary of State that work to deal with the breaches will be carried out; and

(b)   the number of water supply zones which had breaches which were neither trivial nor covered by undertakings.

Zones in the second category may be candidates for enforcement action, or it may be that the Inspectorate is already satisfied that, for some or all of them, remedial work has already been carried out or that the breaches are unlikely to recur. The commentary on water quality in water supply zones provides more detail.

Change to the definition of the coliform parameter

3.35 The term coliform refers to a group of bacteria sharing a limited number of properties and is not taxonomically precise. It has traditionally been defined by reference to the cultural methods used for its enumeration and this has presented an obstacle to the development of novel detection methods. A genetically-based definition was proposed in the "Guidance on Safeguarding the Quality of Drinking Water Supplies" which was published by the Department of the Environment and Welsh Office in 1989 and this definition was adopted in the Standing Committee of Analysts' publication "The Microbiology of Water 1994 - Part 1- Drinking Water". The Inspectorate regards this latter publication as the embodiment of best practice and consequently companies were required to enumerate and report the total coliform parameter using the new definition for 1995. Some companies had already been using the new definition prior to 1995. One consequence of the changed definition is that certain organisms which would not have been regarded as coliforms under the old definition are regarded as coliforms under the new definition. These organisms would be of no less sanitary significance than those which are coliforms by the original definition. The adoption of the new definition represents a tightening of the standard and could give rise to an apparent deterioration in compliance with the total coliform standard which was not representative of the actual quality of water supplied. In order to assess the impact of the change in definition on compliance with the standard in 1995, companies were given the opportunity of reporting results of analysis judged against the definition which applied prior to 1995 in addition to results judged against the definition now in use. Where the information was provided and showed an increase in contraventions of the standard attributable to the change in definition, the number of contraventions judged against the former definition is given in the text of the company section. It must be emphasised that only the new definition applies for the assessment of compliance with the Regulations in 1995.

Fig. 3.1 Water Service Companies of England and Wales
(general areas not showing water supply companies)

Fig. 3.2 Water Supply Companies of England and Wales

Area identification numbers
correspond with the company
section number in this Chapter

2	Bournemouth and West Hampshire Water Plc	14	North East Water Plc
3	Bristol Water Plc	15	North Surrey Water Limited
4	Cambridge Water Company	18	Portsmouth Water Plc
5	Chester Waterworks Company	20	South East Water Limited
6	Cholderton and District Water Company Limited	21	South Staffordshire Water Plc
8	East Surrey Water Plc	24	The Sutton District Water Plc
9	Essex and Suffolk Water Plc	25	Tendring Hundred Water Services Limited
10	Folkestone and Dover Water Services Limited	27	Three Valleys Water Plc
11	Hartlepool Water Plc	29	Wrexham Water Plc
12	Mid Kent Water plc	30	The York Waterworks Plc
13	Mid Southern Water Plc		

ANGLIAN WATER SERVICES LIMITED

Introduction

Anglian Water Services Limited supplies on average approximately 1,117 Ml/d to a resident population of 3.9 million. The area of supply covers East Anglia and Lincolnshire and parts of Essex, Bedfordshire, Buckinghamshire and Northamptonshire. Water is treated at 148 treatment works and is distributed via 392 service reservoirs and 33,000 Km of mains.

Overall water quality

At water treatment works and service reservoirs and in water supply zones, the Company carried out a total of 336,261 determinations in 1995. Of these, 99.8% demonstrated compliance with the relevant water quality standards, but 807 showed a PCV to have been contravened.

Coliforms were not detected at 139 (94%) of the Company's 148 water treatment works. At 391 (>99%) of the Company's 392 service reservoirs, coliforms were absent from at least 95% of samples. Of the Company's 206 water supply zones in 1995, 125 (61%) complied fully with the relevant water quality standards or had breaches of the standards which were either trivial or were fully covered by undertakings. In the other 81 (39%) of the zones, some breaches are regarded as unlikely to recur, but others could result in enforcement action.

Microbiological quality of water leaving treatment works

Table 3.1.1 shows the Company's performance in 1995, with data for 1994 and 1993 for comparison. Differences between the three years are not considered significant.

The Company complied with the sampling frequencies required by regulation 17 at 144 of its 148 treatment works in 1995. Shortfalls at the other four are regarded as trivial or unlikely to recur.

All contraventions of the standards at works are considered trivial.

Table 3.1.1   Anglian Water Services Limited
MICROBIOLOGICAL QUALITY OF WATER LEAVING TREATMENT WORKS

	1995	1994	1993
Number of water treatment works	148	157	150
Works with no sampling shortfall	144	156	150
COLIFORMS			
Total number of determinations	15,281	14,993	16,315
- number containing coliforms	11	15	10
- % containing coliforms	0.1	0.1	<0.1
Treatment works with coliforms detected	**9**	**13**	**10**
- % of all works	6	8	7
FAECAL COLIFORMS			
Total number of determinations	15,281	14,993	16,315
- number containing faecal coliforms	0	2	4
- % containing faecal coliforms	0.0	<0.1	<0.1
Treatment works with faecal coliforms detected	**0**	**2**	**4**
- % of all works	0	1	3

Microbiological quality of water in service reservoirs

Table 3.1.2 shows the Company's performance in 1995, with data for 1994 and 1993 for comparison. Differences between the three years are not considered significant.

The Company complied with the sampling frequencies required by regulation 18 at 390 of its 392 service reservoirs in 1995. Shortfalls at the other two are regarded as trivial or unlikely to recur.

Contraventions of the microbiological quality standards at one service reservoir has resulted in the consideration of enforcement action, as shown in table 3.1.4. All other contraventions of the standards at service reservoirs are considered trivial or unlikely to recur.

Table 3.1.2   Anglian Water Services Limited
MICROBIOLOGICAL QUALITY OF WATER IN SERVICE RESERVOIRS

	1995	1994	1993
Number of service reservoirs	392	389	398
Service reservoirs with no sampling shortfall	390	387	398
COLIFORMS			
Total number of determinations	20,400	21,192	21,074
- number containing coliforms	26	25	53
- % containing coliforms	0.1	0.1	0.3
Service reservoirs with coliforms detected	22	20	41
Service reservoirs with coliforms detected in more than 5% of samples	**1**	**0**	**3**
- % of all service reservoirs	<1	0	<1
FAECAL COLIFORMS			
Total number of determinations	20,400	21,213	21,074
- number containing faecal coliforms	6	6	13
- % containing faecal coliforms	<0.1	<0.1	<0.1
Service reservoirs with faecal coliforms detected	**5**	**5**	**11**
- % of all service reservoirs	1	1	3

Water quality in water supply zones

The Company failed to comply with the required sampling frequencies for some individual pesticides in 31 zones. The shortfalls are considered to be unlikely to recur.

Table 3.1.3 shows the Company's performance in 1995, with data for 1994 and 1993 for comparison. There has been a significant reduction over the three years in the number of zones contravening the standard for the individual pesticide atrazine, iron and nitrate. The apparent significant increase in the number of zones contravening the standard for the individual pesticide isoproturon is a consequence of detection at a supply point serving several zones and is not significant. All other differences between the three years are not considered significant.

Enforcement action is being considered in respect of some contraventions of standards, as shown in tables 3.1.3 and 3.1.4. All other contraventions of the standards in zones are considered trivial or unlikely to recur, or are covered by undertakings or will be covered by the new distribution undertaking.

Table 3.1.3 **Anglian Water Services Limited**
WATER QUALITY IN SUPPLY ZONES

*Columns 'CBU' show, for determinations, contraventions covered by undertakings and, for zones, the total number of zones covered by undertakings in 1995. Column 'E' shows the number of zones for which new enforcement action is under consideration as a result of contraventions of the PCV in 1995. **Please refer to the Introduction to Chapter 3 for more detailed explanation of this table.***

| Parameter | DETERMINATIONS in 1995 | | | | ZONES (206 in 1995)* | | | | |
| | Total | Contravening PCV | | | CBU | E | Non-compliant Number in: | | |
		No.	%	CBU	1995		1995	1994	1993
Coliforms	14,287	44	0.3	0	0	0	0	0	0
Faecal coliforms	14,287	11	<0.1	0	0	0	10	4	12
Colour	4,286	0	0.0	0	0	0	0	0	0
Turbidity	8,100	10	0.1	3	20	0	7	7	9
Odour	2,506	0	0.0	0	0	0	0	0	0
Taste	2,510	1	<0.1	0	0	0	1	0	0
Hydrogen ion	7,876	0	0.0	0	0	0	0	0	0
Nitrate	6,966	65	0.9	59	3	0	5	18	25
Nitrite	7,267	384	5.3	71	7	47	62	66	64
Aluminium	3,935	1	<0.1	0	0	0	1	0	1
Iron	8,479	124	1.5	90	79	0	56	75	95
Manganese	6,993	10	0.1	1	11	0	7	7	16
Lead	1,381	2	0.1	0	0	0	2	2	4
PAH	620	32	5.2	15	18	0	13	17	22
Trihalomethanes	1,230	0	0.0	0	0	0	0	0	5
Total pesticides	5,093	6	0.1	6	17	0	2	2	4
Atrazine	3,333	9	0.3	9	24	0	2	10	25
Chlorotoluron	2,508	5	0.2	4	24	0	3	1	1
Dimethoate	2,562	0	0	0	24	0	0	1	0
Diuron	2,508	0	0	0	24	0	0	2	0
Isoproturon	2,508	43	1.7	13	24	0	40	15	12
MCPB	3,015	0	0	0	24	0	0	1	0
Mecoprop	3,153	0	0	0	24	0	0	1	10
Simazine	3,333	14	0.4	12	24	0	4	2	10
Other pesticides	95,961	0	0.0	0	24	0	0	0	0
Potassium	961	0	0	0	0	0	0	0	2
Ammonium	6,613	2	<0.1	0	7	0	2	0	0
Copper	888	0	0	0	0	0	0	0	1
Phosphorus	6,412	0	0	0	0	0	0	0	5
Temperature	8,986	1	<0.1	0	0	0	1	0	0
Benzo 3,4 pyrene	619	0	0	0	0	0	0	0	2
All others	25,723	0	0.0	0	0	0	0	0	0
Total	**264,899**	**764**	**0.3**	**283**	-	-	-	-	-

* 209 zones in 1994; 214 zones in 1993.

Inspection

Mr W M Waite, Principal Inspector, assisted by Mr M Morgan and Dr K J White, Inspectors, carried out an inspection of Anglian Water Services Limited in a series of visits between 27 September and 31 October 1995. Mr Waite concluded that:

(a)   the general arrangements for sampling satisfied parts IV and V of the Regulations;

(b)   analytical arrangements were generally satisfactory;

(c)   the Company's arrangements for reporting compliance data were generally satisfactory;

(d)   the arrangements for dissemination of results and the information on the public record generally satisfied part VII of the Regulations;

(e)   the Company is on schedule to complete its compliance programmes by the due date;

(f)   the water treatment processes audited complied with regulation 23;

(g)   the Company's arrangements for distributing water are satisfactory;

(h)   the Company has a system of Quality Assurance which is assessed to ISO 9002 by BSi; and

(i)   the Company provides local authorities with the water quality reports required by regulations 30 and 31, but liaison between the company and local authorities could be improved.

Also in October, Mr K Bamford, representing consultants Rofe, Kennard and Lapworth, and working under the general direction of Mr Waite, carried out inspections of selected water treatment works and selected service reservoirs. He concluded that:

(j)   the treatment processes at the three works inspected complied with the requirements of regulation 23; and

(k)   the sampling facilities at the two service reservoirs inspected were satisfactory.

As a result of these inspections 14 recommendations were conveyed to the Company for formal response. 38 suggestions on various matters were also made. The Company has already taken action on most of these recommendations, and is taking action on others. It has also taken action on a number of suggestions.

Improvement programmes

17 undertakings in respect of improvement programmes accepted by the Secretary of State from the Company were due for full completion or the completion of major steps during 1995 and all of these were completed on schedule. A new undertaking given by the Company to carry out improvement works to its distribution system, with a completion date of 31 March 2000, is being considered by the Secretary of State.

Incidents

Three events notified during 1995 by the Company to the Secretary of State under the terms of the Water Undertakers (Information) Direction 1992 are regarded by the Inspectorate as constituting incidents in which drinking water quality demonstrably deteriorated.

One involved the discolouration of supplies to three villages near Felixstowe, as a result of disturbance of deposits in the mains caused by high water demand from consumers. Some of the deposits had been introduced into the system in the past from a water treatment works which was permanently closed 12 years ago. Other deposits were the result of corrosion of the mains in the area. Since the incident the Company has cleaned the trunk main serving the villages, and is replacing the smaller, corroded mains. The mains replacement work is due for completion in October 1996.

A second incident involved the supply of water with an abnormal taste and odour to 220,000 consumers in the Northampton and Daventry area. The incident was caused by a water treatment works being unable to remove exceptionally high levels of naturally occurring taste and odour in the raw water. Since the incident the Company has completed major improvements to treatment at the works, including treatment which should remove naturally occurring taste and odour.

The third incident involved the contamination of a water tower with faecal coliforms. The Company has removed the tower from service and will complete repairs before the tower is returned to service.

Enforcement action

Table 3.1.4 summarises enforcement action under consideration for the Company as a result of the Inspectorate's work in, or pertaining to, the calendar year 1995.

Table 3.1.4	Anglian Water Services Limited **SUMMARY OF ENFORCEMENT ACTION CONSIDERED IN 1995**
Regulation	**Reason for enforcement**
3(3)(c)	Contravention of the standard for nitrite in 47 zones.
3(7)	Contraventions of the standard for faecal coliforms at one service reservoir. (The reservoir has since been taken out of service and assurances given that it will not be returned to service until repairs have been completed)
30(5)	Delay in notifying the relevant local and district health authorities of an incident. (Assurances have been given that procedures have been amended to ensure prompt notification)
Information Direction	
5(1)(b)(ii)	Failure to notify the Inspectorate of significant local publicity associated with an incident. (Assurances have been given that procedures have been amended to ensure notification)
5(2)(a)	Delay in notifying the Inspectorate of an incident. (Assurances have been given that procedures have been amended to ensure prompt notification)

BOURNEMOUTH AND WEST HAMPSHIRE WATER PLC

Introduction

The Company was formed by the merger of Bournemouth Water Plc and West Hampshire Water Plc on 1 July 1994. Bournemouth and West Hampshire Water Plc supplies on average 170 Ml/d to a resident population of about 400,000 consumers in parts of Dorset, Hampshire and Wiltshire. The volume supplied increases substantially during the summer months with the influx of visitors to the area. Almost four fifths of the Company's water supplies come from the Rivers Stour and Avon. The rest comes from boreholes. The Company has nine treatment works on six sites. There are three treatment streams at one site, and two at another. Water is distributed through a network of 2,800 km of pipes and 22 service reservoirs.

Overall water quality

At water treatment works and service reservoirs and in water supply zones, the Company carried out a total of 21,285 determinations in 1995. Of these, 99.7% demonstrated compliance with the relevant water quality standards, but 73 showed a PCV to have been contravened.

Coliforms were not detected at six (67%) of the Company's nine water treatment works. At 20 (91%) of the Company's 22 service reservoirs, coliforms were absent from at least 95% of samples. Of the Company's 15 water supply zones in 1995, 11 (73%) complied fully with the relevant water quality standards or had breaches of the standards which were fully covered by undertakings. In the other four (27%) of the zones, the breaches are regarded as unlikely to recur.

Microbiological quality of water leaving treatment works

Table 3.2.1 shows the Company's performance in 1995, with data for 1994 and 1993 for comparison. The data presented for 1993 represents combined data for the two predecessor companies. The decrease in 1995 in the number of works with coliforms detected is notable but the number is still higher than that in 1993. Had the definition of the coliform parameter not been changed as described in 3.35 above, but remained as it was for 1994 and previous years, the number of determinations containing coliforms would have been four.

Table 3.2.1 Bournemouth and West Hampshire Water Plc
MICROBIOLOGICAL QUALITY OF WATER LEAVING TREATMENT WORKS

	1995	1994	1993[a]
Number of water treatment works	9	6	6
Works with no sampling shortfall	7	5	6
COLIFORMS			
Total number of determinations	2,293	1,857	2,266
- number containing coliforms	6	7	1
- % containing coliforms	0.3	0.4	<0.1
Treatment works with coliforms detected	**3**	**5**	**1**
- % of all works	33	83	17
FAECAL COLIFORMS			
Total number of determinations	2,293	1,857	2,226
- number containing faecal coliforms	1	1	0
- % containing faecal coliforms	<0.1	<0.1	0.0
Treatment works with faecal coliforms detected	**1**	**1**	**0**
- % of all works	11	17	0

[a] Numbers in this column represent combined data for the predecessor companies.

The Company complied with the sampling frequencies required by regulation 17 at seven of its nine treatment works in 1995. Shortfalls at the other two works are regarded as unlikely to recur.

Contraventions of the microbiological quality standards at one works would have resulted in the consideration of enforcement action if it had not already been initiated as a result of a water quality incident, as shown in table 3.2.4. All other contraventions of the standards at works are considered trivial or unlikely to recur.

Microbiological quality of water in service reservoirs

Table 3.2.2 shows the Company's performance in 1995, with data for 1994 and combined data for the two predecessor companies for 1993 for comparison. Differences between the three years are not considered significant. Had the definition of the coliform parameter not been changed as described in 3.35 above, but remained as it was for 1994 and previous years, the number of determinations containing coliforms would have been 10.

Table 3.2.2	Bournemouth and West Hampshire Water Plc MICROBIOLOGICAL QUALITY OF WATER IN SERVICE RESERVOIRS		
	1995	**1994**	**1993[a]**
Number of service reservoirs	22	27	22
Service reservoirs with no sampling shortfall	19	16	22
COLIFORMS			
Total number of determinations	1,140	1,521	1,162
- number containing coliforms	11	6	14
- % containing coliforms	1.0	0.4	1.2
Service reservoirs with coliforms detected	6	4	10
Service reservoirs with coliforms detected in more than 5% of samples	**2**	**1**	**0**
- % of all service reservoirs	9	4	0
FAECAL COLIFORMS			
Total number of determinations	1,140	1,521	1,162
- number containing faecal coliforms	1	2	4
- % containing faecal coliforms	0.1	0.1	0.3
Service reservoirs with faecal coliforms detected	**1**	**2**	**4**
- % of all service reservoirs	5	7	18

[a] Numbers in this column represent combined data for the predecessor companies.

The Company complied with the sampling frequencies required by regulation 18 at 19 of its 22 service reservoirs in 1995. Shortfalls at the other three are regarded as trivial or are unlikely to recur.

Contraventions of the microbiological quality standards at a total of two service reservoirs would have resulted in the consideration of enforcement action if it had not already been initiated as a result of a water quality incident, as shown in table 3.2.4.

Water quality in water supply zones

The Company complied with the required sampling frequencies for all parameters in all zones.

Table 3.2.3 shows the Company's performance in 1995, with data for 1994 and combined data for the two predecessor companies for 1993 for comparison. There has been a significant increase in the number of zones failing the nitrite standard in 1995. All other differences between the three years are not considered significant. Had the definition of the coliform parameter not been changed as described in 3.35 above, but remained as it was for 1994 and previous years, no zones would have contravened the PCV for coliforms and the number of determinations containing coliforms would have been 17.

Table 3.2.3 Bournemouth and West Hampshire Water Plc
WATER QUALITY IN SUPPLY ZONES

Columns 'CBU' show, for determinations, contraventions covered by undertakings and, for zones, the total number of zones covered by undertakings in 1995. Column 'E' shows the number of zones for which new enforcement action is under consideration as a result of contraventions of the PCV in 1995. **Please refer to the Introduction to Chapter 3 for more detailed explanation of this table.**

| Parameter | DETERMINATIONS in 1995 | | | | ZONES (15 in 1995)* | | | | |
| | Total | Contravening PCV | | | CBU | E | Non-compliant Number[a] in: | | |
		No.	%	CBU	1995		1995	1994	1993
Coliforms	1,335	20	1.5	0	0	0	1	0	0
Faecal coliforms	1,350	1	0.1	0	0	0	1	3	5
Colour	197	0	0.0	0	0	0	0	0	2
Turbidity	197	0	0.0	0	0	0	0	0	0
Odour	195	0	0.0	0	0	0	0	1	0
Taste	195	0	0.0	0	0	0	0	0	0
Hydrogen ion	197	0	0.0	0	0	0	0	0	0
Nitrate	195	0	0.0	0	0	0	0	0	0
Nitrite	195	6	3.1	0	0	0	4	0	0
Aluminium	195	0	0	0	0	0	0	0	0
Iron	227	5	2.2	0	0	0	2	0	0
Manganese	195	0	0.0	0	0	0	0	0	0
Lead	60	0	0.0	0	0	0	0	0	0
PAH	98	7	7.1	3	1	0	4	2	1
Trihalomethanes	200	0	0.0	0	0	0	0	4	0
Total pesticides	60	0	0.0	0	0	0	0	0	0
Atrazine	236	10	4.2	10	10	0	10	2	9
Isoproturon	161	0	0.0	0	10	0	0	5	0
Propyzamide	61	1	1.6	1	10	0	1	0	0
Other pesticides	5,610	0	0.0	0	10	0	0	0	0
Benzo 3,4 pyrene	98	4	4.1	0	0	0	0	0	0
All others	3,162	0	0.0	0	0	0	0	0	0
Total	**14,419**	**54**	**0.4**	**14**	-	-	-	-	-

* 15 zones in 1994; 15 zones in 1993.
[a] Numbers in the 1993 column represent combined data for the predecessor companies.

The Company has taken action to prevent further contraventions of the nitrite standard and enforcement action is not required. Enforcement action would have been considered in respect of one contravention of the standards for microbiological parameters if enforcement action had not already been initiated in respect of similar contraventions at the water treatment works supplying the zone following a water quality incident. All other contraventions of the standards in zones are covered by undertakings.

Inspection

Mr W M Waite, Principal Inspector, assisted by Mr M Morgan, Inspector, carried out an inspection of Bournemouth and West Hampshire Water Plc in a series of visits between 27 July and 2 November 1995. On the basis of their findings and observations during the inspection, they concluded that:

(a) the Company had taken appropriate and satisfactory measures to implement most of the recommendations made in the 1994 technical audit inspection reports;

(b) the general arrangements for sampling satisfied parts IV and V of the Regulations, but failures to adhere to the sampling programme resulted in contraventions of regulations 13(10)(b) and 18 (see below);

(c) analytical arrangements were generally satisfactory although there were deficiencies in the arrangements for sample storage prior to transfer to the laboratory;

(d) the Company's arrangements for reporting compliance data were generally satisfactory but improvements could be made in the procedures for handling data;

(e) the arrangements for dissemination of results and the information on the public record generally satisfied part VII of the Regulations except for the absence of some records in contravention of regulation 29 (see below);

(f) the Company was behind schedule with its compliance programmes for pesticide removal, but is able to complete the required works by the due date;

(g) the water treatment processes audited complied with regulation 23;

(h) the Company's arrangements for maintaining the service reservoirs inspected were unsatisfactory;

(i) the Company is currently assessing the effectiveness of its implementation of its policy of turning water over regularly in service reservoirs;

(j) the Company has not yet completed writing its procedures for dealing with incidents and emergencies but a draft has been shown to the Inspectorate;

(k) the Company has a system of Quality Assurance which is assessed to ISO 9001 by BSi, but its internal audits could be more focussed and reporting improved; and

(l) the Company provides local authorities with the water quality reports required by regulations 30 and 31, but liaison between the company and local authorities could be improved.

The Inspectors made 43 recommendations to the Company in the light of the inspection, together with 67 suggestions for the Company to consider.

The Company has already taken action on a number of these recommendations and suggestions, including action to deal with the observed contraventions of regulations 13(10)(b), 18 and 29, and enforcement action is not required.

Improvement programmes

None of the undertakings in respect of improvement programmes accepted by the Secretary of State from the Company were due for full completion or the completion of major steps during 1995. A new undertaking given by the Company to carry out improvement works to its distribution system, with a completion date of 31 March 2000, has been accepted by the Secretary of State.

Incidents

One event notified during 1995 by the Company to the Secretary of State under the terms of the Water Undertakers (Information) Direction 1992 is regarded by the Inspectorate as constituting an incident in which drinking water quality demonstrably deteriorated.

The incident involved the microbiological contamination of water leaving one treatment works and two service reservoirs, and supplied to consumers in one supply zone. Enforcement action was initiated in respect of the contraventions at the treatment works and service reservoirs.

No other events regarded as constituting incidents came to the attention of the Inspectorate in 1995.

Enforcement action

Table 3.2.4 summarises enforcement action under consideration for the Company as a result of the Inspectorate's work in, or pertaining to, the calendar year 1995.

Table 3.2.4	Bournemouth and West Hampshire Water Plc SUMMARY OF ENFORCEMENT ACTION CONSIDERED IN 1995
Regulation	**Reason for enforcement**
3(7)	Contraventions of the standards for microbiological parameters at one water treatment works and two service reservoirs as a result of an incident affecting one zone, probably caused by a leaking service reservoir although the condition of another service reservoir and inadequacies in disinfection at one water treatment works may also be implicated. Enforcement action would have been initiated in respect of contraventions of microbiological parameters at the treatment works, both service reservoirs and in one zone supplied from the treatment works as a result of the compliance assessment if it had not already been initiated as a result of the incident. Undertakings have subsequently been accepted.

BRISTOL WATER PLC

Introduction

The Company supplies on average approximately 325 Ml/d to a population of 1,035,000 in the city of Bristol, parts of Somerset and small areas of Gloucestershire and Wiltshire. The Company's water resources consist of:

(a) springs and surface water from impounding reservoirs in the Mendips (between 25% and 45% of supply, depending on available storage in the impounding reservoirs);

(b) surface water abstracted from the River Severn via the Gloucester and Sharpness Canal (up to 60% of supply); and

(c) groundwater sources from springs, wells and boreholes (about 25% of supply).

The water is treated at 24 treatment works and distributed via 182 service reservoirs and through approximately 6,200 km of water mains. The supply area is divided into 52 water supply zones.

Overall water quality

At water treatment works and service reservoirs and in water supply zones, the Company carried out a total of 53,909 determinations in 1995. Of these, 99.8% demonstrated compliance with the relevant water quality standards, but 120 showed a PCV to have been contravened.

Coliforms were not detected at 19(79%) of the Company's 24 water treatment works. At all of the Company's 182 service reservoirs, coliforms were absent from at least 95% of samples. All of the Company's 52 water supply zones in 1995 complied fully with the relevant water quality standards or had breaches of the standards which were either trivial or were covered by undertakings or will be covered by the new distribution undertaking.

Microbiological quality of water leaving treatment works

Table 3.3.1 shows the Company's performance in 1995, with data for 1994 and 1993 for comparison. Differences between the three years are not considered significant.

Table 3.3.1	Bristol Water Plc MICROBIOLOGICAL QUALITY OF WATER LEAVING TREATMENT WORKS		
	1995	**1994**	**1993**
Number of water treatment works	24	26	26
Works with no sampling shortfall	24	26	26
COLIFORMS			
Total number of determinations	4,162	4,550	4,721
- number containing coliforms	6	6	5
- % containing coliforms	0.1	0.1	0.1
Treatment works with coliforms detected	**5**	**2**	**4**
- % of all works	21	8	15
FAECAL COLIFORMS			
Total number of determinations	4,162	4,550	4,721
- number containing faecal coliforms	0	1	1
- % containing faecal coliforms	0	<0.1	<0.1
Treatment works with faecal coliforms detected	**0**	**1**	**1**
- % of all works	0	4	4

The Company complied with the sampling frequencies required by regulation 17 at all of its treatment works in 1995.

All contraventions of the microbiological quality standards at works are considered trivial or unlikely to recur.

Microbiological quality of water in service reservoirs

Table 3.3.2 shows the Company's performance in 1995, with data for 1994 and 1993 for comparison. Differences between the three years are not considered significant.

Table 3.3.2 Bristol Water Plc
MICROBIOLOGICAL QUALITY OF WATER IN SERVICE RESERVOIRS

	1995	1994	1993
Number of service reservoirs	182	186	182
Service reservoirs with no sampling shortfall	177	186	182
COLIFORMS			
Total number of determinations	8,998	9,194	8,896
- number containing coliforms	20	14	27
- % containing coliforms	0.2	0.2	0.3
Service reservoirs with coliforms detected	19	11	19
Service reservoirs with coliforms detected in more than 5% of samples	**0**	**1**	**1**
- % of all service reservoirs	0	<1	<1
FAECAL COLIFORMS			
Total number of determinations	8,998	9,194	8,896
- number containing faecal coliforms	4	0	2
- % containing faecal coliforms	<0.1	0.0	<0.1
Service reservoirs with faecal coliforms detected	**4**	**0**	**2**
- % of all service reservoirs	2	0	1

The Company complied with the sampling frequencies required by regulation 18 at 177 of its 182 service reservoirs in 1995. Shortfalls at the other five reservoirs are regarded as trivial.

There were no contraventions of the total coliform standard at any of the Company's service reservoirs. The single contraventions of the faecal coliform standard at four reservoirs have been regarded as trivial.

Water quality in water supply zones

The Company failed to comply with the required sampling frequencies for selenium in one zone and sulphate in one zone but these contraventions of regulation 13 are considered unlikely to recur.

Table 3.3.3 shows the Company's performance in 1995, with data for 1994 and 1993 for comparison.

Contraventions of the PAH standard in seven zones are not trivial. These zones are to be included in the new distribution undertaking. All other contraventions of the standards in zones are considered trivial or are covered by undertakings.

Table 3.3.3   **Bristol Water Plc**
WATER QUALITY IN SUPPLY ZONES

Columns 'CBU' show, for determinations, contraventions covered by undertakings and, for zones, the <u>total</u> number of zones covered by undertakings in 1995. Column 'E' shows the number of zones for which new enforcement action is under consideration as a result of contraventions of the PCV in 1995. **Please refer to the Introduction to Chapter 3 for more detailed explanation of this table.**

Parameter	DETERMINATIONS in 1995				ZONES (52 in 1995)*				
	Total	Contravening PCV					Non-compliant		
		No.	%	CBU	CBU	E	Number in:		
					1995		1995	1994	1993
Coliforms	3,095	12	0.4	0	0	0	0	0	0
Faecal coliforms	3,095	0	0.0	0	0	0	0	1	1
Colour	441	0	0.0	0	0	0	0	0	0
Turbidity	612	0	0.0	0	0	0	0	0	0
Odour	444	0	0.0	0	0	0	0	0	0
Taste	440	0	0.0	0	0	0	0	0	0
Hydrogen ion	553	0	0.0	0	0	0	0	0	0
Nitrate	1,088	0	0.0	0	0	0	0	0	1
Nitrite	897	52	5.8	52	21	0	16	13	27
Aluminium	474	0	0.0	0	17	0	0	1	3
Iron	634	1	0.2	1	52	0	1	1	9
Manganese	627	0	0.0	0	0	0	0	0	0
Lead	369	5	1.4	0	0	0	5	9	10
PAH	322	17	5.3	0	0	0	8	9	7
Trihalomethanes	239	0	0.0	0	0	0	0	1	0
Total pesticides	504	0	0.0	0	52	0	0	0	4
Diuron	118	2	1.7	2	52	0	1	0	0
Isoproturon	118	1	0.9	1	52	0	1	1	1
Mecoprop	122	0	0.0	0	52	0	0	1	4
Other pesticides	2,389	0	0.0	0	52	0	0	0	0
Benzo 3,4 pyrene	320	0	0.0	0	0	0	0	1	1
All others	10,688	0	0.0	0	0	0	0	0	0
Total	**27,589**	**90**	**0.3**	**70**	-	-	-	-	-

* 52 zones in 1994; 56 zones in 1993.

Inspection

Dr J Gray, Principal Inspector, assisted by Miss C Y Hill, Inspector, carried out an inspection of Bristol Water Plc in a series of visits between September and November 1995. Dr Gray concluded that:

(a)   appropriate and satisfactory measures have been taken or are being taken to implement the recommendations made in the 1994 technical audit inspection report;

(b)   the arrangements for sampling as audited generally satisfied parts IV and V of the Regulations and accorded with the recommendations of the Guidance Document;

(c)   the requirements of regulation 21(2)(d)(iii) were generally satisfactory in the laboratories where analysis was carried by the Company;

(d)   the Company is aware of the contents of the most recent issue of Report 71 and, in general, action has been taken or is being taken to implement changes to its procedures where appropriate;

(e) the Company's arrangements for reporting compliance data were generally satisfactory and secure although some areas need attention;

(f) the arrangements for the dissemination of water quality data within the Company and to members of the public were generally satisfactory, and the public record satisfied the requirements of regulations 29 and 30, although some areas need attention;

(g) from the information provided, the Company is generally maintaining progress with the compliance programmes examined; and

(h) the Company has taken action or is taking action in respect of recommendations arising from the assessment by the Inspectorate of water quality incidents.

Also, in October, Mr R M Walls, representing consultants Rofe, Kennard and Lapworth and working under the general direction of Dr Gray, carried out inspection of selected water treatment works and selected service reservoirs. He concluded that:

(i) the treatment processes at Barrow and Chelvey water treatment works complied with Regulation 23;

(j) the use of substances and products satisfied the requirements of Regulation 25;

(k) the Company's policy and arrangements for disinfection at Barrow and Chelvey treatment works were satisfactory; and

(l) the Company's arrangements for compliance sampling at Barrow and Chelvey treatment works are generally in accordance with the recommendations of paragraph 2.8 of the Guidance Document and with the requirements of Regulation 21(2)(a); however, there were some deficiencies with the compliance sampling arrangements at Shirehampton and Westbury Pilot service reservoirs.

As a result of these inspections, 13 recommendations were conveyed to the Company for formal response nearly half of which concerned arrangements for water treatment and water distribution. Thirty-nine suggestions on various matters were also made.

Improvement programmes

Six undertakings in respect of improvement programmes accepted by the Secretary of State from the Company was due for full completion during 1995. All six were completed on schedule. A new undertaking given by the Company to carry out improvement works to its distribution system, with a completion date of 31 March 2000, is being considered by the Secretary of State.

Incidents

One event notified during 1995 by the Company to the Secretary of State under the terms of the Water Undertakers (Information) Direction 1992 was regarded by the Inspectorate as constituting an incident in which drinking water quality demonstrably deteriorated. The water supply to a number of properties in the village of Lamyatt became contaminated with microorganisms as a result of backsiphonage via an illegal cross-connection between a private spring supply and the mains supply to a farm in the area. The Inspectorate considered that the Company took prompt action to protect the consumers by issuing advice to boil water and took steps to restore supplies to normal as quickly as possible. However, it was critical of the Company over its failure to carry out a byelaws inspection at the farm following an earlier indication of a problem with the property's supply pipework.

No other events regarded as constituting incidents in which drinking water quality demonstrably deteriorated came to the attention of the Inspectorate in 1995.

Enforcement action

No enforcement action is under consideration for the Company as a result of the technical audit in 1995.

CAMBRIDGE WATER COMPANY

Introduction

The Company supplies on average approximately 74 Ml/d to a population of some 281,000 in the City of Cambridge and surrounding areas. The Company's water resources consist of 26 groundwater sources, of which 23 are deep chalk boreholes (about 97.2% of supply), two are from greensand aquifers (about 2.1% of supply) and one is from river gravels (about 0.7% of supply). These sources are treated at 25 treatment works. The treated water is distributed by pumping and gravity through 36 service reservoirs and some 2,104 km of water mains. The supply area is divided into 14 water supply zones.

Overall water quality

At water treatment works and service reservoirs and in water supply zones, the Company carried out a total of 14,403 determinations in 1995. Of these, 99.8% demonstrated compliance with the relevant water quality standards, but 30 showed a PCV to have been contravened.

Coliforms were not detected at 19 (76%) of the Company's 25 water treatment works. Coliforms were absent from all samples taken at the Company's 36 service reservoirs. Of the Company's 14 water supply zones in 1995, 10 (71%) complied fully with the relevant water quality standards or had breaches of the standards which were either trivial or will be covered by the new distribution undertaking. In the other four zones (29%) breaches are unlikely to recur.

Microbiological quality of water leaving treatment works

Table 3.4.1 shows the Company's performance in 1995, with data for 1994 and 1993 for comparison. There has been a significant increase in the number of water treatment works with coliforms detected over the three years.

Table 3.4.1 Cambridge Water Company MICROBIOLOGICAL QUALITY OF WATER LEAVING TREATMENT WORKS			
	1995	**1994**	**1993**
Number of water treatment works	25	26	26
Works with no sampling shortfall	25	26	26
COLIFORMS			
Total number of determinations	1,782	1,908	2,165
- number containing coliforms	9	6	1
- % containing coliforms	0.5	0.3	<0.1
Treatment works with coliforms detected	**6**	**4**	**1**
- % of all works	24	15	4
FAECAL COLIFORMS			
Total number of determinations	1,782	1,908	2,165
- number containing faecal coliforms	0	0	1
- % containing faecal coliforms	0.0	0.0	<0.1
Treatment works with faecal coliforms detected	**0**	**0**	**1**
- % of all works	0	0	4

The Company complied with the sampling frequencies required by regulation 17 at all its treatment works in 1995.

The Company has identified the probable cause of the contraventions of the standard for total coliforms at three water treatment works and remedial action has been taken. The Inspectorate will assess the results of further monitoring for the first six months of

1996 to confirm that this action has been effective and that the contraventions are unlikely to recur. All other contraventions of the standards at works are considered trivial.

Microbiological quality of water in service reservoirs

Table 3.4.2 shows the Company's performance in 1995, with data for 1994 and 1993 for comparison. Differences between the three years are not considered significant.

Table 3.4.2 Cambridge Water Company
MICROBIOLOGICAL QUALITY OF WATER IN SERVICE RESERVOIRS

	1995	1994	1993
Number of service reservoirs	36	36	34
Service reservoirs with no sampling shortfall	36	35	34
COLIFORMS			
Total number of determinations	1,871	1,867	1,754
- number containing coliforms	0	2	1
- % containing coliforms	0.0	0.1	<0.1
Service reservoirs with coliforms detected	0	2	1
Service reservoirs with coliforms detected in more than 5% of samples	**0**	**0**	**0**
- % of all service reservoirs	0	0	0
FAECAL COLIFORMS			
Total number of determinations	1,871	1,867	1,754
- number containing faecal coliforms	0	0	0
- % containing faecal coliforms	0.0	0.0	0.0
Service reservoirs with faecal coliforms detected	**0**	**0**	**0**
- % of all service reservoirs	0	0	0

The Company complied with the sampling frequencies required by regulation 18 at all its service reservoirs in 1995. There were no contraventions of the microbiological standards at any of the Company's service reservoirs in 1995.

Water quality in water supply zones

The Company complied fully with the required sampling frequencies in all zones.

Table 3.4.3 shows the Company's performance in 1995, with data for 1994 and 1993 for comparison. Differences between the three years are not considered significant.

The contraventions of the standard for nitrite in one zone are not trivial but the Company has taken remedial action to prevent a recurrence. The Inspectorate will assess the results of further monitoring during the first six months of 1996 before deciding on the need for enforcement action. All other contraventions of the standards in zones are considered trivial or are included in the Company's new distribution undertaking.

The substance TCA was found at concentrations above the standard for individual pesticides in one or more samples taken in nine zones. The Company has demonstrated that the TCA is present in one zone as a disinfection by-product and not as the result of pesticide usage. The occurrence of TCA in the other eight zones is under investigation.

Table 3.4.3　Cambridge Water Company
WATER QUALITY IN SUPPLY ZONES

*Columns 'CBU' show, for determinations, contraventions covered by undertakings and, for zones, the <u>total</u> number of zones covered by undertakings in 1995. Column 'E' shows the number of zones for which new enforcement action is under consideration as a result of contraventions of the PCV in 1995. **Please refer to the Introduction to Chapter 3 for more detailed explanation of this table.**

Parameter	DETERMINATIONS in 1995				ZONES (14 in 1995)*				
	Total	Contravening PCV			CBU	E	Non-compliant Number in:		
		No.	%	CBU	1995	1995	1995	1994	1993
Coliforms	872	4	0.5	0	0	0	0	0	0
Faecal coliforms	872	0	0.0	0	0	0	0	0	1
Colour	87	0	0.0	0	0	0	0	0	0
Turbidity	81	0	0.0	0	0	0	0	0	0
Odour	107	0	0.0	0	0	0	0	0	0
Taste	107	0	0.0	0	0	0	0	0	0
Hydrogen ion	97	0	0.0	0	0	0	0	0	0
Nitrate	155	0	0.0	0	0	0	0	0	0
Nitrite	186	2	1.1	0	1	0	1	2	1
Aluminium	94	0	0.0	0	0	0	0	0	0
Iron	227	0	0.0	0	1	0	0	1	1
Manganese	100	0	0.0	0	0	0	0	0	0
Lead	96	0	0.0	0	3	0	0	0	1
PAH	68	3	4.4	0	0	0	3	2	1
Trihalomethanes	26	0	0.0	0	0	0	0	0	0
Total pesticides	333	0	0.0	0	0	0	0	0	0
Chlortoluron	64	0	0.0	0	0	0	0	0	1
Isoproturon	76	0	0.0	0	0	0	0	0	1
Propham	78	0	0.0	0	0	0	0	0	1
TCA	181	11	6.1	0	0	0	8	1	0
Other pesticides	1,594	0	0.0	0	0	0	0	0	0
Hydrocarbons	67	1	1.5	0	0	0	1	0	4
All others	1,529	0	0.0	0	0	0	0	0	0
Total	**7,097**	**21**	**0.3**	**0**	**-**	**-**	**-**	**-**	**-**

* 14 zones in 1994; 13 zones in 1993.

Inspection

Miss C Jackson, Inspector, carried out an inspection of Cambridge Water Company in September 1995. Miss Jackson concluded that:

(a)　the Company had taken appropriate and satisfactory measures to implement the four recommendations made in the 1994 technical audit inspection report;

(b)　the Company's method of defining water supply zones met the requirements of the Regulations and accorded with the recommendations given the Guidance Document;

(c)　the general arrangements for sampling satisfied parts IV and V of the Regulations and accorded with the recommendations of the Guidance Document, although some deficiencies were identified in the sample transport arrangements;

(d)   the Company's contractual arrangements for analytical services were satisfactory and the contracts well managed; however, potential problems were identified with some of the analyses further subcontracted;

(e)   the Company was on target to meet the key stages of its compliance programme by the due dates, although the timescale was tight;

(f)   the Company's procedures for disinfection of the water supply, as audited, were generally satisfactory;

(g)   the Company's operational procedures to ensure adequate turn over of water in its service reservoirs were satisfactory;

(h)   the Company had systems in place for seeking advice in the event of a radioactive release into the environment; and

(j)   the Company's procedures arrangements for communications and liaison with the local authorities in its area of supply were satisfactory.

As a result of this inspection, seven recommendations were conveyed to the Company for formal response. Twelve suggestions on various matters were also made. The Company is taking action or has already taken action on a number of the recommendations.

Improvement programmes

Two undertakings in respect of improvement programmes accepted by the Secretary of State from the Company were due for full completion during 1995. Both of these were completed on schedule. A new undertaking given by the Company to carry out improvement works to its distribution system, with a completion date of 31 March 2000, has been accepted by the Secretary of State.

Incidents

One event notified during 1995 by the Company to the Secretary of State under the terms of the Water Undertakers (Information) Direction 1992 is regarded by the Inspectorate as constituting an incident in which drinking water quality demonstrably deteriorated.

Bacteriological contamination occurred within a private water storage and distribution system supplied by the Company and which was also used to supply water to a small number of the Company's consumers. This incident remains under consideration by the Inspectorate.

No other events regarded as constituting incidents came to the attention of the Inspectorate in 1995.

Enforcement action

No enforcement action needed to be considered for the Company as a result of the Inspectorate's work in, or pertaining to, the calendar year 1995.

CHESTER WATERWORKS COMPANY

Introduction

The Company supplies on average approximately 29 Ml/d of water to a population of some 107,100 in an area centred on the City of Chester and including a small part of Wales. The Company's water resources consist almost entirely of surface water abstracted from the River Dee (95%) with one groundwater source supplying the remainder. The Company also imports treated water from Dŵr Cymru to supply about 170 people in the Old Warren area.

Each source has its own treatment works. Treated water is distributed via three service reservoirs and 563 km of mains. During 1995, the supply area was divided into six water supply zones.

Overall water quality

At water treatment works and service reservoirs and in water supply zones, the Company carried out a total of 5,160 determinations in 1995. All these demonstrated compliance with the relevant water quality standards.

Coliforms were not detected at the Company's two water treatment works and at the Company's three service reservoirs. All the Company's six water supply zones in 1995 complied fully with the relevant water quality standards.

Microbiological quality of water leaving treatment works

Table 3.5.1 shows the Company's performance in 1995, with data for 1994 and 1993 for comparison. There has been full compliance with the relevant regulations in all three years.

**Table 3.5.1   Chester Waterworks Company
MICROBIOLOGICAL QUALITY OF WATER LEAVING TREATMENT WORKS**

	1995	1994	1993
Number of water treatment works	2	2	2
Works with no sampling shortfall	2	2	2
COLIFORMS			
Total number of determinations	469	469	469
- number containing coliforms	0	0	0
- % containing coliforms	0.0	0.0	0.0
Treatment works with coliforms detected	**0**	**0**	**0**
FAECAL COLIFORMS			
Total number of determinations	469	469	469
- number containing faecal coliforms	0	0	0
- % containing faecal coliforms	0.0	0.0	0.0
Treatment works with faecal coliforms detected	**0**	**0**	**0**

Microbiological quality of water in service reservoirs

Table 3.5.2 shows the Company's performance in 1995, with data for 1994 and 1993 for comparison. There has been full compliance with the relevant regulations in all three years.

Table 3.5.2   Chester Waterworks Company
MICROBIOLOGICAL QUALITY OF WATER IN SERVICE RESERVOIRS

	1995	1994	1993
Number of service reservoirs	3	3	3
Service reservoirs with no sampling shortfall	3	3	3
COLIFORMS			
Total number of determinations	154	156	156
- number containing coliforms	0	0	2
- % containing coliforms	0.0	0.0	1.3
Service reservoirs with coliforms detected	0	0	2
Service reservoirs with coliforms detected in more than 5% of samples	**0**	**0**	**0**
FAECAL COLIFORMS			
Total number of determinations	154	156	156
- number containing faecal coliforms	0	0	0
- % containing faecal coliforms	0.0	0.0	0.0
Service reservoirs with faecal coliforms detected	**0**	**0**	**0**

Water quality in water supply zones

The Company complied with the required sampling frequencies for all parameters in all its zones.

Table 3.5.3 shows the Company's performance in 1995, with data for 1994 and 1993 for comparison. The small differences between the three years are not considered significant.

Inspection

Dr P K Marsden, Inspector, carried out an inspection of Chester Waterworks Company in November 1995. Dr Marsden concluded that:

(a)   the Company had implemented or was about to implement all of the recommendations of the 1994 inspection and had made a very positive response to the suggestions;

(b)   the Company's analytical procedures were not inspected in detail but one recommendation was necessary in respect of unsatisfactory performance testing of two methods;

(c)   the Company is generally maintaining adequate records allowing full audit trails of compliance results to be carried out;

(d)   the operation of Plemstall treatment works was generally satisfactory but one recommendation was made in respect of security of disinfection;

(e)   the Company's records of action taken in respect of water quality alarms were inadequate to allow full audit trails to be completed;

(f)   the Company is aware of the advice in the Department's Green Book and is strengthening aspects of its emergency procedures; and

(g)   the Company is committed to a total quality management approach.

As a result of this inspection, two recommendations were conveyed to the Company for formal response. Eleven suggestions on various matters were also made.

Table 3.5.3   Chester Waterworks Company
WATER QUALITY IN SUPPLY ZONES

*Columns 'CBU' show, for determinations, contraventions covered by undertakings and, for zones, the total number of zones covered by undertakings in 1995. Column 'E' shows the number of zones for which new enforcement action is under consideration as a result of contraventions of the PCV in 1995. **Please refer to the Introduction to Chapter 3 for more detailed explanation of this table.***

| Parameter | DETERMINATIONS in 1995 | | | | ZONES (6 in 1995)* | | | | |
| | Total | Contravening PCV | | | | | Non-compliant | | |
		No.	%	CBU	CBU 1995	E	1995	Number in: 1994	1993
Coliforms	312	0	0.0	0	0	0	0	0	0
Faecal coliforms	312	0	0.0	0	0	0	0	0	0
Colour	360	0	0.0	0	0	0	0	0	0
Turbidity	360	0	0.0	0	0	0	0	0	0
Odour	48	0	0.0	0	0	0	0	0	0
Taste	48	0	0.0	0	0	0	0	0	0
Hydrogen ion	360	0	0.0	0	0	0	0	1	0
Nitrate	48	0	0.0	0	0	0	0	0	0
Nitrite	48	0	0.0	0	0	0	0	0	0
Aluminium	48	0	0.0	0	0	0	0	0	0
Iron	56	0	0.0	0	0	0	0	1	0
Manganese	48	0	0.0	0	0	0	0	0	0
Lead	24	0	0.0	0	0	0	0	0	0
PAH	24	0	0.0	0	0	0	0	0	0
Trihalomethanes	24	0	0.0	0	0	0	0	0	0
Total pesticides	24	0	0.0	0	0	0	0	0	0
Individual pesticides	768	0	0.0	0	0	0	0	0	0
All others	1,002	0	0.0	0	0	0	0	0	0
Total	**3,914**	**0**	**0.0**	**0**	-	-	-	-	-

* 6 zones in 1994; 6 zones in 1993.

Improvement programmes

The Company no longer has any other undertakings in place and has no relaxations authorised under regulation 4.

Incidents

No events regarded as constituting incidents in which drinking water quality demonstrably deteriorated came to the attention of the Inspectorate in 1995.

Enforcement action

No breaches of regulations resulting in enforcement action being initiated against the Company were detected as a result of the 1995 technical audit.

CHOLDERTON AND DISTRICT WATER COMPANY LIMITED

Introduction

The Company supplies on average approximately 0.6 Ml/d to a population of some 2,500 in the villages of Cholderton and Shipton Bellinger in Wiltshire. The Company's water resources consist of two deep chalk borehole sources, one operational and one standby. The standby source has not been used for supply purposes during 1995. The treated water is distributed by gravity via a service reservoir and some 44 km of water mains. The Company has one water supply zone.

Overall water quality

At the water treatment works and service reservoir and in the water supply zone, the Company carried out a total of 513 determinations in 1995. The Company achieved 100% compliance with the relevant water quality standards.

Microbiological quality of water leaving treatment works

Table 3.6.1 shows the Company's performance in 1995, with data for 1994 and 1993 for comparison. The Company complied with the sampling frequencies required by regulation 17 at its treatment works in 1995.

Coliforms and faecal coliforms were not detected in the water leaving the treatment works.

Table 3.6.1 Cholderton and District Water Company Limited MICROBIOLOGICAL QUALITY OF WATER LEAVING TREATMENT WORKS

	1995	1994	1993
Number of water treatment works	1	1	1
Works with no sampling shortfall	1	1	1
COLIFORMS			
Total number of determinations	53	53	54
- number containing coliforms	0	0	0
- % containing coliforms	0	0	0
Treatment works with coliforms detected	**0**	**0**	**0**
- % of all works	0	0	0
FAECAL COLIFORMS			
Total number of determinations	53	53	54
- number containing faecal coliforms	0	0	0
- % containing faecal coliforms	0	0	0
Treatment works with faecal coliforms detected	**0**	**0**	**0**
- % of all works	0	0	0

Microbiological quality of water in service reservoirs

Table 3.6.2 shows the Company's performance in 1995, with data for 1994 and 1993 for comparison. The Company complied fully with the required sampling frequencies at its service reservoir.

Coliforms and faecal coliforms were not detected in any samples taken from the service reservoir.

Table 3.6.2   Cholderton and District Water Company Limited
MICROBIOLOGICAL QUALITY OF WATER IN SERVICE
RESERVOIRS

	1995	1994	1993
Number of service reservoirs	1	1	1
Service reservoirs with no sampling shortfall	1	1	1
COLIFORMS			
Total number of determinations	53	53	54
- number containing coliforms	0	0	0
- % containing coliforms	0	0	0
Service reservoirs with coliforms detected	0	0	0
Service reservoirs with coliforms detected in more than 5% of samples	**0**	**0**	**0**
- % of all service reservoirs	0	0	0
FAECAL COLIFORMS			
Total number of determinations	53	53	54
- number containing faecal coliforms	0	0	0
- % containing faecal coliforms	0	0	0
Service reservoirs with faecal coliforms detected	**0**	**0**	**0**
- % of all service reservoirs	0	0	0

Water quality in water supply zones

The Company complied with the sampling frequencies required by regulation 13 for all parameters in the zone.

Table 3.6.3 gives a summary of water quality in the water supply zone in 1995 with some data for 1994 and 1993 for comparison. The small differences between the three years are not considered significant. The regulatory standards were met throughout 1995.

Inspection

The inspection of the Company was carried out in July 1995 by Miss C Jackson, Inspector. Miss Jackson concluded that:

(a)   the Company had not take action on the recommendation made in the 1994 technical audit inspection report because the standby source has not been used for domestic supply during the interim period;

(b)   the Company's contractual arrangements for sampling, analytical and reporting services, as audited, were satisfactory and the contract was well managed;

(c)   the Company's arrangements for the dissemination of water quality data generally satisfied the requirements of regulations 29 and 30;

(d)   the Company was on target to meet the key stages of its compliance programme by the due dates;

(e)   the Company's procedures for disinfection of the water supply, as audited, were generally satisfactory;

(f)   the Company's operational procedures to ensure adequate turn over of water in its service reservoirs were satisfactory;

(g)   the Company had systems in place for seeking advice in the event of a radioactive release into the environment; and

(h)   the Company's procedures and arrangements for communications and liaison with the local authorities in its area of supply were satisfactory.

Table 3.6.3   Cholderton and District Water Company Limited
WATER QUALITY IN SUPPLY ZONES

Columns 'CBU' show, for determinations, contraventions covered by undertakings and, for zones, the total number of zones covered by undertakings in 1995. Column 'E' shows the number of zones for which new enforcement action is under consideration as a result of contraventions of the PCV in 1995. **Please refer to the Introduction to Chapter 3 for more detailed explanation of this table.**

| Parameter | DETERMINATIONS in 1995 | | | | ZONES (1 in 1995)* | | | | |
| | Total | Contravening PCV | | | | | Non-compliant | | |
		No.	%	CBU	CBU 1995	E	Number in: 1995	1994	1993
Coliforms	14	0	0.0	0	0	0	0	0	1
Faecal coliforms	14	0	0.0	0	0	0	0	0	0
Colour	12	0	0.0	0	0	0	0	0	0
Turbidity	12	0	0.0	0	0	0	0	0	0
Odour	1	0	0.0	0	0	0	0	0	0
Taste	1	0	0.0	0	0	0	0	0	0
Hydrogen ion	12	0	0.0	0	0	0	0	0	0
Nitrate	13	0	0.0	0	0	0	0	0	0
Nitrite	13	0	0.0	0	0	0	0	0	0
Aluminium	4	0	0.0	0	0	0	0	0	0
Iron	4	0	0.0	0	0	0	0	0	0
Manganese	4	0	0.0	0	0	0	0	0	0
Lead	1	0	0.0	0	0	0	0	0	0
PAH	4	0	0.0	0	0	0	0	0	0
Trihalomethanes	1	0	0.0	0	0	0	0	0	0
Total pesticides	14	0	0.0	0	0	0	0	0	0
Atrazine	14	0	0.0	0	1	0	0	1	1
Other pesticides	58	0	0.0	0	0	0	0	0	0
All others	105	0	0.0	0	0	0	0	0	0
Total	**301**	**0**	**0.0**	**0**	-	-	-	-	-

* 1 zone in 1994; 1 zone in 1993.

Miss Jackson made three recommendations to the Company in the light of the inspection, together with six suggestions for the Company to consider. Assurances have been given that these have all been acted upon.

Improvement programmes

The Company's one undertaking in respect of an improvement programme accepted by the Secretary of State was due for the completion of a major step at the end of 1995. Miss Jackson reviewed this during the course of the 1995 inspection and concluded that the undertaking was on schedule.

Incidents

The Inspectorate was not notified during 1995 of any incidents under the terms of the Water Undertakers (Information) Direction 1992.

Enforcement action

No enforcement action is under consideration for the Company as a result of the technical audit in 1995.

DŴR CYMRU CYFYNGEDIG

Introduction

The Company supplies on average 1,026 Ml/d of water to a resident population of approximately 2.8 million people in an area covering most of Wales and parts of Hereford and Worcester and Gloucestershire.

Approximately 48% of the Company's water resources is derived from impounding reservoirs, 43% from river abstractions and 9% from boreholes and springs.

The Company operates 156 water treatment works and also imports a small amount of treated water from Chester Water Company, Severn Trent Water Limited and Wrexham Water plc. The treated water is distributed via 658 service reservoirs and some 24,900 km of water mains. The supply area is divided into 224 water supply zones.

Overall water quality

At water treatment works and service reservoirs and in water supply zones, the Company carried out a total of 201,282 determinations in 1995. Of these, 99.6% demonstrated compliance with the relevant water quality standards, but 828 showed a PCV to have been contravened.

Coliforms were not detected at 118 (76%) of the Company's 156 water treatment works. At 652 (99%) of the Company's 658 service reservoirs, coliforms were absent from at least 95% of samples. Of the Company's 224 water supply zones in 1995, 201 (90%) complied fully with the relevant water quality standards or had breaches of the standards which were either trivial or were fully covered by undertakings. In the other 23 (10%) of the zones, most breaches are regarded as unlikely to recur, but others could result in enforcement action.

Microbiological quality of water leaving treatment works

Table 3.7.1 shows the Company's performance in 1995, with data for 1994 and 1993 for comparison. Differences between the three years are not considered significant.

The Company complied with the sampling frequencies required by regulation 17 at 129 of its 156 treatment works in 1995. Shortfalls at the other 27 are regarded as trivial or unlikely to recur.

Table 3.7.1 Dŵr Cymru Cyfyngedig
MICROBIOLOGICAL QUALITY OF WATER LEAVING TREATMENT WORKS

	1995	1994	1993
Number of water treatment works	156	159	170
Works with no sampling shortfall	129	153	141
COLIFORMS			
Total number of determinations	17,810	19,071	20,684
- number containing coliforms	52	28	94
- % containing coliforms	0.3	0.1	0.5
Treatment works with coliforms detected	**38**	**22**	**60**
- % of all works	24	14	35
FAECAL COLIFORMS			
Total number of determinations	17,813	19,071	20,684
- number containing faecal coliforms	17	9	24
- % containing faecal coliforms	<0.1	<0.1	0.1
Treatment works with faecal coliforms detected	**15**	**8**	**21**
- % of all works	10	5	12

Contraventions of the microbiological quality standards at one works has resulted in the consideration of enforcement action, as shown in table 3.7.4. The Company has taken remedial action at one works and the Inspectorate will assess the results of further monitoring before deciding whether enforcement action is required. All other contraventions of the standards at works are considered trivial or unlikely to recur, or are covered by undertakings.

Microbiological quality of water in service reservoirs

Table 3.7.2 shows the Company's performance in 1995, with data for 1994 and 1993 for comparison. Differences between the three years are not considered significant.

The Company complied with the sampling frequencies required by regulation 18 at 536 of its 658 service reservoirs in 1995. Shortfalls at the other 122 are regarded as trivial or unlikely to recur.

Contraventions of the microbiological quality standards at one service reservoir has resulted in the consideration of enforcement action, as shown in table 3.7.4. All other contraventions of the standards at service reservoirs are considered trivial or unlikely to recur, or are covered by undertakings.

Table 3.7.2 Dŵr Cymru Cyfyngedig MICROBIOLOGICAL QUALITY OF WATER IN SERVICE RESERVOIRS	1995	1994	1993
Number of service reservoirs	658	665	672
Service reservoirs with no sampling shortfall	536	649	624
COLIFORMS			
Total number of determinations	32,910	33,438	33,361
- number containing coliforms	152	92	257
- % containing coliforms	0.5	0.3	0.8
Service reservoirs with coliforms detected	122	74	202
Service reservoirs with coliforms detected in more than 5% of samples	**6**	**6**	**10**
- % of all service reservoirs	1	1	2
FAECAL COLIFORMS			
Total number of determinations	32,918	33,438	33,361
- number containing faecal coliforms	45	35	61
- % containing faecal coliforms	0.1	0.1	0.2
Service reservoirs with faecal coliforms detected	**41**	**31**	**51**
- % of all service reservoirs	6	5	8

Water quality in water supply zones

The Company failed to comply fully with the required sampling frequencies for various parameters in 50 zones but these breaches of regulation 13 are considered either trivial or unlikely to recur. Nonetheless the Inspectorate is critical of the number of shortfalls that were attributed to administrative errors and anticipates an improved performance in 1996.

Table 3.7.3 shows the Company's performance in 1995, with data for 1994 and 1993 for comparison. Differences between the three years are not considered significant.

Table 3.7.3   Dŵr Cymru Cyfyngedig
WATER QUALITY IN SUPPLY ZONES

Columns 'CBU' show, for determinations, contraventions covered by undertakings and, for zones, the <u>total</u> *number of zones covered by undertakings in 1995. Column 'E' shows the number of zones for which new enforcement action is under consideration as a result of contraventions of the PCV in 1995.* **Please refer to the Introduction to Chapter 3 for more detailed explanation of this table.**

| Parameter | DETERMINATIONS in 1995 | | | | ZONES (224 in 1995)* | | | | |
| | Total | Contravening PCV | | | | Non-compliant | | | |
		No.	%	CBU	CBU 1995	E 1995	Number in: 1995	1994	1993
Coliforms	9,486	70	0.7	0	24	0	2	0	5
Faecal coliforms	9,489	15	0.2	3	5	0	12	5	6
Colour	1,483	1	<0.1	1	224	0	1	1	4
Turbidity	1,542	3	0.2	3	224	0	3	7	3
Odour	1,812	7	0.4	0	0	0	6	3	9
Taste	1,778	11	0.6	0	0	0	8	13	21
Hydrogen ion	1,538	6	0.4	6	224	0	6	4	11
Nitrate	1,230	0	0.0	0	0	0	0	2	2
Nitrite	1,664	69	4.1	41	4	3	16	9	6
Aluminium	1,828	30	1.6	0	5	0	16	17	22
Iron	2,949	122	4.1	122	224	0	63	51	53
Manganese	2,059	31	1.5	31	224	0	18	9	14
Lead	1,359	38	2.8	0	224	0	24	33	29
PAH	1,486	101	6.8	0	0	1	45	38	35
Trihalomethanes	1,133	15	1.3	0	1	0	0	0	17
Total pesticides	1,750	2	0.1	0	0	0	2	5	0
Asulam	851	1	0.1	0	0	0	1	1	0
Atrazine	793	0	0.0	0	3	0	0	3	0
Carbendazim	331	0	0.0	0	0	0	0	3	0
Diuron	877	0	0.0	0	0	0	0	0	1
Fenpropimorph	609	2	0.3	0	0	0	2	0	0
Fentin	320	0	0.0	0	0	0	0	1	0
Glyphosate	904	1	0.1	0	0	0	1	2	3
Isoproturon	855	0	0.0	0	0	0	0	2	0
MCPA	819	3	0.4	0	0	0	3	6	2
Mecoprop	763	3	0.4	0	0	0	2	2	3
Methabenzthiazuron	880	0	0.0	0	0	0	0	2	0
Oxadixyl	602	0	0.0	0	0	0	0	1	0
Simazine	803	2	0.2	0	4	0	2	5	3
Other pesticides	22,876	0	0.0	0	0	0	0	0	0
Conductivity	4,940	0	0.0	0	0	0	0	1	0
Nickel	240	0	0.0	0	0	0	0	1	0
Oxidizability	246	0	0.0	0	0	0	0	1	3
Phosphorus	418	1	0.2	CBU	0	0	1	0	1
Temperature	9,427	1	<0.1	0	0	0	1	0	0
Tetrachloroethene	540	4	0.7	0	0	0	1	0	1
Tetrachloromethane	524	0	0.0	0	0	0	0	0	1
Trichloroethene	486	0	0.0	0	0	0	0	0	1
Benzo 3,4 pyrene	1,482	23	1.6	0	0	0	6	0	3
All others	6,659	0	0.0	0	0	0	0	0	0
Total	**99,831**	**562**	**0.6**	**207**	**-**	**-**	**-**	**-**	**-**

* 230 zones in 1994; 237 zones in 1993.

The Company has identified the probable cause of contraventions of four standards and has taken remedial action. The Inspectorate will consider the results of further monitoring before deciding whether enforcement action is required. Enforcement action is being considered in respect of some contraventions of two standards, as shown in tables 3.7.3 and 3.7.4. All other contraventions of the standards in zones are considered trivial or unlikely to recur, or are covered by undertakings or will be covered by the new distribution undertaking.

Inspection

Mr D F Drury, Principal Inspector, assisted by Dr P K Marsden, Inspector, carried out an inspection of Dŵr Cymru in November 1995. Mr Drury concluded that:

(a) the Company generally made a very positive response to the recommendations made in the 1994 inspection;

(b) on the basis of inspection in each Division and of other specific items, the Company continues to maintain sound arrangements for sampling and is satisfying the requirements of parts IV and V of the Regulations and is generally in accord with the recommendations in the Guidance Document. A recommendation was necessary in respect of reviewing the time elapsing between sampling and analysis for some microbiological samples;

(c) the Company is now making good progress towards developing a sound monitoring strategy for Cryptosporidium;

(d) on the basis of inspection of analytical quality control performance at its contract laboratories, the Company is generally meeting the requirements of regulation 21(2)(d), results are generally good, action is being taken as a result of identified problems but noted the number of flags attributed to avoidable mistakes by laboratory staff such as dilution error, spiking error and incorrect calculation in respect of non-microbiological distributions and a recommendation was necessary;

(e) on the basis of detailed audit trails of thirty one randomly selected samples and of other specific items, with minor exceptions, arrangements for reporting compliance data are generally satisfactory and secure and that the Company is taking appropriate action in respect of contraventions of standards but recommendations were necessary on analysis, reporting and follow up times;

(f) the Company's Public Record at Brecon met the requirements of regulation 29 and 30 except for an isolated contravention of regulation 29(1)(f) which is being corrected;

(g) the Company has a prudent policy for monitoring chlorate levels at water supply works where OSEC plant is installed and there is no evidence to suggest that the approval condition has been breached;

(h) the Company was now making good progress towards achieving failsafe disinfection at all its water treatment works and the programme was almost complete;

(i) based on an audit of its Swansea Control Room, the Company could not demonstrate readily the action taken in response to water quality alarms although there was no evidence to suggest that the Company was not taking appropriate and timely action;

(j) on the basis of his examination of records in South Western Division, the Company is generally epoxy resin lining in accordance with the Operational Guidelines and Code of Practice;

(k) the Company had a very extensive programme of improvements to water treatment works which was largely completed by the end of 1995. Of the schemes due for completion in 1995 a small number overran. Whilst appreciating the amount of improvement work undertaken by the Company, he is very critical that it allowed schemes to overrun and expects the

Company to ensure that more management emphasis is directed towards achieving the due dates in its obligations. The Inspectorate considered the issue of a Notice of Intention to make a Final Enforcement Order but the Company satisfactorily completed the necessary works and a Notice was not required;

(l)   the Company failed to achieve consistent phosphate dosing at a number of works where treatment was installed. He is highly critical of the Company for the inadequate operation of these works. The Company has been required to provide the Inspectorate with frequent and regular reports which show that operation is now satisfactory; and

(m)   the Company has sound arrangements for dealing with emergencies and incidents and liaison with local authorities and district health authorities and is keeping these under review in the light of experience.

In October 1995, Mr R Kidson from the consultants Rofe, Kennard and Lapworth, working under the general direction of Mr Drury, carried out inspection of Felindre, Schwyll and Llanybydder water treatment works and Cefn Llan and Hen Gaer service reservoirs. Mr Kidson concluded that:

(n)   the treatment processes complied with Regulation 23;

(o)   the use of substances and products satisfied the requirements of Regulation 25;

(p)   the Company's policy and arrangements for disinfection at treatment works were satisfactory; and

(q)   the Company's arrangements for compliance sampling at treatment works and service reservoirs are generally in accordance with the recommendations of paragraph 2.8 of the Guidance Document and the requirements of Regulation 21(2)(a).

As a result of these inspections, 14 recommendations on various matters were conveyed to the Company for formal response. 14 suggestions on various matters were also made.

Improvement programmes

The Company had a very extensive programme of improvements to water treatment works which was largely completed by the end of 1995. Some of the schemes were required under the terms of undertakings others were conditions of authorised relaxations and some were required by both relaxations and undertakings. Of the 56 schemes due for completion in 1995, most were completed by the due date but a small number of schemes overran, one for reasons beyond the control of the Company. Further comments are given above in the section on inspection. A new undertaking given by the Company to carry out improvement works to its distribution system, with a completion date of 31 March 2000, is being considered by the Secretary of State.

Incidents

Twelve events notified during 1995 by the Company to the Secretary of State under the terms of the Water Undertakers (Information) Direction 1992 are regarded by the Inspectorate as constituting incidents in which drinking water quality demonstrably deteriorated.

These incidents concerned:

(a)   supply of discoloured water to about 1000 properties in the Aberystwyth following a planned interruption to supply to install new valves;

(b)   complaints of discoloured water and one unsubstantiated allegation of illness from consumers in Pembroke and associated press coverage;

(c)   the issue on two separate occasions of advice to boil water to consumers in parts of Tredegar and Llangwm respectively following mains bursts in those areas;

(d) a taste problem and high pH affecting 300 properties in the Morriston area of Swansea following commissioning of a cement mortar lined main;

(e) the issue on four separate occasions of advice to boil water to consumers in Brynamman, Nantymoel, a rural area on the borders of Pembrokeshire and Carmarthenshire, and Abergorlech respectively following the detection of coliform bacteria in the supplies to those areas;

(f) the issue of advice to boil water to 150 consumers living in the Leominster area following chlorination failure at Byton treatment works;

(g) complaints of discoloured water following failure of Sluvad treatment works to remove increased levels of naturally occurring manganese; and

(h) deterioration in water quality following the failure of part of the treatment stream at Bryncoch water treatment works.

The Company generally took appropriate action to restore normal supplies as soon as possible in the incidents in Pembroke and Tredegar. The other ten incidents are still under consideration.

No other events regarded as constituting incidents came to the attention of the Inspectorate in 1995.

Following assessment of one incident from 1994 the Inspectorate considered enforcement action for breaches of the standard for colour. Subsequently the Company was able to demonstrate that it had taken appropriate remedial action and the contraventions were unlikely to recur.

Enforcement action

Table 3.7.4 summarises enforcement action under consideration for the Company as a result of the Inspectorate's work in, or pertaining to, the calendar year 1995.

Table 3.7.4	Dŵr Cymru Cyfyngedig SUMMARY OF ENFORCEMENT ACTION CONSIDERED IN 1995
Regulation	**Reason for enforcement**
3(3)(c)	Contravention of the standard for colour in one zone as a result of an incident, nitrite in three zones and PAH in one zone.
3(7)	Contravention of the coliforms standard at one water treatment works.
3(7)	Contravention of the coliforms standard at one service reservoir.

EAST SURREY WATER PLC

Introduction

East Surrey Water Plc, an independent water company not allied to any other water group, supplies on average 97 Ml/d of water to a population of about 328,000 people in an area around the M25 motorway in the counties of Surrey and Kent.

Approximately 65% of the Company's water is abstracted from boreholes in the chalk aquifer, 10% from boreholes in the greensand strata and 25% is surface derived from the River Eden and stored in Bough Beech reservoir. The water is treated at eight treatment works. Treated water is distributed via 26 service reservoirs and some 2,260 km of water mains. The supply area is divided into 16 water supply zones.

Overall water quality

At water treatment works and service reservoirs and in water supply zones, the Company carried out a total of 17,589 determinations in 1995. Of these, 97.8% demonstrated compliance with the relevant water quality standards, but 394 showed a PCV to have been contravened.

Coliforms were not detected at four of the Company's eight water treatment works. At all of the Company's 26 service reservoirs, coliforms were absent from at least 95% of samples. Of the Company's 16 water supply zones in 1995, 13 (81%) complied fully with the relevant water quality standards or had breaches of the standards which were either trivial or were fully covered by undertakings. In the other three zones, breaches are regarded as unlikely to recur.

Microbiological quality of water leaving treatment works

Table 3.8.1 shows the Company's performance in 1995, with data for 1994 and 1993 for comparison. There has been a significant increase in 1995 in the number of determinations containing coliforms.

The Company complied with the sampling frequencies required by regulation 17 at six of its eight treatment works in 1995. Shortfalls at the other two treatment works are regarded as trivial.

The Inspectorate will consider the results of further monitoring at three works to determine whether enforcement action is required. The contraventions of the standards at one other works are covered by an undertaking.

Table 3.8.1 East Surrey Water Plc
MICROBIOLOGICAL QUALITY OF WATER LEAVING TREATMENT WORKS

	1995	1994	1993
Number of water treatment works	8	8	8
Works with no sampling shortfall	6	7	8
COLIFORMS			
Total number of determinations	1,662	1,663	1,763
- number containing coliforms	18	4	3
- % containing coliforms	1.1	0.2	0.2
Treatment works with coliforms detected	**4**	**2**	**2**
- % of all works	50	25	25
FAECAL COLIFORMS			
Total number of determinations	1,662	1,663	1,763
- number containing faecal coliforms	1	1	0
- % containing faecal coliforms	<0.1	<0.1	0.0
Treatment works with faecal coliforms detected	**1**	**1**	**0**
- % of all works	12	12	0

Microbiological quality of water in service reservoirs

Table 3.8.2 shows the Company's performance in 1995, with data for 1994 and 1993 for comparison. Differences between the three years are not considered significant.

The Company complied with the sampling frequencies required by regulation 18 at all its service reservoirs in 1995.

There were no contraventions of the microbiological standards at any of the Company's service reservoirs in 1995.

Table 3.8.2 East Surrey Water Plc MICROBIOLOGICAL QUALITY OF WATER IN SERVICE RESERVOIRS	1995	1994	1993
Number of service reservoirs	26	26	26
Service reservoirs with no sampling shortfall	26	26	26
COLIFORMS			
Total number of determinations	1,402	1,368	1,352
- number containing coliforms	5	0	2
- % containing coliforms	0.4	0.0	0.1
Service reservoirs with coliforms detected	4	0	2
Service reservoirs with coliforms detected in more than 5% of samples	**0**	**0**	**0**
- % of all service reservoirs	0	0	0
FAECAL COLIFORMS			
Total number of determinations	1,402	1,368	1,352
- number containing faecal coliforms	0	0	0
- % containing faecal coliforms	0	0	0
Service reservoirs with faecal coliforms detected	**0**	**0**	**0**
- % of all service reservoirs	0	0	0

Water quality in water supply zones

Table 3.8.3 shows the Company's performance in 1995 with data for 1994 and 1993 for comparison. Differences between the three years are not considered significant.

The Company complied with the required sampling frequencies for all parameters in 13 of its 16 supply zones. Shortfalls for the total coliform and faecal coliform parameters in 3 zones have been regarded as trivial.

All contraventions of the standards in zones are considered trivial or unlikely to recur, or are covered by undertakings.

Inspection

Mr P L Jiggins, Inspector, carried out an inspection of East Surrey Water Plc in December 1995. He concluded that:

(a) the Company has taken appropriate and satisfactory measures to implement most of the recommendations made in the 1994 technical audit inspection reports;

(b) the Company's pesticide sampling policy continues to evolve in a satisfactory manner and that it has appropriate arrangements for the delineation of water supply zones;

(c) the arrangements for microbiological analysis are generally satisfactory but could benefit from some improvements to quality control procedures;

Table 3.8.3   East Surrey Water Plc
WATER QUALITY IN SUPPLY ZONES

Columns 'CBU' show, for determinations, contraventions covered by undertakings and, for zones, the <u>total</u> number of zones covered by undertakings in 1995. Column 'E' shows the number of zones for which new enforcement action is under consideration as a result of contraventions of the PCV in 1995. **Please refer to the Introduction to Chapter 3 for more detailed explanation of this table.**

Parameter	DETERMINATIONS in 1995				ZONES (16 in 1995)*				
	Total	Contravening PCV			CBU	E	Non-compliant		
		No.	%	CBU	1995		Number in:		
							1995	1994	1993
Coliforms	993	5	0.5	0	0	0	0	0	1
Faecal coliforms	993	0	0.0	0	0	0	0	0	4
Colour	632	0	0.0	0	0	0	0	0	0
Turbidity	632	3	0.5	3	16	0	3	4	5
Odour	119	0	0.0	0	0	0	0	0	0
Taste	119	0	0.0	0	0	0	0	0	0
Hydrogen ion	632	0	0.0	0	0	0	0	0	0
Nitrate	314	0	0.0	0	0	0	0	0	0
Nitrite	458	41	9.0	41	6	0	5	6	6
Aluminium	314	0	0.0	0	0	0	0	0	0
Iron	636	12	1.9	12	16	0	7	11	9
Manganese	109	1	0.9	0	0	0	1	0	0
Lead	104	1	1.0	0	0	0	1	1	5
PAH	163	7	4.3	0	0	0	3	3	1
Trihalomethanes	152	32	21.1	32	4	0	4	4	0
Total pesticides	271	42	15.5	42	9	0	5	6	5
Atrazine	264	62	23.5	62	9	0	4	5	3
Chlorotoluron	261	30	11.5	30	9	0	5	5	5
Diuron	261	0	0.0	0	9	0	0	0	3
Isoproturon	261	43	16.5	43	9	0	5	5	5
Mecoprop	262	56	21.4	56	9	0	5	5	1
Simazine	264	35	13.3	35	9	0	5	0	2
Other pesticides	712	0	0.0	0	9	0	0	0	0
All others	2,535	0	0.0	0	0	0	0	0	0
Total	**11,461**	**370**	**3.2**	**356**	-	-	-	-	-

* 15 zones in 1994; 15 zones in 1993.

(d)   the Company's arrangements for recording compliance sampling, analysis and reporting are generally satisfactory but that some attention to aspects of analytical quality control, calibration procedures and documentation would result in further improvement;

(e)   the Company's arrangements for maintaining the public record are satisfactory and comply with the requirements of regulation 29;

(f)   the Company has made satisfactory progress with two schemes however, the scheme for pesticide removal at Kenley WTW was subject to slight delay, and the operation of the scheme for THM removal at Bough Beech WTW was considerably delayed by the need for the installation of noise reduction measures and further enforcement action should be considered;

(g)   the Company has a satisfactory system of Quality Assurance which is assessed to ISO 9002 by BSi in relation to water treatment and distribution systems;

(h) the Company's arrangements for dealing with incidents and events are generally satisfactory but that arrangements for rehearsals of emergency procedures require improvement; and

(i) the Company provides local authorities with the water quality reports required by regulations 30 and 31 and communications between the Company and Reigate and Banstead Borough Council are generally satisfactory, but the provision for liaison meetings should be reviewed.

In November, Dr A K Hughes representing consultants Rofe, Kennard and Lapworth carried out inspections of water treatment works and service reservoirs.

(j) the Company has maintained the quality of water supplied by Westwood water treatment works;

(k) water has been adequately disinfected to meet the requirements of regulation 23(1) and equipment failure should not result in unchlorinated water entering supply;

(l) Alderstead Reservoir is maintained to a satisfactory standard; and

(m) sampling points are installed such that it is possible that an unrepresentative sample is obtained at times, which does not meet the requirement of regulation 21(2)(a). The Company took prompt remedial action and enforcement was not required.

As a result of these inspections, 24 recommendations were conveyed to the Company for formal response. 28 suggestions were also made for the Company to consider.

The Company has already taken action on a number of the recommendations and suggestions.

Improvement programmes

Six undertakings in respect of improvement programmes accepted by the Secretary of State from the Company were due for full completion or the completion of major steps during 1995 and of these, four were completed on schedule. The pesticide scheme at Kenley was delayed because of hydraulic problems beyond the Company's control experienced during commissioning. Further enforcement was not required as the work was completed early in 1996.

A delay in completion of the trihalomethane scheme at Bough Beech treatment works was not beyond the Company's control. The Company considered the necessary work would be completed by March 1996. The Inspectorate issued a Notice of Intention to make a Final Enforcement Order requiring the Company to complete the installation of appropriate treatment. The Company ensured that treatment was installed and fully operational and an Order was not required.

A new undertaking given by the Company to carry out improvement works to its distribution system, with a completion date of 31 March 2000, has been accepted by the Secretary of State.

Relaxations

An authorised relaxation for the iron parameter in the zone supplied by Cliftons Lane treatment works was granted to the Company by the Secretary of State, which was to be further reviewed by the end of 1995. The relaxation is currently being reviewed.

Incidents

No events regarded by the Inspectorate as constituting incidents in which drinking water quality demonstrably deteriorated were notified during 1995 by the Company to the Secretary of State under the terms of the Water Undertakers (Information) Direction 1992.

Enforcement action

No new enforcement action needed to be considered for the Company as a result of the Inspectorate's work in, or pertaining to, the calendar year 1995.

ESSEX AND SUFFOLK WATER PLC

Introduction

Essex and Suffolk Water Plc was formed on 1 April 1994 by the merger of Essex Water Company and Suffolk Water Company. The Company is a wholly owned subsidiary of the Lyonnaise Des Eaux group.

The Company supplies on average 508 Ml/d of water to a population of some 1.7 million people in Essex, south Norfolk and north Suffolk. The bulk of the Company's water is surface derived from rivers in Suffolk and Essex. A bulk supply of raw surface water representing approximately 20% of the Company's water is obtained from Thames Water. The remainder of the water is derived from underground sources, principally chalk boreholes. The water from these sources is treated at 24 treatment works. Treated water is distributed through 110 water towers and service reservoirs and 8,000 km of water mains. The supply area is divided into 64 water supply zones.

Overall water quality

At water treatment works and service reservoirs and in water supply zones, the Company carried out a total of 163,967 determinations in 1995. Of these, 98.0% demonstrated compliance with the relevant water quality standards, but 3,294 showed a PCV to have been contravened. Of these contraventions 3,182 were due to infringements of the pesticide standards and all were covered by existing undertakings.

Coliforms were not detected at 21 (88%) of the Company's 24 water treatment works. At all of the Company's 110 service reservoirs, coliforms were absent from at least 95% of samples. Of the Company's 64 water supply zones in 1995, all complied fully with the relevant water quality standards or had breaches of the standards which were either trivial or were fully covered by undertakings.

Microbiological quality of water leaving treatment works

Table 3.9.1 shows the Company's performance in 1995, with data for 1994 and 1993 for comparison. The data presented for 1993 represents combined data for the two predecessor companies. Differences between the three years are not regarded as significant.

Table 3.9.1	Essex and Suffolk Water Plc MICROBIOLOGICAL QUALITY OF WATER LEAVING TREATMENT WORKS			
		1995	**1994**	**1993**[a]
Number of water treatment works		24	24	25
Works with no sampling shortfall		21	15	25
COLIFORMS				
Total number of determinations		3,765	3,995	4,197
- number containing coliforms		7	12	8
- % containing coliforms		0.2	0.3	0.2
Treatment works with coliforms detected		**3**	**8**	**7**
- % of all works		13	33	28
FAECAL COLIFORMS				
Total number of determinations		3,765	3,995	4,197
- number containing faecal coliforms		1	4	1
- % containing faecal coliforms		<0.1	0.1	<0.1
Treatment works with faecal coliforms detected		**1**	**4**	**1**
- % of all works		4	17	4

[a] Numbers in this column represent combined data for the predecessor companies.

Had the definition of the coliform parameter not been changed as described in 3.35 above, but remained as it was for 1994 and previous years, the number of treatment works with coliforms detected would have been two and the number of determinations containing coliforms six.

The Company complied with the sampling frequencies required by regulation 17 at 21 of its 24 treatment works in 1995. Shortfalls at the other three are regarded as trivial or unlikely to recur.

The contraventions of the microbiological quality standards at three works are considered trivial or unlikely to recur.

Microbiological quality of water in service reservoirs

Table 3.9.2 shows the Company's performance in 1995, with data for 1994 and combined data for the two predecessor companies for 1993 for comparison. There have been significant reductions over the three years in the numbers of service reservoirs failing to comply with the microbiological standards.

Had the definition of the coliform parameter not been changed as described in 3.35 above, but remained as it was for 1994 and previous years, there would have been seven determinations containing coliforms.

The Company complied with the sampling frequencies required by regulation 18 at all of its 110 service reservoirs in 1995.

All contraventions of the standards at service reservoirs are considered trivial or unlikely to recur.

Table 3.9.2 Essex and Suffolk Water Plc MICROBIOLOGICAL QUALITY OF WATER IN SERVICE RESERVOIRS	1995	1994	1993[a]
Number of service reservoirs	110	111	105
Service reservoirs with no sampling shortfall	110	109	105
COLIFORMS			
Total number of determinations	5,434	5,029	5,100
- number containing coliforms	11	18	30
- % containing coliforms	0.2	0.4	0.6
Service reservoirs with coliforms detected	9	18	24
Service reservoirs with coliforms detected in more than 5% of samples	**0**	**2**	**1**
- % of all service reservoirs	0	2	1
FAECAL COLIFORMS			
Total number of determinations	5,434	5,029	5,100
- number containing faecal coliforms	2	11	12
- % containing faecal coliforms	<0.1	0.2	0.2
Service reservoirs with faecal coliforms detected	**2**	**11**	**12**
- % of all service reservoirs	2	10	11

[a] Numbers in this column represent combined data for the predecessor companies.

Water quality in water supply zones

The Company failed to comply with the required sampling frequencies in five zones. The Company breached regulation 13 in respect of temperature, iron and trihalomethanes. The Inspectorate will assess further performance in respect of the temperature contraventions in three zones to confirm that appropriate action has been taken by the Company to prevent the shortfalls recurring. The remaining contraventions of regulation 13 are considered trivial or unlikely to recur.

Table 3.9.3 shows the Company's performance in 1995, with data for 1994 and combined data for the two predecessor companies for 1993 for comparison. The changes from year to year in the numbers of zones failing to comply with the individual pesticides standard for specific substances are magnified by the use of authorised supply points for monitoring as described in 3.21. Differences between the three years for all parameters are not regarded as significant.

Had the definition of the coliform parameter not been changed as described in 3.35 above, but remained as it was for 1994 and previous years, the number of determinations containing coliforms would have been 15.

All contraventions of the standards in zones are considered trivial or unlikely to recur, or are covered by undertakings.

Inspection

The inspection of Essex and Suffolk Water Plc was led by Mr M J Purcell and carried out by Mr R F Millar, Inspector, assisted by Mr B S Bell, Inspector, in a series of visits between 18 August and 1 December 1995. Mr Millar concluded that:

(a) a review of the Company's arrangements for water supply confirmed that data provided was an accurate record of the Company's current water supply arrangements;

(b) the Company had made significant progress in addressing the recommendations made by the Inspectors and consultants in the 1994 inspection report;

(c) audits of compliance data carried out by the Inspectors identified some areas which required attention, most of which have already been satisfactorily addressed;

(d) the Company has in place satisfactory arrangements for inter- and intra-company transfer of bulk supplies of water;

(e) the Company has in place liaison arrangements for dealing with radioactivity monitoring;

(f) the Company has satisfactory procedures for the analysis of microbiological parameters, incorporating the recommendations of the new Report 71;

(g) the Company is developing various internal quality assurance initiatives including third party accreditation for the majority of the Company functions;

(h) the Company has in place satisfactory arrangements for liaison with local authorities on issues concerning water quality;

(i) progress with capital schemes related to undertakings was generally satisfactory, although three schemes had been delayed, one significantly; and

(j) the water treatment processes and records reviewed at Chigwell were generally maintained and operated satisfactorily, but some areas required attention.

Mr Millar noted contraventions of regulations 29(1)(d) and 29(1)(f) concerning the Public Record. However, remedial action was taken speedily in each case and consideration of enforcement action was not necessary.

Table 3.9.3   Essex and Suffolk Water Plc
WATER QUALITY IN SUPPLY ZONES

Columns 'CBU' show, for determinations, contraventions covered by undertakings and, for zones, the <u>total</u> *number of zones covered by undertakings in 1995. Column 'E' shows the number of zones for which new enforcement action is under consideration as a result of contraventions of the PCV in 1995.* **Please refer to the Introduction to Chapter 3 for more detailed explanation of this table.**

| Parameter | DETERMINATIONS in 1995 | | | | ZONES (64 in 1995)* | | | | |
| | Total | Contravening PCV | | | CBU | E | Non-compliant Number[a] in: | | |
		No.	%	CBU	1995		1995	1994	1993
Coliforms	4,433	24	0.5	0	0	0	0	0	0
Faecal coliforms	4,433	5	0.1	0	0	0	5	4	6
Colour	523	0	0.0	0	0	0	0	0	0
Turbidity	582	1	0.2	0	0	0	1	0	0
Odour	727	0	0.0	0	0	0	0	1	0
Taste	723	0	0.0	0	0	0	0	0	0
Hydrogen ion	524	0	0.0	0	0	0	0	0	0
Nitrate	620	0	0.0	0	0	0	0	0	0
Nitrite	1,025	2	0.2	1	39	0	2	2	4
Aluminium	665	0	0.0	0	0	0	0	0	1
Iron	1,768	21	1.2	21	64	0	15	23	20
Manganese	830	5	0.6	0	0	0	3	1	4
Lead	544	3	0.6	0	0	0	3	5	4
PAH	308	1	0.3	0	0	0	1	0	0
Trihalomethanes	568	28	4.9	28	41	0	13	13	2
Total pesticides	3,804	725	19.1	725	55	0	46	45	37
Atrazine	4,297	68	1.6	68	55	0	41	45	43
Chlorotoluron	4,062	91	2.2	91	55	0	46	40	25
2,4-D	4,069	39	1.0	39	55	0	13	0	1
Dimethoate	275	22	8.0	22	55	0	11	11	0
Diuron	4,017	35	0.9	35	55	0	24	11	35
Isoproturon	4,067	1,044	25.7	1,044	55	0	48	49	41
MCPA	4,041	0	0.0	0	55	0	0	1	0
Mecoprop	4,061	161	4.0	161	55	0	42	46	36
Propazine	4,242	0	0.0	0	55	0	0	0	1
Propham	311	0	0.0	0	55	0	0	0	1
Simazine	4,297	997	23.2	997	55	0	46	47	37
Trifluralin	1,881	0	0.0	0	55	0	0	1	0
Other pesticides	75,474	0	0.0	0	55	0	0	0	0
Phosphorus	471	0	0.0	0	0	0	0	0	1
Sulphate	109	0	0.0	0	0	0	0	2	2
Tetrachloromethane	568	1	0.2	0	0	0	0	0	0
All others	7,250	0	0.0	0	0	0	0	0	0
Total	**145,569**	**3,273**	**2.2**	**3,232**	-	-	-	-	-

*   64 zones in 1994; 54 zones in 1993 refers to the total in the predecessor companies.
[a]   Numbers in the 1993 column represent combined data for the predecessor companies.

Mr Millar recommended that the Inspectorate considers the making of an Enforcement Order to secure the completion of the outstanding steps to be taken for a compliance scheme at one water treatment works.

In October 1995 a consultant from Rofe, Kennard & Lapworth and working under Mr Purcell's general direction, carried out inspection of selected water treatment works and service reservoirs. The inspection was carried out by Mr K Bamford, appointed as Temporary Technical Assessor by the Secretary of State for the duration of the inspection. He concluded that:

(k) the treatment processes complied with Regulation 23;

(l) the use of substances and products satisfied the requirements of Regulation 25;

(m) the Company's policy and arrangements for disinfection at treatment works were satisfactory; and

(n) the Company's arrangements for compliance sampling at treatment works and service reservoirs are generally in accordance with the recommendations of paragraph 2.8 of the Guidance Document and with the requirements of Regulation 21(2)(a).

As a result of these inspections, 11 recommendations were conveyed to the Company for formal response, mainly in respect of water treatment and maintenance of the Public Record. Twenty-two suggestions on various matters were also made. The Company is taking action or has already taken action on a number of the recommendations.

Improvement programmes

Ten undertakings in respect of improvement programmes accepted by the Secretary of State from the Company were due for full completion or the completion of major steps during 1995 and eight of these were completed on schedule.

A major improvement scheme at Hanningfield water treatment works was completed slightly behind the scheduled target completion date for reasons beyond the Company's control.

At Barsham water treatment works, construction problems occuring late in the contract and which could not have been reasonably foreseen by the Company resulted in a major improvement scheme overrunning by approximately 10 weeks. To secure compliance with regulation 3(3)(c), the Inspectorate issued a Notice of Intention to make a Final Enforcement Order in respect of the construction and commissioning of the treatment plant. However, the Company satisfactorily completed the improvement scheme within the period of notice and a final Enforcement Order was not necessary. The Company made provision to achieve or facilitate compliance by other means during this period of delay. A new undertaking given by the Company to carry out improvement works to its distribution system, with a completion date of 31 March 2000, is being considered by the Secretary of State.

Incidents

Two events notified during 1995 by the Company to the Secretary of State under the terms of the Water Undertakers (Information) Direction 1992 were regarded by the Inspectorate as constituting incidents in which drinking water quality demonstrably deteriorated. The first involved the supply of discoloured water to the Canvey Island area of Essex. This incident remains under consideration by the Inspectorate. The second incident involved a disinfection failure at Linford water treatment works. The Inspectorate concluded that the Company had taken all reasonable steps to protect consumers following the incident, but was critical of the Company's disinfection monitoring and control arrangements.

No other events regarded as constituting incidents came to the attention of the Inspectorate in 1995.

Enforcement action

Apart from the Notice referred above, which was subsequently not required, no other enforcement action needed to be considered for the Company as a result of the Inspectorate's work in, or pertaining to, the calendar year 1995.

FOLKESTONE AND DOVER WATER SERVICES LIMITED

Introduction

The Company supplies approximately 53 Ml/d to a population of some 152,000 in the coastal strip from Dungeness to Dover on the Kent coast. Principal population centres are Dover, Folkestone, Hythe and New Romney in the Dover and Shepway districts. The Company also supplies local industry including the Dungeness Nuclear Power Stations, Dover and Folkestone Harbours and the Channel Tunnel.

The Company's water resources consist of 26 groundwater sources which are treated at 18 treatment works. Some 75% of water supplies are derived from chalk aquifers and over 20% from the Dungeness shingle headland. The remainder is derived from the Folkestone and Hythe beds of the Lower Greensand aquifer.

Treated water is distributed by gravity via 14 service reservoirs through approximately 1,019 km of mains. The supply area is divided into 12 water supply zones.

Overall water quality

At water treatment works and service reservoirs and in water supply zones, the Company carried out a total of 9,862 determinations in 1995. Of these, 99.8% demonstrated compliance with the relevant water quality standards, but 16 showed a PCV to have been contravened.

Coliforms were not detected at 17 (94.4%) of the Company's 18 water treatment works. At all of the Company's 14 service reservoirs, coliforms were absent from at least 95% of samples. Of the Company's 12 water supply zones in 1995, 11 (91.7%) complied fully with the relevant water quality standards or had breaches of the standards which were either trivial or were fully covered by undertakings. In the other zone, breaches are regarded as unlikely to recur.

Microbiological quality of water leaving treatment works

Table 3.10.1 shows the Company's performance in 1995, with data for 1994 and 1993 for comparison. Differences between the three years are not regarded as significant.

**Table 3.10.1 Folkestone and Dover Water Services Limited
MICROBIOLOGICAL QUALITY OF WATER LEAVING
TREATMENT WORKS**

	1995	1994	1993
Number of water treatment works	18	18	20
Works with no sampling shortfall	18	16	20
COLIFORMS			
Total number of determinations	1,227	1,077	1,133
- number containing coliforms	1	1	2
- % containing coliforms	<0.1	<0.1	0.2
Treatment works with coliforms detected	**1**	**1**	**2**
- % of all works	6	6	10
FAECAL COLIFORMS			
Total number of determinations	1,227	1,077	1,126
- number containing faecal coliforms	0	0	2
- % containing faecal coliforms	0.0	0.0	0.2
Treatment works with faecal coliforms detected	**0**	**0**	**2**
- % of all works	0	0	10

The Company complied with the sampling frequencies required by regulation 17 at all of its treatment works in 1995. The contravention of the coliform standard at one works is considered trivial.

Microbiological quality of water in service reservoirs

Table 3.10.2 shows the Company's performance in 1995, with data for 1994 and 1993 for comparison.

The Company complied with the sampling frequencies required by regulation 18 at all of its service reservoirs in 1995, at which there were no contraventions of the microbiological standards. Differences between the three years are not regarded as significant.

**Table 3.10.2   Folkestone and Dover Water Services Limited
MICROBIOLOGICAL QUALITY OF WATER IN SERVICE RESERVOIRS**

	1995	1994	1993
Number of service reservoirs	14	14	14
Service reservoirs with no sampling shortfall	14	14	14
COLIFORMS			
Total number of determinations	678	649	668
- number containing coliforms	1	0	2
- % containing coliforms	0.2	0.0	0.3
Service reservoirs with coliforms detected	1	0	2
Service reservoirs with coliforms detected in more than 5% of samples	**0**	**0**	**0**
- % of all service reservoirs	0	0	0
FAECAL COLIFORMS			
Total number of determinations	678	649	664
- number containing faecal coliforms	0	0	1
- % containing faecal coliforms	0.0	0.0	0.2
Service reservoirs with faecal coliforms detected	**0**	**0**	**1**
- % of all service reservoirs	0	0	7

Water quality in water supply zones

The Company complied with the required sampling frequencies for all parameters in all of its zones.

Table 3.10.3 shows the Company's performance in 1995, with data for 1994 and 1993 for comparison. Differences between the three years are not regarded as significant.

All contraventions of the standards in zones are considered trivial or unlikely to recur or covered by undertakings.

Inspection

Dr M J Gray, Principal Inspector, assisted by Miss C Y Hill, Inspector, carried out an inspection of Folkestone and Dover Water Services Limited during visits in July and August 1995. Dr Gray concluded that:

(a)   appropriate and satisfactory measures have been taken or are being taken to implement the recommendations made in the 1994 technical audit inspection report;

(b)   the arrangements for sampling as audited generally satisfied parts IV and V of the Regulations and accorded with the recommendations of the Guidance Document;

Table 3.10.3 Folkestone and Dover Water Services Limited
WATER QUALITY IN SUPPLY ZONES

*Columns 'CBU' show, for determinations, contraventions covered by undertakings and, for zones, the <u>total</u> number of zones covered by undertakings in 1995. Column 'E' shows the number of zones for which new enforcement action is under consideration as a result of contraventions of the PCV in 1995. **Please refer to the Introduction to Chapter 3 for more detailed explanation of this table.***

| Parameter | DETERMINATIONS in 1995 | | | | ZONES (12 in 1995)* | | | | |
| | Total | Contravening PCV | | | Non-compliant | | | | |
		No.	%	CBU	CBU 1995	E 1995	Number in: 1995	1994	1993
Coliforms	637	1	0.2	0	0	0	0	0	1
Faecal coliforms	637	0	0.0	0	0	0	0	0	0
Colour	72	0	0.0	0	0	0	0	0	0
Turbidity	101	1	1.0	1	12	0	1	0	0
Odour	72	0	0.0	0	0	0	0	0	0
Taste	72	0	0.0	0	0	0	0	0	0
Hydrogen ion	259	0	0.0	0	0	0	0	0	0
Nitrate	72	0	0.0	0	0	0	0	0	0
Nitrite	72	0	0.0	0	0	0	0	0	0
Aluminium	72	0	0.0	0	0	0	0	0	0
Iron	98	2	2.0	2	12	0	1	1	1
Manganese	72	0	0.0	0	0	0	0	0	0
Lead	56	2	3.6	0	0	0	1	0	2
PAH	101	6	5.9	2	3	0	5	5	4
Trihalomethanes	48	0	0.0	0	0	0	0	0	0
Total pesticides	127	0	0.0	0	12	0	0	0	0
Atrazine	88	2	2.3	2	12	0	1	2	2
Other pesticides	2,352	0	0.0	0	5	0	0	0	0
Total hardness	12	0	0.0	0	0	0	0	0	0
All others	1,032	0	0.0	0	0	0	0	0	0
Total	**6,052**	**14**	**0.2**	**7**	-	-	-	-	-

* 12 zones in 1994; 12 zones in 1993.

(c) the Company's analytical arrangements satisfied the requirements of regulation 21(2)(d)(iii);

(d) the Company is aware of the contents of the most recent issue of Report 71 and, in general, action has been taken or is being taken to implement changes to its procedures where appropriate;

(e) the Company's arrangements for reporting compliance data were satisfactory and secure;

(f) the arrangements for the dissemination of water quality data both within the Company and to members of the public were satisfactory and the public record satisfies the requirements of regulation 29;

(g) from the information provided, the Company is on target to meet all key stages of its compliance programmes by the due dates;

(h) the Company has a satisfactory policy and procedure for the automatic shut-down of treatment works in the event of a disinfection failure;

(i)   from an audit of a representative selection of data charts and logs, the Company has a satisfactory system in place for checking that information provided by on-site continuous residual disinfection monitors is consistent with the result of on-site testing;

(j)   the Company is aware of the advice provided in the document "Civil Emergencies involving Radioactive Substances: The Department's Role and Arrangements" published June 1995 and its role in the event of a radioactive release to the environment; and

(k)   the Company has a satisfactory system for liaising with and reporting to local authorities and is meeting the requirements of regulations 30(4), 30(5) and 31.

There were no recommendations arising from these inspections. Seven suggestions on various matters were made.

Improvement programmes

No undertakings were due for full completion during 1995. A new undertaking given by the Company to carry out improvement works to its distribution system, with a completion date of 31 March 2000, is being considered by the Secretary of State.

Incidents

No events regarded as constituting incidents in which drinking water quality demonstrably deteriorated were notified during 1995 by the Company to the Secretary of State under the terms of the Water Undertakers (Information) Direction 1992.

Enforcement action

No enforcement action needed to be considered for the Company as a result of the Inspectorate's work in, or pertaining to, the calendar year 1995.

HARTLEPOOL WATER PLC

Introduction

The Company supplies on average 34 Ml/d of water to a population of approximately 92,000 people centred on the town of Hartlepool. The Company's water resources for potable supply consist of 20 boreholes operating at depths between 70 m and 200 m in the Magnesian limestone. Water is treated at a single site at Dalton Piercy which has two treatment streams. This is a central blending station where all water is subject to disinfection. Treated water is distributed via six service reservoirs and 466 km of mains. The supply area is divided into three water supply zones.

Overall water quality

At water treatment works and service reservoirs and in water supply zones, the Company carried out a total of 2,468 determinations in 1995. Of these, 99.7% demonstrated compliance with the relevant water quality standards, but seven showed a PCV to have been contravened.

Coliforms were not detected at the Company's water treatment works. At all of the Company's six service reservoirs, coliforms were absent from at least 95% of samples. In 1995 two of the Company's three water supply zones had breaches of the standards which were regarded as trivial. One zone had breaches of a standard which were not regarded as trivial.

Microbiological quality of water leaving treatment works

Table 3.11.1 shows the Company's performance in 1995, with data for 1994 and 1993 for comparison. Differences between the three years are not considered significant.

In 1995 the Company complied with the sampling frequency required by regulation 17 and had no contraventions of the microbiological standards at the water treatment works.

Table 3.11.1 Hartlepool Water Plc
MICROBIOLOGICAL QUALITY OF WATER LEAVING TREATMENT WORKS

	1995	1994	1993
Number of water treatment works	2	1	1
Works with no sampling shortfall	2	1	1
COLIFORMS			
Total number of determinations	312	312	312
- number containing coliforms	0	0	2
- % containing coliforms	0.0	0.0	0.6
Treatment works with coliforms detected	**0**	**0**	**1**
% of all works			
FAECAL COLIFORMS	0	0	100
Total number of determinations	312	312	312
- number containing faecal coliforms	0	0	1
- % containing faecal coliforms	0.0	0.0	0.3
Treatment works with faecal coliforms detected	**0**	**0**	**1**
% of all works	0	0	100

Microbiological quality of water in service reservoirs

Table 3.11.2 shows the Company's performance in 1995, with data for 1994 and 1993 for comparison. Differences between the three years are not considered significant.

The Company complied with the required sampling frequencies at all of its service reservoirs.

Coliforms were detected in one sample taken from one service reservoir, but regulation 3(7) was not breached at this site.

Table 3.11.2 Hartlepool Water Plc MICROBIOLOGICAL QUALITY OF WATER IN SERVICE RESERVOIRS	1995	1994	1993
Number of service reservoirs	6	6	6
Service reservoirs with no sampling shortfall	6	6	6
COLIFORMS			
Total number of determinations	312	312	317
- number containing coliforms	1	3	3
- % containing coliforms	0.3	1.0	0.9
Service reservoirs with coliforms detected	1	3	3
Service reservoirs with coliforms detected in more than 5% of samples	**0**	**0**	**0**
% of all service reservoirs	0	0	0
FAECAL COLIFORMS			
Total number of determinations	312	312	317
- number containing faecal coliforms	0	1	0
- % containing faecal coliforms	0.0	0.3	0.0
Service reservoirs with faecal coliforms detected	**0**	**1**	**0**
% of all service reservoirs	0	17	0

Water quality in water supply zones

The Company complied with the required sampling frequencies in all of its zones. Table 3.11.3 gives a summary of water quality in water supply zones in 1995, with data for 1994 and 1993 for comparison. Differences between the three years are not considered significant.

Enforcement action is being considered for contravention of the standard for PAH in one zone, as shown in Tables 3.11.3 and 3.11.4. All other contraventions of the standards in zones are considered trivial.

Inspection

The Inspection of Hartlepool Water Plc was led by Mr M J Purcell and carried out by Mr B S Bell, Inspector, in September 1995. Mr Bell concluded that:

(a) the Company had satisfactorily addressed, or was in the process of addressing, the recommendations made in the 1994 inspection report;

(b) the Company has satisfactory procedures for the analysis of microbiological parameters, although it needs to take account of the latest edition of Report 71;

(c) audits of analytical methods identified some areas which require attention;

Table 3.11.3 Hartlepool Water Plc
WATER QUALITY IN SUPPLY ZONES

Columns 'CBU' show, for determinations, contraventions covered by undertakings and, for zones, the <u>total</u> number of zones covered by undertakings in 1995. Column 'E' shows the number of zones for which new enforcement action is under consideration as a result of contraventions of the PCV in 1995. **Please refer to the Introduction to Chapter 3 for more detailed explanation of this table.**

Parameter	DETERMINATIONS in 1995				ZONES (3 in 1995)*				
	Total	Contravening PCV			Non-compliant				
		No.	%	CBU	CBU 1995	E	1995	1994	1993
Coliforms	240	0	0.0	0	0	0	0	0	0
Faecal coliforms	240	0	0.0	0	0	0	0	0	1
Colour	12	0	0.0	0	0	0	0	0	0
Turbidity	12	0	0.0	0	0	0	0	0	0
Odour	4	0	0.0	0	0	0	0	0	0
Taste	4	0	0.0	0	0	0	0	0	0
Hydrogen ion	12	0	0.0	0	0	0	0	0	0
Nitrate	12	0	0.0	0	0	0	0	0	0
Nitrite	12	0	0.0	0	0	0	0	0	0
Aluminium	12	0	0.0	0	0	0	0	0	0
Iron	120	2	1.7	0	0	0	2	0	2
Manganese	120	1	0.8	0	0	0	1	0	3
Lead	6	0	0.0	0	0	0	0	0	0
PAH	9	3	33.3	0	0	1	1	0	0
Trihalomethanes	3	0	0.0	0	0	0	0	0	0
Total pesticides	3	0	0.0	0	0	0	0	0	0
Individual pesticides	126	0	0.0	0	0	0	0	0	0
All others	273	0	0.0	0	0	0	0	0	0
Total	**1,220**	**6**	**0.5**	**0**	-	-	-	-	-

* 3 zones in 1994; 3 zones in 1993.

(d) an audit of the telemetry system at the Company's water treatment works indicated that the Company had satisfactory procedures in place to effectively monitor water treatment processes;

(e) there was no evidence of shortcomings in service reservoir operations;

(f) the Company had in place liaison arrangements for dealing with radioactivity monitoring;

(g) the Company has in place procedures which comply with the requirements of regulation 30(4) and 31(3) and satisfactory arrangements for communications with local authorities on issues of water quality and compliance with regulation 30(5); and

(h) the Company is developing various internal quality assurance initiatives and will keep open the option of third party accreditation in the future.

Mr Bell noted contraventions of regulation 21(2)(d)(iii) in respect of contracted laboratory procedures. However, remedial action was taken speedily and enforcement action was not necessary. As a result of the inspection one recommendation was conveyed to the Company for formal response. 12 suggestions on various matters were also made.

Improvement programmes

No undertakings in respect of improvement programmes were due for full completion or the completion of major steps during 1995.

Incidents

No events regarded as constituting incidents in which drinking water quality demonstrably deteriorated came to the attention of the Inspectorate in 1995.

Enforcement action

Table 3.11.4 summarises enforcement action under consideration for the Company as a result of the Inspectorate's work in, or pertaining to, the calendar year 1995.

Table 3.11.4 Hartlepool Water Plc
SUMMARY OF ENFORCEMENT ACTION CONSIDERED IN 1995

Regulation	Reason for enforcement
3(3)(c)	Contravention of the standard for PAH in one zone.

MID KENT WATER PLC

Introduction

The Company supplies on average approximately 172 Ml/d of treated water to a population of some 528,000 in Maidstone, Ashford, Canterbury and the surrounding areas. The Company's water resources consist of:

(a)   groundwater sources in the chalk, greensands and Ashdown sands aquifers (approximately 82% of supply);

(b)   a lowland pumped storage reservoir (approximately 6% of supply); and

(c)   bulk supplies of treated water from Southern Water Services Limited (approximately 12% of supply).

The water is treated at 29 water treatment works. The treated water is distributed by pumping and gravity through 73 service reservoirs and some 4,100 km of water mains. The Company has 21 designated water supply zones.

Overall water quality

At water treatment works and service reservoirs and in water supply zones, the Company carried out a total of 25,719 determinations in 1995. Of these, 99.6% demonstrated compliance with the relevant water quality standards, but 115 showed a PCV to have been contravened.

Coliforms were not detected at 28 (97%) of the Company's 29 water treatment works. Coliforms were absent from at least 95% of samples taken from each of the Company's 73 service reservoirs. All the Company's 21 water supply zones in 1995 (100%) complied fully with the relevant water quality standards or had breaches of the standards which were either trivial or were fully covered by undertakings.

Microbiological quality of water leaving treatment works

Table 3.12.1 shows the Company's performance in 1995, with data for 1994 and 1993 for comparison. Differences between the three years are not considered significant.

Table 3.12.1   Mid Kent Water plc
MICROBIOLOGICAL QUALITY OF WATER LEAVING TREATMENT WORKS

	1995	1994	1993
Number of water treatment works	29	31	33
Works with no sampling shortfall	29	31	33
COLIFORMS			
Total number of determinations	2,270	2,020	2,238
- number containing coliforms	1	0	3
- % containing coliforms	<0.1	0.0	0.1
Treatment works with coliforms detected	**1**	**0**	**3**
- % of all works	3	0	9
FAECAL COLIFORMS			
Total number of determinations	2,270	2,009	2,238
- number containing faecal coliforms	1	0	1
- % containing faecal coliforms	<0.1	0.0	<0.1
Treatment works with faecal coliforms detected	**1**	**0**	**1**
- % of all works	3	0	3

The Company complied with the sampling frequencies required by regulation 17 at all its treatment works in 1995.

All contraventions of the standards at works are considered trivial.

Microbiological quality of water in service reservoirs

Table 3.12.2 shows the Company's performance in 1995, with data for 1994 and 1993 for comparison. Differences between the three years are not considered significant.

Table 3.12.2 Mid Kent Water plc MICROBIOLOGICAL QUALITY OF WATER IN SERVICE RESERVOIRS	1995	1994	1993
Number of service reservoirs	73	73	79
Service reservoirs with no sampling shortfall	73	73	79
COLIFORMS			
Total number of determinations	3,666	3,775	3,836
- number containing coliforms	15	14	8
- % containing coliforms	0.4	0.4	0.2
Service reservoirs with coliforms detected	13	9	7
Service reservoirs with coliforms detected in more than 5% of samples	**0**	**1**	**0**
- % of all service reservoirs	0	1	0
FAECAL COLIFORMS			
Total number of determinations	3,666	3,760	3,836
- number containing faecal coliforms	9	7	3
- % containing faecal coliforms	0.2	0.2	<0.1
Service reservoirs with faecal coliforms detected	**8**	**4**	**3**
- % of all service reservoirs	11	5	4

Had the definition of the coliform parameter not been changed as described in 3.35 above, but remained as it was for 1994 and previous years, only 14 samples from service reservoirs would have been reported as containing coliforms.

The Company complied with the sampling frequencies required by regulation 18 at all its service reservoirs in 1995.

The Company has identified the probable cause of the contraventions of the standard for faecal coliforms at two service reservoirs and remedial action is being taken. The Inspectorate will assess the results of further monitoring for the first six months of 1996 to determine whether this action has been effective and that the contraventions are unlikely to recur or whether enforcement action is required. All other contraventions of the standards at service reservoirs are considered trivial or unlikely to recur.

Water quality in water supply zones

The Company failed to comply with the required sampling frequencies for arsenic, barium, boron and chromium in one zone. The Company has identified the reasons for these shortfalls and taken appropriate action to prevent a recurrence.

Table 3.12.3 shows the Company's performance in 1995, with data for 1994 and 1993 for comparison. Differences between the three years are not considered significant. Had the definition of the coliform parameter not been changed as described in 3.35

above, but remained as it was for 1994 and previous years, only 14 samples from water supply zones would have been reported as containing coliforms.

The Inspectorate will assess the results of further monitoring during the first six months of 1996 for lead in one zone before deciding on the need for enforcement action. All other contraventions of the standards in zones are considered trivial or are covered by undertakings or will be covered by the new distribution undertaking.

Table 3.12.3 Mid Kent Water plc
WATER QUALITY IN SUPPLY ZONES

*Columns 'CBU' show, for determinations, contraventions covered by undertakings and, for zones, the <u>total</u> number of zones covered by undertakings in 1995. Column 'E' shows the number of zones for which new enforcement action is under consideration as a result of contraventions of the PCV in 1995. **Please refer to the Introduction to Chapter 3 for more detailed explanation of this table.**

Parameter	DETERMINATIONS in 1995				ZONES (21 in 1995)*				
	Total	Contravening PCV					Non-compliant		
		No.	%	CBU	CBU	E	Number in:		
					1995		1995	1994	1993
Coliforms	1,453	16	1.1	0	0	0	0	2	1
Faecal coliforms	1,453	2	0.1	0	1	0	2	5	2
Colour	172	0	0.0	0	0	0	0	0	0
Turbidity	172	0	0.0	0	0	0	0	0	0
Odour	210	0	0.0	0	0	0	0	1	0
Taste	210	0	0.0	0	0	0	0	0	0
Hydrogen ion	230	0	0.0	0	0	0	0	0	0
Nitrate	172	0	0.0	0	0	0	0	0	0
Nitrite	254	0	0.0	0	1	0	0	2	1
Aluminium	172	0	0.0	0	0	0	0	0	0
Iron	695	17	2.4	17	21	0	9	17	20
Manganese	338	3	0.9	3	21	0	2	3	2
Lead	86	1	1.2	0	0	0	1	1	0
PAH	300	24	8.0	0	0	0	11	18	16
Trihalomethanes	84	0	0.0	0	0	0	0	0	0
Total pesticides	648	0	0.0	0	8	0	0	1	5
Atrazine	212	1	0.5	1	8	0	1	1	2
Chlorotoluron	129	4	3.1	4	8	0	2	2	2
2,4-D	136	0	0.0	0	8	0	0	2	1
Diuron	129	0	0.0	0	8	0	0	0	4
Flutriafol	7	2	28.6	2	8	0	2	0	0
Isoproturon	129	5	3.9	5	8	0	2	2	3
MCPA	136	0	0.0	0	8	0	0	1	0
Mecoprop	136	1	0.7	1	8	0	1	4	3
Simazine	212	12	5.7	12	8	0	4	4	10
2,4,5-T	136	0	0.0	0	8	0	0	0	1
Other pesticides	3,465	0	0.0	0	8	0	0	0	0
Benzo 3,4 pyrene	300	1	0.3	0	0	0	0	0	1
Temperature	172	0	0.0	0	0	0	0	0	1
Zinc	84	0	0.0	0	0	0	0	0	1
All others	1,815	0	0.0	0	0	0	0	0	0
Total	**13,847**	**89**	**0.6**	**45**	-	-	**18**	-	-

* 34 zones in 1994; 34 zones in 1993.

Inspection

Mr A Hallas, Principal Inspector, carried out an inspection of Mid Kent Water plc in two visits on 25 July 1995 and between 20 and 23 November 1995. Miss C R Jackson, Inspector, and Mr M D Wright, Temporary Technical Assessor, assisted in the first part of the inspection. Mr Hallas concluded that:

(a)   the Company had responded positively to the recommendations on analytical requirements made in the 1994 technical audit inspection report;

(b)   the general arrangements for sampling satisfied parts IV and V of the Regulations and accorded with the recommendations of the Guidance Document;

(c)   the Company's sampling procedures as audited during the inspection met the requirements of regulation 21(2)(a)(b) and (c);

(d)   the Company's contract laboratory had made significant progress towards meeting fully the requirements of regulation 21, although a number of further deficiencies were identified in respect of samples audited in detail during the inspection;

(e)   the Company's contract laboratory was following most of the recommendations given in the new Report 71;

(f)   progress with capital schemes related to undertakings was generally satisfactory, except that the pesticide removal plant at Burham (managed by Southern Water) would not be fully operational by the due date;

(g)   the Company is continuing to take a positive approach in respect of water treatment policies audited;

(h)   the Company's procedure for disinfection of water supplied, as audited, were satisfactory;

(i)   the Company's operational procedures to ensure adequate turnover of water in its service reservoirs were satisfactory;

(j)   the Company's operational procedures for the disinfection of new mains was satisfactory, as audited;

(k)   the Company had systems in place for seeking advice in the event of a radioactive release into the environment;

(l)   the Company's procedures and arrangements for communications and liaison with the local authorities in its area of supply were satisfactory; and

(m)   satisfactory progress is being made by the Company in becoming a quality organisation.

Mr Hallas found contraventions of regulation 21(2)(d) in respect of one parameter and enforcement action was considered. However the Company took appropriate action to prevent recurrence and enforcement was not required.

In October, Mr R M Walls, representing consultants Rofe, Kennard and Lapworth, and working under the general direction of Mr Hallas, carried out inspection of selected water treatment works and selected service reservoirs. He concluded that:

(n)   the treatment processes complied with Regulation 23;

(o)   the use of substances and products satisfied the requirements of Regulation 25;

(p)   the Company's policy and arrangements for disinfection at treatment works were satisfactory; and

(q)   the Company's arrangements for compliance sampling at treatment works and service reservoirs are generally in accordance with the recommendations of paragraph 2.8 of the Guidance Document and with the requirements of Regulation 21(2)(a).

As a result of these inspections, 17 recommendations were conveyed to the Company for formal response, mainly associated with water treatment practices. Twenty-nine suggestions on various matters were also made. Mr Hallas is satisfied that the Company has taken appropriate and satisfactory measures to implement the four recommendations made in Part 1 of technical audit inspection report and is taking action or has already taken action on the other recommendations.

Improvement programmes

Two undertakings in respect of improvement programmes accepted by the Secretary of State from the Company were due for full completion during 1995 and one of these was completed on schedule. The final completion date of the other scheme was delayed for reasons beyond the Company's control but action was taken to ensure compliance was achieved pending completion of the works. A new undertaking given by the Company to carry out improvement works to its distribution system, with a completion date of 31 March 2000, is being considered by the Secretary of State.

Incidents

No events regarded as constituting incidents in which drinking water quality demonstrably deteriorated came to the attention of the Inspectorate in 1995.

Enforcement action

Table 3.12.4 summarises enforcement action under consideration for the Company as a result of the Inspectorate's work in, or pertaining to, the calendar year 1995.

Table 3.12.4	Mid Kent Water plc **SUMMARY OF ENFORCEMENT ACTION CONSIDERED IN 1995**
Regulation	**Reason for enforcement**
21(2)(d)	Samples were not analysed as soon as maybe after being taken.

MID SOUTHERN WATER PLC

Introduction

The Company supplies on average 229 Ml/d to a population of 722,000 in the counties of Berkshire, Surrey, West Sussex and Hampshire. Approximately 86% of the Company's water is obtained from boreholes; the remainder is obtained from North Surrey Water Limited as a bulk supply of treated water obtained from the River Thames. The water is treated at 28 treatment works sites, two of which have multiple sampling points for the purposes of compliance assessment. Treated water is distributed via 73 service reservoirs and 4,400 km of water mains. The supply area is divided into 44 water supply zones.

Overall water quality

At water treatment works and service reservoirs and in water supply zones, the Company carried out a total of 43,751 determinations in 1995. Of these, 99.3% demonstrated compliance with the relevant water quality standards, but 303 showed a PCV to have been contravened.

Coliforms were not detected at 25 (83%) of the Company's 30 water treatment works. At 72 (97%) of the Company's 73 service reservoirs, coliforms were absent from at least 95% of samples. Of the Company's 44 water supply zones in 1995, 40 (90%) complied fully with the relevant water quality standards or had breaches of the standards which were either trivial or were fully covered by undertakings. In the other four (10%) of the zones, some breaches could result in enforcement action.

Microbiological quality of water leaving treatment works

Table 3.13.1 shows the Company's performance in 1995, with data for 1994 and 1993 for comparison. Differences between the three years are not considered significant. Had the definition of the coliform parameter not been changed as described in 3.35 above, but remained as it was for 1994 and previous years, the number of treatment works with coliforms detected would have been three and the number of determinations containing coliforms three.

Table 3.13.1 Mid Southern Water Plc
MICROBIOLOGICAL QUALITY OF WATER LEAVING TREATMENT WORKS

	1995	1994	1993
Number of water treatment works	30	29	30
Works with no sampling shortfall	29	26	30
COLIFORMS			
Total number of determinations	3,182	3,068	3,056
- number containing coliforms	5	3	1
- % containing coliforms	0.2	<0.1	<0.1
Treatment works with coliforms detected	**5**	**1**	**1**
- % of all works	17	3	3
FAECAL COLIFORMS			
Total number of determinations	3,182	3,068	3,056
- number containing faecal coliforms	2	0	0
- % containing faecal coliforms	<0.1	0.0	0.0
Treatment works with faecal coliforms detected	**2**	**0**	**0**
- % of all works	7	0	0

The Company complied with the sampling frequencies required by regulation 17 at 29 of its 30 treatment works in 1995. The shortfall at a single works is regarded as trivial.

Contraventions of the microbiological quality standards at Hawkley water treatment works have resulted in the consideration of enforcement action, as shown in table 3.13.4. All other contraventions of the standards at works are considered trivial.

Microbiological quality of water in service reservoirs

Table 3.13.2 shows the Company's performance in 1995, with data for 1994 and 1993 for comparison. Differences between the three years are not considered significant. Had the definition of the coliform parameter not been changed as described in 3.35 above, but remained as it was for 1994 and previous years, there would have been no service reservoirs with coliforms detected in more than 5% of samples and the number of determinations containing coliforms would have been eight.

Table 3.13.2 Mid Southern Water Plc
MICROBIOLOGICAL QUALITY OF WATER IN SERVICE RESERVOIRS

	1995	1994	1993
Number of service reservoirs	73	72	74
Service reservoirs with no sampling shortfall	58	72	74
COLIFORMS			
Total number of determinations	3,840	3,832	3,878
- number containing coliforms	17	8	10
- % containing coliforms	0.4	0.2	0.3
Service reservoirs with coliforms detected	13	7	7
Service reservoirs with coliforms detected in more than 5% of samples	**2**	**0**	**1**
- % of all service reservoirs	3	0	1
FAECAL COLIFORMS			
Total number of determinations	3,840	3,832	3,878
- number containing faecal coliforms	4	1	4
- % containing faecal coliforms	0.1	<0.1	0.1
Service reservoirs with faecal coliforms detected	**4**	**1**	**3**
- % of all service reservoirs	5	1	4

The Company complied with the sampling frequencies required by regulation 18 at 58 of its 73 service reservoirs in 1995. Shortfalls at the other 15 are regarded as unlikely to recur.

Contraventions of the microbiological quality standards at two service reservoirs have resulted in the consideration of enforcement action, as shown in table 3.13.4. All other contraventions of the standards at service reservoirs are considered trivial or unlikely to recur.

Water quality in water supply zones

The Company complied with the required sampling frequencies of regulation 13 in all of its supply zones.

Table 3.13.3 shows the Company's performance in 1995, with data for 1994 and 1993 for comparison. Several substances have given rise to changing patterns of compliance of zones with the individual pesticides standard; of these changes the decrease in the number of zones failing to comply in respect of atrazine and simazine are significant. The Company has provided evidence to show that the main reason for the detection of dalapon and TCA is as by-products of disinfection rather than their use as pesticides.

Table 3.13.3 **Mid Southern Water Plc**
WATER QUALITY IN SUPPLY ZONES

Columns 'CBU' show, for determinations, contraventions covered by undertakings and, for zones, the total *number of zones covered by undertakings in 1995. Column 'E' shows the number of zones for which new enforcement action is under consideration as a result of contraventions of the PCV in 1995.* **Please refer to the Introduction to Chapter 3 for more detailed explanation of this table.**

Parameter	DETERMINATIONS in 1995				ZONES (44 in 1995)*				
	Total	Contravening PCV			CBU	E	Non-compliant Number in:		
		No.	%	CBU	1995		1995	1994	1993
Coliforms	2,783	65	2.3	0	0	3	3	0	0
Faecal coliforms	2,332	9	0.4	0	0	2	7	1	3
Colour	307	0	0.0	0	0	0	0	0	0
Turbidity	344	0	0.0	0	0	0	0	2	0
Odour	308	1	0.3	0	0	0	1	0	0
Taste	308	0	0.0	0	0	0	0	0	0
Hydrogen ion	1,620	0	0.0	0	0	0	0	0	0
Nitrate	307	0	0.0	0	0	0	0	0	0
Nitrite	307	0	0.0	0	0	0	0	0	2
Aluminium	330	2	0.6	0	0	0	2	0	0
Iron	467	5	1.1	0	0	0	3	5	1
Manganese	319	0	0.0	0	0	0	0	1	1
Lead	184	0	0.0	0	0	0	0	1	0
PAH	275	22	8.0	0	0	0	13	9	8
Trihalomethanes	183	0	0.0	0	0	0	0	0	0
Total pesticides	266	2	0.8	2	11	0	2	5	2
Atrazine	390	5	1.3	2	11	0	5	10	16
Carbetamide	330	1	0.3	0	11	0	1	0	0
Chlorotoluron	330	0	0.0	0	11	0	0	3	0
Dalapon	266	43	16.1	37	11	0	14	11	1
Diuron	330	2	0.6	2	11	0	2	1	1
Glyphosate	84	2	2.4	2	11	0	2	0	0
Isoproturon	330	3	0.9	3	11	0	2	7	1
Linuron	330	4	1.2	0	11	0	4	0	0
Mecoprop	267	0	0.0	0	11	0	0	2	0
Simazine	390	0	0.0	0	11	0	0	3	5
TCA	266	109	41.0	73	11	0	30	29	11
Other pesticides	9,284	0	0.0	0	11	0	0	0	0
Temperature	334	0	0.0	0	0	0	0	1	0
Benzo 3,4 pyrene	275	0	0.0	0	0	0	0	0	1
All others	5,861	0	0.0	0	0	0	0	0	0
Total	**29,707**	**275**	**0.9**	**121**	**-**	**-**	**-**	**-**	**-**

* 44 zones in 1994; 42 zones in 1993.

Had the definition of the coliform parameter not been changed as described in 3.35 above, but remained as it was for 1994 and previous years, the number of zones contravening the PCV for would have been one and the number of determinations containing coliforms 48.

Enforcement action is being considered in respect of some contraventions of standards, as shown in tables 3.13.3 and 3.13.4. All other contraventions of the standards in zones are considered trivial or covered by undertakings.

Inspection

Mr R J Vincent, Principal Inspector, assisted by Mr P L Jiggins, Inspector, carried out an inspection of Mid Southern Water Plc in a series of visits between 6 October and 30 November 1995. Mr Vincent concluded that:

(a) the Company has initiated action in respect of the recommendations made in the 1994 Inspection Report;

(b) analytical arrangements were generally satisfactory, although regulation 21(2)(d)(iii) has been breached trivially in regard to some parameters;

(c) the Company's arrangements for recording compliance sampling and reporting are generally satisfactory;

(d) the Company's arrangements for maintaining and providing a Public Record are satisfactory;

(e) the Company will achieve compliance with the pesticide standards by the due dates of its two current undertakings, but that full completion of the schemes may be marginally delayed;

(f) the Company's arrangements for mains rehabilitation using epoxy resin relining are generally satisfactory, but provision for training and validation of records could be improved;

(g) the Company's arrangements for rehearsals of emergency procedures are generally satisfactory; and

(h) communications between the Company and Basingstoke and Deane District Council are satisfactory.

Mr Vincent found contraventions of regulation 21(2)(d)(iii) in respect of some parameters, however remedial action was taken speedily in each case and enforcement action was not necessary.

In October, Mr R M Walls, representing consultants Rofe, Kennard and Lapworth, and working under the general direction of Mr Vincent, carried out inspection of selected water treatment works and selected service reservoirs. He concluded that:

(i) the treatment processes at Hawkley water treatment works complied with Regulation 23;

(j) the use of substances and products satisfied the requirements of Regulation 25;

(k) the Company's arrangements for compliance sampling at Hawkley water treatment are generally in accordance with the recommendations of paragraph 2.8 of the Guidance Document and with the requirements of Regulation 21(2)(a); and

(l) Claypits service reservoir is maintained to a satisfactory standard and the sampling arrangements are in accord with the recommendations of paragraph 2.8 of the Guidance Document and with the requirements of Regulation 21(2)(a).

As a result of these inspections, 26 recommendations were conveyed to the Company for formal response, together with 37 suggestions for the Company to consider. The Company has already taken action on most of these recommendations, and is taking action on others.

Improvement programmes

Two undertakings in respect of improvement programmes accepted by the Secretary of State from the Company were due for full completion during 1995. The necessary treatment plant was installed by the due date of 31 December at Bray and Windmill Hill treatment works but commissioning was slightly delayed for reasons beyond the Company's control. In both cases the Company made alternative supply arrangements to ensure compliance with the pesticide standard until commissioning was completed. A new undertaking given by the Company to carry out improvement works to its distribution system, with a completion date of 31 March 2000, is being considered by the Secretary of State.

Incidents

One event notified during 1995 by the Company to the Secretary of State under the terms of the Water Undertakers (Information) Direction 1992 is regarded by the Inspectorate as constituting an incident in which drinking water quality demonstrably deteriorated.

In May, an incident involving discolouration of the water supply in Farnham affecting some 2,500 consumers occurred, following the isolation of a trunk main prior to lining operations. Advice not to consume discoloured water was issued to the public and alternative supplies in bowsers and bottles were made available. The Inspectorate concluded that the Company took appropriate action to minimise the discolouration and provide alternative supplies.

During the course of the inspection the Inspectorate became aware of an event at Tilford Meads water treatment works, in which drinking water quality demonstrably deteriorated. The event occurred in March, when the works was taken out of supply following the detection of increased turbidity. Investigations by the Company revealed that the borehole had become contaminated by backwash water from the filters via a blocked overflow. The Inspectorate considered that the contamination event at Tilford Meads represented a significant health risk, although subsequent bacteriological monitoring indicated satisfactory water quality. The Inspectorate is critical of the Company for its failure to notify the event formally and has made recommendations accordingly.

No other events regarded as constituting incidents came to the attention of the Inspectorate in 1995.

Enforcement action

Table 3.13.4 summarises enforcement action under consideration for the Company as a result of the Inspectorate's work in, or pertaining to, the calendar year 1995.

Table 3.13.4	Mid Southern Water Plc SUMMARY OF ENFORCEMENT ACTION CONSIDERED IN 1995
Regulation	**Reason for enforcement**
3(3)(c)	Contravention of the standard for coliforms in three zones and faecal coliforms in two zones.
3(7)	Contravention of the coliforms standard at one water treatment works.
3(7)	Contravention of the faecal coliforms standard at one service reservoir and both faecal and total coliform standards at a further service reservoir.

NORTH EAST WATER PLC

Introduction

The Company supplies on average 364 Ml/d of water to a population of approximately 1.3 million people in the urban areas of Tyneside and Wearside and a largely rural area of Northumberland.

The majority of the Company's water is abstracted from surface water sources including the rivers Coquet, North Tyne, Tyne and Wear and from the upland reservoirs at Catcleugh, Derwent and Burnhope. In addition there are a number of borehole sources in the south east of its area and a number of springs and borehole sources in the rural area of Northumberland.

The water is treated at 39 treatment works and distributed via 157 service reservoirs and some 7,700 km of mains. The supply area is divided into 70 supply zones.

Overall water quality

At water treatment works and service reservoirs and in water supply zones, the Company carried out a total of 88,151 determinations in 1995. Of these, 99.7% demonstrated compliance with the relevant water quality standards, but 253 showed a PCV to have been contravened.

Coliforms were not detected at 31 (79%) of the Company's 39 water treatment works. Coliforms were absent from at least 95% of samples from each of the Company's 157 service reservoirs. Of the Company's 70 water supply zones in 1995, 65 (93%) complied fully with the relevant water quality standards or had breaches of the standards which were either trivial or were fully covered by undertakings. In the other five (7%) of the zones, some breaches are regarded as unlikely to recur.

Microbiological quality of water leaving treatment works

Table 3.14.1 shows the Company's performance in 1995, with data for 1994 and 1993 for comparison. Differences between the three years are not considered significant.

Table 3.14.1 North East Water Plc
MICROBIOLOGICAL QUALITY OF WATER LEAVING TREATMENT WORKS

	1995	1994	1993
Number of water treatment works	39	41	41
Works with no sampling shortfall	38	40	38
COLIFORMS			
Total number of determinations	5,151	4,887	5,297
- number containing coliforms	10	8	24
- % containing coliforms	0.2	0.2	0.5
Treatment works with coliforms detected	**8**	**6**	**15**
- % of all works	21	15	37
FAECAL COLIFORMS			
Total number of determinations	5,151	4,887	5,281
- number containing faecal coliforms	4	6	15
- % containing faecal coliforms	<0.1	0.1	0.3
Treatment works with faecal coliforms detected	**3**	**4**	**11**
- % of all works	8	10	27

The Company complied with the sampling frequencies required by regulation 17 at 38 of its 39 treatment works in 1995. The shortfall at the remaining works is regarded as not trivial, however, the Company has taken remedial action to prevent a recurrence and enforcement action is not being considered.

Contraventions of the microbiological quality standards occurred at a total of eight works. Contraventions at five works were considered trivial and contraventions at three works were considered as not trivial but were covered by undertakings.

Microbiological quality of water in service reservoirs

Table 3.14.2 shows the Company's performance in 1995, with data for 1994 and 1993 for comparison. There has been a significant reduction over the three years in the number of determinations containing coliforms and faecal coliforms, and in the number of reservoirs with coliforms detected in more than 5% of samples.

Table 3.14.2 North East Water Plc
MICROBIOLOGICAL QUALITY OF WATER IN SERVICE RESERVOIRS

	1995	1994	1993
Number of service reservoirs	157	155	151
Service reservoirs with no sampling shortfall	144	152	142
COLIFORMS			
Total number of determinations	7,873	7,736	7,377
- number containing coliforms	28	35	49
- % containing coliforms	0.4	0.5	0.7
Service reservoirs with coliforms detected	23	31	32
Service reservoirs with coliforms detected in more than 5% of samples	**0**	**1**	**6**
- % of all service reservoirs	0	1	4
FAECAL COLIFORMS			
Total number of determinations	7,873	7,735	7,351
- number containing faecal coliforms	8	14	22
- % containing faecal coliforms	0.1	0.2	0.3
Service reservoirs with faecal coliforms detected	**8**	**12**	**16**
- % of all service reservoirs	5	8	11

The Company complied with the sampling frequencies required by regulation 18 at 144 of its 157 service reservoirs in 1995. Shortfalls at three reservoirs were regarded as not trivial but unlikely to recur as the Company has taken corrective action. Shortfalls at the remaining ten reservoirs were regarded as trivial.

All contraventions of the standards at service reservoirs are considered trivial.

Water quality in water supply zones

The Company failed to comply with the required sampling frequencies for odour and taste in two zones, however the Company has taken corrective action and contraventions are unlikely to recur.

Table 3.14.3 shows the Company's performance in 1995, with data for 1994 and 1993 for comparison. There has been a significant increase in the number of zones contravening the standard for manganese and PAH but these will be covered by the new distribution undertaking. The apparent significant increase in the number of zones contravening the standard for total pesticides and the individual pesticide isoproturon

Table 3.14.3   North East Water Plc
WATER QUALITY IN SUPPLY ZONES

*Columns 'CBU' show, for determinations, contraventions covered by undertakings and, for zones, the <u>total</u> number of zones covered by undertakings in 1995. Column 'E' shows the number of zones for which new enforcement action is under consideration as a result of contraventions of the PCV in 1995. **Please refer to the Introduction to Chapter 3 for more detailed explanation of this table.***

Parameter	DETERMINATIONS in 1995				ZONES (70 in 1995)*				
	Total	Contravening PCV			CBU	E	Non-compliant		
		No.	%	CBU	1995		Number in:		
							1995	1994	1993
Coliforms	3,733	35	0.9	0	0	0	1	0	1
Faecal coliforms	3,733	4	0.1	0	0	0	4	6	5
Colour	488	0	0.0	0	0	0	0	1	1
Turbidity	531	1	0.2	0	0	0	1	1	1
Odour	533	1	0.2	0	0	0	1	1	0
Taste	938	22	2.3	0	0	0	10	14	0
Hydrogen ion	480	0	0.0	0	0	0	0	0	0
Nitrate	480	0	0.0	0	0	0	0	0	0
Nitrite	526	5	1.0	0	0	0	1	2	1
Aluminium	1,704	3	0.2	3	55	0	3	7	7
Iron	1,932	38	2.0	38	70	0	25	23	29
Manganese	1,512	15	1.0	15	55	0	10	8	2
Lead	898	18	2.0	13	36	0	17	11	12
PAH	322	5	1.6	0	0	0	5	3	0
Trihalomethanes	296	0	0.0	0	0	0	0	0	1
Total pesticides	836	25	3.0	0	0	0	25	0	1
Chlorotoluron	836	0	0.0	0	0	0	0	0	1
2,4-D	844	0	0.0	0	0	0	0	1	1
Dieldrin	836	0	0.0	0	0	0	0	0	1
Diuron	836	0	0.0	0	0	0	0	0	24
Isoproturon	836	25	3.0	0	0	0	25	0	24
Simazine	836	0	0.0	0	0	0	0	0	1
Other pesticides	30,932	0	0.0	0	0	0	0	0	0
Ammonium	480	0	0.0	0	0	0	0	0	1
Barium	70	0	0.0	0	0	0	0	0	1
Benzo 3,4 pyrene	314	3	1.0	0	0	0	0	0	0
Mercury	81	0	0.0	0	0	0	0	1	0
Potassium	74	1	1.4	0	0	0	1	0	0
Selenium	74	1	1.4	0	0	0	1	0	0
Tetrachloroethene	280	1	0.4	0	0	0	0	0	0
All others	5,832	0	0.0	0	0	0	0	0	0
Total	**62,103**	**203**	**0.3**	**69**	-	-	-	-	-

* 73 zones in 1994; 74 zones in 1993.

is a consequence of detection at a supply point serving several zones and is not significant. All other differences between the three years are not considered significant.

Contraventions of the quantitative taste standard in one zone are not considered trivial. However the Company discovered an error in its analytical technique for quantitative taste, which it corrected and as a result contraventions are unlikely to recur. All other contraventions of the standards in zones are considered trivial or unlikely to recur, or are covered by undertakings or will be covered by the new distribution undertaking.

Inspection

Mr B S Bell, Inspector led by Mr M J Purcell, Principal Inspector and assisted by Dr D Westwood, Principal Inspector, carried out an inspection of North East Water Plc in a series of visits between 31 July and 15 December 1995. Mr Bell concluded that:

(a) the Company needs to review its procedures for dealing with radioactivity monitoring;

(b) the Company has in place satisfactory procedures for microbiological sampling and analysis based on those of the previous edition of Report 71 and which have subsequently been amended to take account of the latest edition of Report 71;

(c) in general audit trails of compliance data indicated that the Company's contractor laboratory was maintaining satisfactory records, the performance of some pesticide methods did not meet fully the requirements of regulation 21 but these methods have since been revalidated, and the contractor laboratory had also encountered problems with retrieving some stored analytical data which has since been rectified;

(d) progress with capital schemes relating to undertakings was satisfactory;

(e) an audit of the telemetry system at Warkworth water treatment works indicated that the Company had satisfactory procedures in place to effectively monitor water treatment processes;

(f) the Company makes significant bulk transfers of water; it has procedures in place to deal with water quality issues relating to these transfers;

(g) the Company is undertaking in situ epoxy resin lining of its mains in a satisfactory manner; and

(h) the Company is consolidating its substantial achievements in obtaining accreditation to ISO 9002 for most of its water treatment works and looks to be making considerable progress in achieving accreditation in other areas of the Company's activities.

Mr Bell found contraventions of regulation 21(2)(d)(iii) in respect of certain pesticide analysis and the retrieval of analytical data for pesticides. However, remedial action was taken speedily in each case and so enforcement action was not necessary.

Also on 10 October 1995, Mr P Durrant, representing consultants Rofe, Kennard and Lapworth, and working under the general direction of Mr M J Purcell, carried out inspection of selected water treatment works and selected service reservoirs. He concluded that at Henderson and Cockershield water treatment works:

(i) the treatment processes complied with Regulation 23;

(j) the use of substances and products satisfied the requirements of Regulation 25;

(k) the Company's policy and arrangements for disinfection at treatment works were generally satisfactory; and

(l) the Company's arrangements for compliance sampling at treatment works and service reservoirs are generally in accordance with the recommendations of paragraph 2.8 of the Guidance Document and with the requirements of Regulation 21(2)(a).

As a result of these inspections, eight recommendations were conveyed to the Company for formal response, nearly half of them concerning reporting arrangements. Seventeen suggestions on various matters were also made.

Improvement programmes

One undertaking in respect of an improvement programme for lead accepted by the Secretary of State from the Company was due for full completion during 1995 and was completed on schedule. A new undertaking given by the Company to carry out improvement works to its distribution system, with a completion date of 31 March 2000, is being considered by the Secretary of State.

Incidents

Four events notified during 1995 by the Company to the Secretary of State under the terms of the Water Undertakers (Information) Direction 1992 are regarded by the Inspectorate as constituting incidents in which drinking water quality demonstrably deteriorated.

The first involved a treatment failure at Mosswood water treatment works which resulted in the supply of discoloured water with a below normal residual chlorine content to most of Washington. This also affected the bulk supply to Northumbrian Water which supplies Durham City and outlying districts. The second involved detection of bacteriological contamination, following routine sampling of a service reservoir, in water supplies to part of the village of Riding Mill which resulted in the Company issuing advice to boil water to about 150 properties. The third involved the bacteriological contamination in a rural spring supply known as Park Allotments, in Allendale, Hexham. This resulted in the Company issuing advice to boil water to about 28 properties. The fourth involved the detection of microbiological contamination in routine samples from a compartment of Whalton service reservoir, Northumberland. The contamination was also confirmed in the distribution system by samples taken from properties supplied by the service reservoir. These incidents remain under consideration by the Inspectorate.

Enforcement action

No enforcement action needed to be considered for the Company as a result of the Inspectorate's work in, or pertaining to, the calendar year 1995.

NORTH SURREY WATER LIMITED

Introduction

The Company supplies on average approximately 145 Ml/d to a population of some 472,000 in parts of Surrey and Middlesex. Approximately 85% of the water supplied is derived from the River Thames, with the remainder drawn from underground sources and two bulk supplies of treated water from Thames Water Utilities. The Company in turn provides a bulk supply of approximately 36 Ml/d treated water to Mid Southern Water.

The river derived water is treated at three treatment works. Ground water is treated at two works. Treated water is distributed by pumping and gravity through 23 service reservoirs and some 2,459 km of water mains. The supply area is divided into 14 water supply zones.

Overall water quality

At water treatment works and service reservoirs and in water supply zones, the Company carried out a total of 24,661 determinations in 1995. Of these, 98.8% demonstrated compliance with the relevant water quality standards, but 289 showed a PCV to have been contravened.

Coliforms were not detected at four of the Company's five water treatment works. At all of the Company's 23 service reservoirs, coliforms were absent from at least 95% of samples. Of the Company's 14 water supply zones in 1995, 13 (93%) complied fully with the relevant water quality standards or had breaches of the standards which were either trivial or were fully covered by undertakings. In the other zone, breaches have been regarded as unlikely to recur.

Microbiological quality of water leaving treatment works

Table 3.15.1 shows the Company's performance in 1995, with data for 1994 and 1993 for comparison. Differences between the three years are not regarded as significant.

The Company complied with the sampling frequencies required by regulation 17 at four of its five treatment works in service in 1995. The shortfalls at the other works have been regarded as unlikely to recur.

Contraventions of the microbiological standards at one works in 1995 have resulted in the consideration of enforcement action as shown in table 3.15.4.

Table 3.15.1   North Surrey Water Limited
MICROBIOLOGICAL QUALITY OF WATER LEAVING TREATMENT WORKS

	1995	1994	1993
Number of water treatment works	5	4	3
Works with no sampling shortfall	4	4	3
COLIFORMS			
Total number of determinations	1,113	1,130	1,095
- number containing coliforms	5	0	4
- % containing coliforms	0.5	0.0	0.4
Treatment works with coliforms detected	**1**	**0**	**1**
- % of all works	20	0	33
FAECAL COLIFORMS			
Total number of determinations	1,113	1,130	1,095
- number containing faecal coliforms	4	0	2
- % containing faecal coliforms	0.4	0.0	0.2
Treatment works with faecal coliforms detected	**1**	**0**	**1**
- % of all works	20	0	33

Microbiological quality of water in service reservoirs

Table 3.15.2 shows the Company's performance in 1995, with data for 1994 and 1993 for comparison. Differences between the three years are not regarded as significant.

The Company complied with the sampling frequencies required by regulation 18 at all its service reservoirs in 1995.

There were no contraventions of the microbiological standards at any of the Company's service reservoirs in 1995.

Table 3.15.2 North Surrey Water Limited MICROBIOLOGICAL QUALITY OF WATER IN SERVICE RESERVOIRS			
	1995	**1994**	**1993**
Number of service reservoirs	23	23	22
Service reservoirs with no sampling shortfall	23	22	22
COLIFORMS			
Total number of determinations	1,133	1,134	1,116
- number containing coliforms	7	11	4
- % containing coliforms	0.6	1.0	0.4
Service reservoirs with coliforms detected	7	9	3
Service reservoirs with coliforms detected in more than 5% of samples	**0**	**0**	**0**
- % of all service reservoirs	0	0	0
FAECAL COLIFORMS			
Total number of determinations	1,133	1,134	1,116
- number containing faecal coliforms	0	5	0
- % containing faecal coliforms	0.0	0.4	0.0
Service reservoirs with faecal coliforms detected	**0**	**5**	**0**
- % of all service reservoirs	0	21	0

Water quality in water supply zones

The Company failed to comply with the required sampling frequencies for the parameter PAH in one of its zones. The shortfall has been regarded as unlikely to recur.

Table 3.15.3 shows the Company's performance in 1995, with data for 1994 and 1993 for comparison.

All contraventions of the standards in zones are considered trivial or unlikely to recur, or are covered by undertakings.

Inspection

Dr J Gray, Principal Inspector, assisted by Miss C Y Hill, Inspector, carried out an inspection of North Surrey Water Limited during visits in July and October 1995. Dr Gray concluded that:

(a) the Company had taken appropriate and satisfactory measures to implement the recommendations made in the 1994 technical audit inspection report;

(b) the general arrangements for sampling satisfied parts IV and V of the Regulations and accorded with the recommendations of the Guidance Document;

Table 3.15.3   North Surrey Water Limited
WATER QUALITY IN SUPPLY ZONES

Columns 'CBU' show, for determinations, contraventions covered by undertakings and, for zones, the <u>total</u> number of zones covered by undertakings in 1995. Column 'E' shows the number of zones for which new enforcement action is under consideration as a result of contraventions of the PCV in 1995. **Please refer to the Introduction to Chapter 3 for more detailed explanation of this table.**

| Parameter | DETERMINATIONS in 1995 | | | | ZONES (14 in 1995)* | | | | |
| | Total | Contravening PCV | | | | | Non-compliant | | |
		No.	%	CBU	CBU 1995	E	Number in: 1995	1994	1993
Coliforms	1,274	10	0.8	0	0	0	0	0	0
Faecal coliforms	1,274	1	<0.1	0	0	0	1	3	1
Colour	147	0	0.0	0	0	0	0	0	0
Turbidity	146	0	0.0	0	14	0	0	0	0
Odour	367	0	0.0	0	0	0	0	0	0
Taste	367	0	0.0	0	0	0	0	0	0
Hydrogen ion	677	0	0.0	0	0	0	0	0	0
Nitrate	147	0	0.0	0	9	0	0	0	0
Nitrite	195	3	1.5	3	4	0	2	1	1
Aluminium	203	1	0.5	1	7	0	1	2	1
Iron	149	1	0.7	0	14	0	1	0	2
Manganese	146	0	0.0	0	0	0	0	0	0
Lead	56	0	0.0	0	0	0	0	0	0
PAH	56	1	1.8	0	0	0	1	0	0
Trihalomethanes	56	0	0.0	0	0	0	0	0	0
Total pesticides	565	39	6.9	39	14	0	11	10	14
Atrazine	488	8	1.6	8	14	0	4	10	14
Chlorotoluron	490	15	3.1	15	14	0	7	7	0
2,4-D	275	0	0.0	0	14	0	0	7	7
Diuron	560	63	11.3	63	14	0	11	14	14
Iprodione	163	0	0.0	0	14	0	0	0	1
Isoproturon	560	76	13.6	76	14	0	14	14	14
Linuron	560	42	7.5	42	14	0	7	0	0
MCPA	275	0	0.0	0	14	0	0	0	7
MCPP (Mecoprop)	275	0	0.0	0	14	0	0	7	7
Methabenzthiazuron	560	7	1.3	7	14	0	7	0	0
Simazine	488	4	0.8	4	14	0	4	10	14
Trietazine	484	0	0.0	0	14	0	0	0	7
Other pesticides	8,181	0	0.0	0	14	0	0	0	0
Nickel	39	2	5.1	0	0	0	2	2	0
Oxidizability	14	0	0.0	0	0	0	0	0	1
All others	932	0	0.0	0	0	0	0	0	0
Total	**20,169**	**273**	**1.4**	**258**	-	-	-	-	-

* 14 zones in 1994; 14 zones in 1993.

(c)   the Company's arrangements for reporting compliance data were satisfactory and secure although there were some deficiencies in confirming the integrity of the compliance data in some of the laboratories in which analysis was carried out on behalf of the Company;

(d)   the public record satisfies the requirements of regulation 29;

(e)   the Company is on target to meet all key stages of its compliance programmes by the due dates;

(f)   the Company has defined policies and procedures on the reliability of disinfection processes and on the use of products and substances, which are robust and satisfactory;

(g)   the Company's procedures for reporting events and incidents are well defined and satisfactory;

(h)   the Company is aware of the advice provided in the DOE document "Civil Emergencies involving Radioactive Substances: The Department's Role and Arrangements" published in June 1995 and the action to take in the event of a radioactive release to the environment; and

(i)   the Company has a satisfactory system for liaising with and reporting to local authorities and is meeting the requirements of regulations 30(4), 30(5) and 31(3).

Also, in November, Mr R M Walls representing consultants Rofe, Kennard and Lapworth, and working under the general direction of Dr Gray, carried out inspection of selected water treatment works and selected service reservoirs. He concluded that:

(j)   the treatment process at Chertsey water treatment works complied with Regulation 23;

(k)   the use of substances and products satisfied the requirements of Regulation 25;

(l)   the Company's policy and arrangements for disinfection at Chertsey water treatment works were satisfactory; and

(m)   the Company's arrangements for compliance sampling at Chertsey treatment works and Blackhill and St Georges service reservoirs are generally in accordance with the recommendations of paragraph 2.8 of the Guidance Document and with the requirements of regulation 21(2)(a).

As a result of these inspections, five recommendations were conveyed to the Company for formal response. Thirty-one suggestions on various matters were also made.

Since the inspection, the Company has taken action in respect of all five recommendations.

Improvement programmes

Five undertakings in respect of improvement programmes were due for full completion or the completion of major steps during 1995. All were completed on schedule. A new undertaking given by the Company to carry out improvement works to its distribution system, with a completion date of 31 March 2000, is being considered by the Secretary of State.

Incidents

One event notified during 1995 by the Company to the Secretary of State under the terms of the Water Undertakers (Information Direction) 1992 is regarded by the Inspectorate as constituting an incident in which drinking water quality demonstrably deteriorated.

The supply of water to approximately 126,000 consumers in Surrey was found to contain concentrations of phosphorus above the prescribed standard. The cause of the problem was traced to recently installed GAC at the Company's Chertsey water treatment works which had been activated with orthophosphoric acid prior to dispatch from the manufacturers. The Inspectorate considered that, once the cause of the problem had been identified, the Company acted promptly to restore supplies to normal. However, it was critical of the delay in initiating investigations following reports of unusual water quality occurrences.

No other events regarded as constituting incidents in which drinking water quality demonstrably deteriorated came to the attention of the Inspectorate in 1995.

Enforcement action

Table 3.15.4 summarises enforcement action under consideration for the Company as a result of the Inspectorate's work in, or pertaining to, the calendar year 1995.

Table 3.15.4	North Surrey Water Limited SUMMARY OF ENFORCEMENT ACTION CONSIDERED IN 1995
Regulation	**Reason for enforcement**
3(7)	Contravention of the coliform standard at one water treatment works.

NORTH WEST WATER LIMITED

Introduction

The Company supplies on average approximately 2,400 Ml/d to a population of some 6.8 million in an area covering the Lake District, the Western Pennines, and the major conurbations of Merseyside and Greater Manchester, Lancashire, Cumbria and Cheshire. Approximately 67% of the Company's water resources derive from impounding reservoirs. A further 25% derive from direct river abstraction and the remaining 8% from boreholes and springs.

In 1995, water was treated at 175 treatment works and distributed through 408 service reservoirs and approximately 40,000 km of water mains, including aqueducts conveying water from the Lake District to Manchester and from Wales to Liverpool. The Company has 306 designated water supply zones.

Overall water quality

At water treatment works and service reservoirs and in water supply zones, the Company carried out a total of 350,921 determinations in 1995. Of these, 99.5% demonstrated compliance with the relevant water quality standards, but 1,791 showed a PCV to have been contravened.

Coliforms were not detected at 132 (75%) of the Company's 175 water treatment works. At 402 (98.5%) of the Company's 408 service reservoirs, coliforms were absent from at least 95% of samples. Of the Company's 306 water supply zones in 1995, 288 (94%) complied fully with the relevant water quality standards or had breaches of the standards which were either trivial or were fully covered by undertakings. In the other 18 (6%) zones, some breaches are regarded as unlikely to recur and others will be covered by an undertaking currently under consideration

Microbiological quality of water leaving treatment works

Table 3.16.1 shows the Company's performance in 1995, with data for 1994 and 1993 for comparison. Differences between the three years are not regarded as significant.

The Company complied with the sampling frequencies required by regulation 17 at 166 of its 175 treatment works in 1995. Shortfalls at nine works are regarded as unlikely to recur.

Table 3.16.1 North West Water Limited MICROBIOLOGICAL QUALITY OF WATER LEAVING TREATMENT WORKS			
	1995	**1994**	**1993**
Number of water treatment works	175	176	194
Works with no sampling shortfall	166	153	189
COLIFORMS			
Total number of determinations	27,950	27,717	28,488
- number containing coliforms	80	81	81
- % containing coliforms	0.3	0.3	0.3
Treatment works with coliforms detected	**43**	**52**	**49**
- % of all works	25	30	25
FAECAL COLIFORMS			
Total number of determinations	27,949	27,696	28,491
- number containing faecal coliforms	16	18	16
- % containing faecal coliforms	<0.1	<0.1	<0.1
Treatment works with faecal coliforms detected	**9**	**16**	**14**
- % of all works	5	9	8

The Inspectorate will consider the results of further monitoring during the first six months of 1995 for coliforms at 26 works and for faecal coliforms at four of these works before deciding on the need for enforcement action. All other contraventions of the standards at works are considered trivial or unlikely to recur.

Microbiological quality of water in service reservoirs

Table 3.16.2 shows the Company's performance in 1995, with data for 1994 and 1993 for comparison. There has been a significant decrease over the three years in the number of service reservoirs with faecal coliforms detected.

The Company complied with the sampling frequencies required by regulation 18 at 399 of its 408 service reservoirs in 1995. Shortfalls at the other 10 are regarded as unlikely to recur.

All contraventions of the standards at service reservoirs are considered trivial or unlikely to recur.

Table 3.16.2 North West Water Limited
MICROBIOLOGICAL QUALITY OF WATER IN SERVICE RESERVOIRS

	1995	1994	1993
Number of service reservoirs	408	417	429
Service reservoirs with no sampling shortfall	398	399	428
COLIFORMS			
Total number of determinations	22,025	22,370	23,050
- number containing coliforms	77	84	100
- % containing coliforms	0.4	0.4	0.4
Service reservoirs with coliforms detected	57	60	78
Service reservoirs with coliforms detected in more than 5% of samples	**6**	**7**	**3**
- % of all service reservoirs	2	2	<1
FAECAL COLIFORMS			
Total number of determinations	22,025	22,338	23,051
- number containing faecal coliforms	6	17	24
- % containing faecal coliforms	<0.1	<0.1	0.1
Service reservoirs with faecal coliforms detected	**6**	**13**	**20**
- % of all service reservoirs	2	3	5

Water quality in water supply zones

The Company failed to comply with the required sampling frequencies for a number of parameters in 120 zones. These shortfalls were due to problems with sample scheduling and coding. The Inspectorate has been advised that action has been taken to ensure the shortfalls do not recur. A decision on enforcement action has been deferred until the compliance data for the first six months of 1996 has been assessed.

Table 3.16.3 shows the Company's performance in 1995, with data for 1994 and 1993 for comparison. There has been a significant reduction over the three years in the number of zones contravening the standards for hydrogen ion, faecal coliforms, the individual pesticide atrazine, and trihalomethanes. However there have been significant increases in the number of zones contravening the standards for iron and PAH. All other differences between the three years are not regarded as significant.

Contraventions of the hydrogen ion and PAH standards in 14 zones are not trivial. However, the Company has submitted an undertaking which is currently under consideration. All other contraventions of the standards in zones are considered trivial or unlikely to recur, or are covered by undertakings.

Table 3.16.3   North West Water Limited
WATER QUALITY IN SUPPLY ZONES

*Columns 'CBU' show, for determinations, contraventions covered by undertakings and, for zones, the <u>total</u> number of zones covered by undertakings in 1995. Column 'E' shows the number of zones for which new enforcement action is under consideration as a result of contraventions of the PCV in 1995. **Please refer to the Introduction to Chapter 3 for more detailed explanation of this table.***

| Parameter | DETERMINATIONS in 1995 | | | | ZONES (306 in 1995)* | | | | |
| | Total | Contravening PCV | | | | | Non-compliant | | |
		No.	%	CBU	CBU 1995	E	1995	Number in: 1994	1993
Coliforms	22,588	145	0.6	0	0	0	1	2	1
Faecal coliforms	22,642	7	<0.1	0	0	0	6	14	17
Colour	11,942	3	<0.1	3	306	0	3	1	1
Turbidity	11,695	27	0.2	27	306	0	26	15	21
Odour	3,070	0	0.0	0	0	0	0	2	3
Taste	3,012	0	0.0	0	0	0	0	1	1
Hydrogen ion	18,148	45	0.3	0	0	0	33	36	67
Nitrate	2,857	0	0.0	0	0	0	0	3	3
Nitrite	3,610	3	0.1	0	0	0	3	9	2
Aluminium	11,768	48	0.4	11	12	0	36	18	50
Iron	11,786	373	3.2	372	306	0	168	132	115
Manganese	11,781	123	1.0	119	306	0	83	57	60
Lead	14,744	738	5.0	733	305	0	201	196	197
PAH	1,861	34	1.8	0	0	0	19	8	3
Trihalomethanes	3,613	34	0.9	0	3	0	6	15	27
Total pesticides	3,496	1	<0.1	1	73	0	1	1	5
Atrazine	2,042	2	0.1	2	73	0	2	3	25
Chlorfenvinphos	1,990	3	0.2	1	73	0	3	0	0
2,4-D	1,951	2	0.1	1	73	0	2	0	0
Diuron	1,741	0	0.0	0	73	0	0	0	1
Gamma-HCH (Lindane)	2,034	0	0.0	0	73	0	0	0	2
Isoproturon	1,742	0	0.0	0	73	0	0	0	1
Linuron	1,743	1	<0.1	0	73	0	1	0	0
MCPA	1,965	1	<0.1	0	73	0	1	1	7
MCPP (Mecoprop)	1,965	4	0.2	3	73	0	4	7	5
Simazine	2,036	0	0.0	0	73	0	0	2	1
Other pesticides	17,436	0	0.0	0	73	0	0	0	0
Ammonium	3,404	4	0.1	0	0	0	4	6	4
Benz 3,4 pyrene	1,870	5	0.3	CBU	0	0	1	0	0
Copper	1,582	0	0.0	0	0	0	0	1	1
Mercury	402	0	0.0	0	0	0	0	1	0
Oxidizability	435	6	1.4	0	0	0	6	2	0
Phosphorus	2,644	2	<0.1	0	0	0	2	0	0
Potassium	372	1	0.3	0	0	0	1	0	0
Selenium	353	0	0.0	0	0	0	0	0	1
Sulphate	379	0	0.0	0	0	0	0	1	0
All others	44,273	0	0.0	0	0	0	0	0	0
Total	**250,972**	**1,612**	**0.6**	**1,273**	-	-	-	-	-

* 301 zones in 1994; 301 zones in 1993.

Inspection

Dr M J Gray, Principal Inspector, assisted by Dr D Westwood, Principal Inspector, Mr P White, Principal Inspector and Miss C Y Hill, Inspector, carried out an inspection of North West Water Limited in August 1995. Additional matters were inspected during separate visits by Dr Gray and Miss Hill in October and December 1995. Dr Gray concluded that:

(a) the Company had taken appropriate and satisfactory measures to implement the recommendations made in the 1994 technical audit inspection report;

(b) the general arrangements for sampling satisfied parts IV and V of the Regulations and accorded with the recommendations of the Guidance Document;

(c) the requirements of regulation 21(2)(d)(iii) were generally satisfied in the laboratories where analysis was carried out on behalf of the Company;

(d) the Company is aware of the contents of the most recent issue of Report 71 and in general, action has been taken or is being taken to implement changes to its procedures where appropriate;

(e) the Company's arrangements for reporting compliance data were generally satisfactory and secure although some areas need attention;

(f) the arrangements for the dissemination of water quality data within the Company and to members of the public were satisfactory, and the public record satisfied the requirements of regulation 29;

(g) the Company is generally maintaining progress with the compliance programmes examined;

(h) the Company's arrangements for water treatment were generally satisfactory;

(i) the Company in general has adequate provisions for water quality monitoring at Watchgate and Ulpha water treatment works although some areas need attention;

(j) the provision of alarm signals and the telemetry of water quality monitors to the control room were adequate;

(k) the Company has taken or is taking action to implement recommendations made in the Inspectorate's letters of assessment of water quality incidents;

(l) the Company's arrangements for liaison with the NRA in the event of pollution incidents were satisfactory;

(m) the Company's arrangements for communicating with local authorities were generally satisfactory; and

(n) the Company has a satisfactory approach to dealing with complaints on water quality although its system of recording complaints requires attention.

In November, Mr R Kidson representing consultants Rofe, Kennard and Lapworth and working under the general direction of Dr Gray, carried out inspection of selected water treatment works and service reservoirs. He concluded that:

(o) although the arrangements for managing water quality were complex, the tasks of the various groups were well-defined and in general well-performed;

(p) the treatment processes complied with Regulation 23;

(q) the use of substances and products satisfied the requirements of Regulation 25;

(r) the Company's policy and arrangements for disinfection at treatment works were satisfactory;

(s) the Company's arrangements for compliance sampling at treatment works and service reservoirs were, or were planned to be, generally in accordance with the requirements of Regulation 21(2)(a) and the recommendations of the Guidance Document;

(t)   there was no consistently-applied policy for service reservoir management in respect of some key functions relating to water quality;

(u)   Ludworth and Hollins service reservoirs appeared to be maintained adequately and well designed; and

(v)   quality assurance procedures set by the Company were comprehensive and were almost fully implemented.

As a result of these inspections, 15 recommendations were conveyed to the Company for formal response, mainly concerned with arrangements for water treatment and water distribution. Fifty-seven suggestions on various matters were also made.

Improvement programmes

One undertaking in respect of improvement programmes accepted by the Secretary of State from the Company was due for completion in 1995 and was completed on schedule. A new undertaking given by the Company to carry out improvement works to its distribution system, with a completion date of 31 March 2000, is being considered by the Secretary of State.

Incidents

Five events notified during 1995 by the Company to the Secretary of State under the terms of the Water Undertakers (Information) Direction 1992 are regarded by the Inspectorate as constituting incidents in which drinking water quality demonstrably deteriorated. The Inspectorate has completed its assessment of these and has concluded in all cases that the Company has taken action to prevent the incidents from recurring.

One incident, which occurred in May, involved the supply of "blue" coloured water to approximately 22 consumers in Brindley, Cheshire. The problem was caused by an illegal connection from a service pipe to a cattle feed trough on a farm through which a blue coloured magnesium chloride cattle feed supplement was being dosed. The water contravened regulation 3(3)(c) with respect to magnesium.

Another incident occurred in October as a result of a partial treatment failure at Lightshaw treatment works, near Wigan. A fault with the dechlorination equipment led to water containing lower than the normal concentration of chlorine being supplied to approximately 135,000 consumers.

Two incidents involved the supply of discoloured water to consumers. One of these incidents occurred in the Fylde coastal area in August and was due to an increase in flows through the distribution system following the opening of a service reservoir bypass main. The water supplied contained concentrations of manganese and turbidity values above the prescribed concentrations in contravention of regulation 3(3)(c). The other incident involving discolouration of water supplies occurred in November and affected consumers in Blackburn. An increase in flows through the distribution system in the area disturbed sediment accumulated in the mains. The Company has taken appropriate action to prevent recurrence and enforcement action is not required.

In December, an incident occurred which affected the water supply to approximately 8,000 consumers in Rochdale. Following a major mains burst in the area, consumers complained of a "TCP-like" taste to their water supply. The problem was considered to be caused by the reaction of chlorine with organic deposits in the distribution system which had been disturbed by the burst. Traces of TCP were found in samples of water taken from the distribution system but at concentrations below that prescribed by regulation 3(3)(c).

Enforcement action

No enforcement action needed to be considered for the Company as a result of the Inspectorate's work in, or pertaining to, the calendar year 1995.

NORTHUMBRIAN WATER LIMITED

Introduction

The Company supplies on average approximately 425 Ml/d of treated water to a population of 1.19 million in the north east part of England. Approximately 96% of the Company's water is obtained from impounding reservoirs and abstractions from the Rivers Tees and Tyne and the remaining 4% from groundwater sources. The water is treated at 19 water treatment works and distributed via 104 service reservoirs and 8,200 km of water mains. The supply area is divided into 75 water supply zones.

Overall water quality

At water treatment works and service reservoirs and in water supply zones, the Company carried out a total of 82,858 determinations in 1995. Of these, 99.8% demonstrated compliance with the relevant water quality standards, but 170 showed a PCV to have been contravened.

Coliforms were not detected at 12 (63%) of the Company's 19 water treatment works. Coliforms were absent from at least 95% of samples at all of the Company's 104 service reservoirs. All of the Company's 75 water supply zones in 1995 complied fully with the relevant water quality standards or had breaches of the standards which were either trivial or were fully covered by undertakings or will be covered by the new distribution undertaking.

Microbiological quality of water leaving treatment works

Table 3.17.1 shows the Company's performance in 1995, with data for 1994 and 1993 for comparison. Differences between the three years are not considered significant. Had the definition of the coliform parameter not been changed as described in 3.35 above, but remained as it was for 1994 and previous years, the number of treatment works with coliforms detected would have been five and the number of determinations containing coliforms seven.

Table 3.17.1   Northumbrian Water Limited
MICROBIOLOGICAL QUALITY OF WATER LEAVING TREATMENT WORKS

	1995	1994	1993
Number of water treatment works	19	19	20
Works with no sampling shortfall	18	11	20
COLIFORMS			
Total number of determinations	4,144	4,129	4,350
- number containing coliforms	10	5	8
- % containing coliforms	0.2	0.1	0.2
Treatment works with coliforms detected	**7**	**4**	**5**
- % of all works	37	21	25
FAECAL COLIFORMS			
Total number of determinations	4,144	4,129	4,361
- number containing faecal coliforms	1	3	3
- % containing faecal coliforms	<0.1	<0.1	<0.1
Treatment works with faecal coliforms detected	**1**	**2**	**3**
- % of all works	5	11	15

The Company complied with the sampling frequencies required by regulation 17 at 18 of its 19 treatment works in 1995. Shortfalls at the other one are regarded as trivial.

Contraventions of the microbiological quality standards at a total of three works were considered as not trivial. However the Company has carried out remedial action and enforcement action is not being considered. All other contraventions of the standards at works are considered trivial.

Microbiological quality of water in service reservoirs

Table 3.17.2 shows the Company's performance in 1995, with data for 1994 and 1993 for comparison. Differences between the three years are not considered significant. The Company complied with the sampling frequencies required by regulation 18 at 103 of its 104 service reservoirs in 1995. Shortfalls at the other one are regarded as trivial.

All contraventions of the standards at service reservoirs are considered trivial.

Table 3.17.2 Northumbrian Water Limited MICROBIOLOGICAL QUALITY OF WATER IN SERVICE RESERVOIRS	1995	1994	1993
Number of service reservoirs	104	106	107
Service reservoirs with no sampling shortfall	103	83	103
COLIFORMS			
Total number of determinations	5,676	5,688	5,873
- number containing coliforms	24	16	45
- % containing coliforms	0.4	0.3	0.8
Service reservoirs with coliforms detected	23	14	25
Service reservoirs with coliforms detected in more than 5% of samples	**0**	**0**	**3**
- % of all service reservoirs	0	0	3
FAECAL COLIFORMS			
Total number of determinations	5,676	5,688	5,882
- number containing faecal coliforms	4	3	9
- % containing faecal coliforms	0.1	<0.1	0.2
Service reservoirs with faecal coliforms detected	**4**	**3**	**6**
- % of all service reservoirs	4	3	6

Water quality in water supply zones

The Company complied with the required sampling frequencies in all of its zones.

Table 3.17.3 shows the Company's performance in 1995, with data for 1994 and 1993 for comparison. Differences between the three years are not considered significant. Had the definition of the coliform parameter not been changed as described in 3.35 above, but remained as it was for 1994 and previous years the number of determinations containing coliforms would have been 17.

All contraventions of the standards in zones are considered trivial or unlikely to recur, or are covered by undertakings.

Inspection

Mr B S Bell, Inspector led by Mr M J Purcell, Principal Inspector and assisted by Dr D Westwood, Principal Inspector, carried out an inspection of Northumbrian Water Limited in a series of visits between 2 August and 7 December 1995. Mr Bell concluded that:

(a) the Company needs to review its procedures for dealing with radioactivity monitoring;

**Table 3.17.3   Northumbrian Water Limited
WATER QUALITY IN SUPPLY ZONES**

*Columns 'CBU' show, for determinations, contraventions covered by undertakings and, for zones, the <u>total</u> number of zones covered by undertakings in 1995. Column 'E' shows the number of zones for which new enforcement action is under consideration as a result of contraventions of the PCV in 1995. **Please refer to the Introduction to Chapter 3 for more detailed explanation of this table.**

| Parameter | DETERMINATIONS in 1995 | | | | ZONES (75 in 1995)* | | | | |
| | Total | Contravening PCV | | | | | Non-compliant | | |
		No.	%	CBU	CBU 1995	E	Number in: 1995	1994	1993
Coliforms	4,080	23	0.6	0	0	0	0	1	4
Faecal coliforms	4,080	2	<0.1	0	0	0	2	5	6
Colour	4,078	1	<0.1	0	0	0	1	5	2
Turbidity	4,078	3	0.1	0	0	0	3	4	10
Odour	4,088	0	0.0	0	0	0	0	0	0
Taste	4,088	1	0.0	0	0	0	1	1	0
Hydrogen ion	4,078	3	0.1	0	0	0	2	6	3
Nitrate	569	0	0.0	0	0	0	0	0	0
Nitrite	569	0	0.0	0	0	0	0	0	0
Aluminium	1,988	2	0.1	0	0	0	2	2	6
Iron	1,988	34	1.7	34	75	0	22	17	22
Manganese	1,988	13	0.7	13	75	0	10	5	8
Lead	1,076	24	2.2	24	75	0	19	14	27
PAH	348	4	1.1	0	0	0	3	3	2
Trihalomethanes	324	0	0.0	0	0	0	0	0	0
Total pesticides	297	2	0.7	0	0	0	2	5	0
Chlorotoluron	317	0	0.0	0	0	0	0	1	0
2,4-D	417	1	0.2	0	0	0	1	0	1
pp-DDT	315	2	0.6	0	0	0	2	0	0
op-DDT	315	2	0.6	0	0	0	2	0	0
pp-DDE	315	2	0.6	0	0	0	2	0	0
MCPA	417	1	0.2	0	0	0	1	5	0
Mecoprop	417	6	1.4	0	0	0	6	7	7
Propetamos	307	0	0.0	0	0	0	0	1	0
pp-DDD	315	2	0.6	0	0	0	2	0	0
op-DDD	315	2	0.6	0	0	0	2	0	0
Trichlopyr	417	0	0.0	0	0	0	0	0	2
Other pesticides	8,612	0	0.0	0	0	0	0	0	0
Benz 3,4 pyrene	348	1	0.3	0	0	0	0	1	0
Phosphorus	74	0	0.0	0	0	0	0	1	1
All others	12,600	0	0.0	0	0	0	0	0	0
Total	**63,218**	**131**	**0.2**	**71**	-	-	-	-	-

* 76 zones in 1994; 77 zones in 1993.

(b)   progress with capital schemes relating to undertakings and a relaxation were generally satisfactory, although there were some areas of concern;

(c)   the water treatment processes and records reviewed at Lartington water treatment works were generally maintained and operated satisfactorily;

(d) compliance data audits carried out by the Inspectors identified some areas which required attention, all of which have already been satisfactorily addressed;

(e) the Company is reliant on significant bulk transfers of water; it has procedures in place to deal with water quality issues relating to these transfers;

(f) the Company is undertaking in situ epoxy resin lining of its mains in a satisfactory manner;

(g) an audit of the telemetry system at the Company's water treatment works indicated that the Company had satisfactory procedures in place to effectively monitor water treatment processes but that the Company should consider critical review of these process parameters;

(h) the Company has in place procedures which comply with the requirements of regulation 30(4) and 31(3) and satisfactory arrangements for communications with local authorities on issues of water quality and compliance with regulation 30(5); and

(i) the Company is well on the way to achieving accreditation and implementing environmental management systems in most of the Company's districts.

In October 1995 Mr P Durrant, representing consultants Rofe, Kennard & Lapworth and working under Mr Purcell's general direction, carried out inspection of selected water treatment works and service reservoirs. He concluded that:

(j) the treatment processes complied with Regulation 23;

(k) the use of substances and products satisfied the requirements of Regulation 25;

(l) the Company's policy and arrangements for disinfection at Lockwood treatment works were generally satisfactory, but some improvements were identified as necessary at Oven Close treatment works. (Since the inspection the Company has abandoned both sites); and

(m) the Company's arrangements for compliance sampling at treatment works and service reservoirs are generally in accordance with the recommendations of paragraph 2.8 of the Guidance Document and with the requirements of Regulation 21(2)(a).

As a result of these inspections, eight recommendations were conveyed to the Company for formal response, nearly half of them concerning reporting arrangements. Sixteen suggestions on various matters were also made.

Improvement programmes

At Broken Scar water treatment works, an improvement scheme to reduce plumbo solvency was not completed by its target completion date. To secure compliance with regulation 3(3)(c), the Inspectorate issued a Notice of Intention to make a Final Enforcement Order in respect of the construction and commissioning of the treatment plant. However, the Company satisfactorily completed the improvement scheme within the period of notice, thus a final Enforcement Order was not necessary. A new undertaking given by the Company to carry out improvement works to its distribution system, with a completion date of 31 March 2000, is being considered by the Secretary of State.

Incidents

Four events notified during 1995 by the Company to the Secretary of State under the terms of the Water Undertakers (Information) Direction 1992 are regarded by the Inspectorate as constituting incidents in which drinking water quality demonstrably deteriorated.

The first involved the transient detection of high concentrations of isomers of DDT in routine samples from drinking water supplies supplied by two spring sources in the Wear Valley. The second incident involved a bulk supply received from Mosswood water treatment works, which is operated by North East Water Plc. Following a treatment failure, discoloured water with a below normal residual chlorine level was supplied. The Company carried out remedial chlorination in the distribution system to Durham City and surrounding areas. The third concerned detection of hydrocarbons in precautionary samples taken from properties downstream of the repair of an asbestos main in ground contaminated with petrol. The fourth concerned the supply of discoloured water to about 33,000 properties in the Darlington area which gave rise to some 800 consumer complaints. These incidents remain under consideration by the Inspectorate.

No other events regarded as constituting incidents came to the attention of the Inspectorate in 1995.

Enforcement action

No enforcement action needed to be considered for the Company as a result of the Inspectorate's work in, or pertaining to, the calendar year 1995.

PORTSMOUTH WATER PLC

Introduction

The Company supplies on average 188 Ml/d of water to a resident population of approximately 647,000 people in Hampshire and West Sussex including the City of Portsmouth and parts of the Districts of Havant, Gosport, Fareham, Eastleigh, Winchester, Arun, Chichester and East Hampshire.

Approximately 87% of the Company's water resources are derived from springs, boreholes and wells. The remainder is abstracted from the River Itchen and is stored in a raw water storage reservoir before treatment.

The water from these sources is treated at 19 water treatment works and is distributed via 42 service reservoirs and some 3,200 km of water mains. The supply area is divided into 23 water supply zones.

Overall water quality

At water treatment works and service reservoirs and in water supply zones, the Company carried out a total of 26,570 determinations in 1995. Of these, greater than 99.9% demonstrated compliance with the relevant water quality standards, but 20 showed a PCV to have been contravened.

Coliforms were not detected at 18 (95%) of the Company's 19 water treatment works. At all of the Company's 42 service reservoirs, coliforms were absent from at least 95% of samples. Of the Company's 23 water supply zones in 1995, 20 (87%) complied fully with the relevant water quality standards or had breaches of the standards which were either trivial or were fully covered by undertakings. In the other three (17%) of the zones, the breaches are regarded as unlikely to recur.

Microbiological quality of water leaving treatment works

Table 3.18.1 shows the Company's performance in 1995, with data for 1994 and 1993 for comparison. Differences between the three years are not considered significant.

The Company complied with the sampling frequencies required by regulation 17 at all 19 treatment works in 1995 with one very minor exception which is considered trivial.

Table 3.18.1 Portsmouth Water Plc
MICROBIOLOGICAL QUALITY OF WATER LEAVING TREATMENT WORKS

	1995	1994	1993
Number of water treatment works	19	19	19
Works with no sampling shortfall	18	19	15
COLIFORMS			
Total number of determinations	2,894	2,697	2,731
- number containing coliforms	1	4	0
- % containing coliforms	<0.1	0.1	0.0
Treatment works with coliforms detected	**1**	**4**	**0**
- % of all works	5	21	1
FAECAL COLIFORMS			
Total number of determinations	2,898	2,697	2,731
- number containing faecal coliforms	0	1	0
- % containing faecal coliforms	0.0	<0.1	0.0
Treatment works with faecal coliforms detected	**0**	**1**	**0**
- % of all works	0	5	0

The single contravention of the microbiological standard at a works is considered a trivial breach of regulation 3(7).

Microbiological quality of water in service reservoirs

Table 3.18.2 shows the Company's performance in 1995, with data for 1994 and 1993 for comparison. Differences between the three years are not considered significant.

The Company complied with the sampling frequencies required by regulation 18 at 39 of its 42 service reservoirs in 1995. The three minor contraventions of regulation 18 are considered trivial.

Table 3.18.2 Portsmouth Water Plc
MICROBIOLOGICAL QUALITY OF WATER IN SERVICE RESERVOIRS

	1995	1994	1993
Number of service reservoirs	42	42	36
Service reservoirs with no sampling shortfall	42	42	25
COLIFORMS			
Total number of determinations	2,060	2,087	1,854
- number containing coliforms	0	1	9
- % containing coliforms	0.0	<0.1	0.6
Service reservoirs with coliforms detected	0	1	8
Service reservoirs with coliforms detected in more than 5% of samples	**0**	**0**	**0**
- % of all service reservoirs	0	0	0
FAECAL COLIFORMS			
Total number of determinations	2,064	2,087	1,854
- number containing faecal coliforms	0	1	0
- % containing faecal coliforms	0.0	<0.1	0.0
Service reservoirs with faecal coliforms detected	**0**	**1**	**0**
- % of all service reservoirs	0	2	0

Water quality in water supply zones

The Company failed to comply fully with the required sampling frequencies in 14 of its 23 zones in 1995 for the sodium and potassium parameters when samples were not rescheduled after an instrument breakdown. This contravention of regulation 13(1) is considered unlikely to recur. An additional missed sample for the qualitative taste and odour parameters is considered trivial.

Table 3.18.3 shows the Company's performance in 1995, with data for 1994 and 1993 for comparison. Apart from the significant reduction in the number of zones contravening the standard for the individual pesticide atrazine, differences between the three years are not considered significant. All contraventions in 1995 of the standards in zones are considered trivial, unlikely to recur or are covered by undertakings.

Inspection

David Drury, Principal Inspector, carried out an inspection of Portsmouth Water Plc in December 1995. He concluded that:

(a)   the Company made a positive response to the recommendations made in the 1994 inspection;

(b)   on the basis of the inspection of a sampling round and of other specific items, the Company has arrangements for sampling and monitoring that generally satisfy the requirements of parts IV and V of the Regulations;

Table 3.18.3 Portsmouth Water Plc
WATER QUALITY IN SUPPLY ZONES

Columns 'CBU' show, for determinations, contraventions covered by undertakings and, for zones, the <u>*total*</u> *number of zones covered by undertakings in 1995. Column 'E' shows the number of zones for which new enforcement action is under consideration as a result of contraventions of the PCV in 1995.* **Please refer to the Introduction to Chapter 3 for more detailed explanation of this table.**

| Parameter | DETERMINATIONS in 1995 | | | | ZONES (23 in 1995)* | | | | |
| | Total | Contravening PCV | | | | | Non-compliant | | |
		No.	%	CBU	CBU 1995	E	Number in: 1995	1994	1993
Coliforms	1,878	2	0.1	0	0	0	0	0	0
Faecal coliforms	1,879	0	0.0	0	0	0	0	1	3
Colour	251	0	0.0	0	0	0	0	0	0
Turbidity	349	0	0.0	0	0	0	0	0	0
Odour	338	0	0.0	0	0	0	0	0	0
Taste	338	0	0.0	0	0	0	0	2	0
Hydrogen ion	1,720	0	0.0	0	0	0	0	0	0
Nitrate	388	4	1.0	0	0	0	3	1	0
Nitrite	386	0	0.0	0	0	0	0	0	0
Aluminium	177	0	0.0	0	0	0	0	0	0
Iron	160	0	0.0	0	0	0	0	0	0
Manganese	148	0	0.0	0	0	0	0	0	0
Lead	261	1	0.4	1	23	0	1	3	6
PAH	117	6	5.1	5	2	0	2	5	3
Trihalomethanes	92	0	0.0	0	0	0	0	0	0
Total pesticides	276	0	0.0	0	0	0	0	0	0
Atrazine	36	0	0.0	0	0	0	0	5	5
Azinphos methyl	36	0	0.0	0	0	0	0	0	1
Carbophenothion	9	1	11.1	0	0	0	1	0	0
Diuron	27	0	0.0	0	0	0	0	0	1
Methabenzthiazuron	100	2	2.0	0	0	0	2	0	0
Other pesticides	1,703	0	0.0	0	0	0	0	0	0
Benzo 3,4 pyrene	117	3	2.6	0	0	0	0	0	0
All others	5,868	0	0.0	0	0	0	0	0	0
Total	**16,654**	**19**	**0.1**	**6**	**-**	**-**	**-**	**-**	**-**

* 23 zones in 1994; 23 zones in 1993.

(c) on the basis of his inspection of laboratories and other specific items, that the Company is generally meeting the requirements of regulation 21(2)(d) but a recommendation is necessary in respect of following procedures relating to an aspect of analytical quality control;

(d) the sample audit trails showed that arrangements for reporting compliance data are generally satisfactory and secure and that the Company is taking appropriate action in respect of contraventions of standards but recommendations are made in respect of the validity and timeliness of reporting a small number of results;

(e) the Public Record met the requirements of regulations 29 and 30;

(f) based on an audit of records at its control room, it is possible to audit trail action in the event of a water quality alarm but the information is scattered around the Company and record keeping could benefit from a review. The planned new software system that will allow notes to be added to historic computer records should strengthen the system;

(g)   on the basis of examination of records and a site visit, that the Company is generally applying epoxy resin lining in accordance with the Operational Guidelines and Code of Practice but two recommendations were made on aspects of the operation, on which the Company has taken action;

(h)   the Company has taken appropriate action in respect of its PAH undertaking and, where necessary, completed work on schedule;

(i)   the Company has sound arrangements for dealing with emergencies and incidents and is keeping these under review; and

(j)   the Company continues to maintain good procedures for liaising with local authorities and district health authorities.

Also, in November 1995, Mr R M Walls from the consultants Rofe, Kennard and Lapworth, working under the general direction of Mr Drury, carried out an inspection of River Itchen and Brickkiln water treatment works and Slindon and Lavant service reservoirs. Mr Walls concluded that, in respect of the sites inspected:

(k)   the Company has a robust system for maintaining the quality of water supplied by water treatment works; water is adequately disinfected and equipment failure should not result in unchlorinated water entering supply; and

(l)   the reservoirs are maintained to a satisfactory standard and sampling points provide representative samples.

As a result of these inspections, six recommendations were conveyed to the Company for formal response, mainly relating to analytical arrangements and procedures for mains relining using epoxy resin. Nine suggestions on various matters were also made.

Improvement programmes

The Company completed all the steps in its undertaking in respect of the lead parameter well ahead of the due date.

Incidents

No events regarded as constituting incidents in which drinking water quality demonstrably deteriorated came to the attention of the Inspectorate in 1995.

Enforcement action

No enforcement action was considered for the Company as a result of the Inspectorate's work in, or pertaining to, the calendar year 1995.

SEVERN TRENT WATER LIMITED

Introduction

The Company supplies on average 2,082 Ml/d of water to a population of approximately 7.2 million people within a region which broadly covers the catchment areas of the Rivers Severn and Trent and their tributaries. The region thus stretches from the Humber estuary in the north to the Bristol Channel in the south and from Llyn Clywedog in Wales in the west to Lincolnshire in the east. The region includes the cities of Birmingham, Coventry, Derby, Gloucester, Leicester, Nottingham, Shrewsbury, Stoke-on-Trent and Worcester.

Underground sources, river derived sources and impounding reservoirs each provide 35%, 39% and 26% respectively of the total volume of water put into supply.

The Company operated 202 water treatment works in 1995. The average volumes of water treated at works ranges from 300 Ml/d at Frankley, which supplies Birmingham, to small plants which treat less than 1 Ml/d. Treated water is distributed via 718 service reservoirs and 41,000 km of water mains. The area is divided into 347 water supply zones.

Overall water quality

At water treatment works and service reservoirs and in water supply zones, the Company carried out a total of 318,423 determinations in 1995. Of these, 99.8% demonstrated compliance with the relevant water quality standards, but 531 showed a PCV to have been contravened.

Coliforms were not detected at 184 (91%) of the Company's 202 water treatment works. At all of the Company's 718 service reservoirs in 1995, coliforms were absent from at least 95% of samples although faecal coliforms were detected in nine reservoirs. Of the Company's 347 water supply zones in 1995, 303 (87%) complied fully with the relevant water quality standards or had breaches of the standards which were either trivial or were fully covered by undertakings. In the other 44 zones (13%) most breaches are considered unlikely to recur but some could result in enforcement action.

Microbiological quality of water leaving treatment works

Table 3.19.1 shows the Company's performance in 1995, with data for 1994 and 1993 for comparison. Differences between the three years are not considered significant.

The Company complied with the sampling frequencies required by regulation 17 at 197 of its 202 treatment works in 1995. Shortfalls at the other five are regarded as trivial.

All contraventions of the microbiological standards at works are considered trivial, unlikely to recur, or are covered by undertakings.

Microbiological quality of water in service reservoirs

Table 3.19.2 shows the Company's performance in 1995, with data for 1994 and 1993 for comparison. There has been a significant reduction over the three years in the number of service reservoirs with coliforms detected in more than 5% of samples and in the number of determinations containing coliforms.

The Company complied with the sampling frequencies required by regulation 18 at 717 of its 718 service reservoirs in 1995. A minor shortfall at the other one is regarded as trivial. All contraventions of the microbiological standards at service reservoirs are considered trivial or unlikely to recur.

Water quality in water supply zones

The Company complied with the required sampling frequencies in 341 of its 347 water supply zones in 1995. Shortfalls at the other six are regarded as trivial.

Table 3.19.3 shows the Company's performance in 1995, with data for 1994 and 1993 for comparison. There have been significant reductions over the three years in the numbers of zones variously failing to comply with the standards for turbidity, hydrogen ion, aluminium, iron, trihalomethanes, total pesticides and individual pesticides in respect of atrazine, chlorotoluron, diuron, and mecoprop. There has been a significant increase in the number of zones failing to comply for odour.

Enforcement action is being considered in respect of some contraventions of standards, as shown in tables 3.19.3 and 3.19.4. All other contraventions of the standards in zones are considered trivial or unlikely to recur, or are covered by undertakings or will be covered by the new distribution undertaking.

Table 3.19.1 Severn Trent Water Limited
MICROBIOLOGICAL QUALITY OF WATER LEAVING TREATMENT WORKS

	1995	1994	1993
Number of water treatment works	202	209	211
Works with no sampling shortfall	197	203	204
COLIFORMS			
Total number of determinations	22,719	29,293	29,616
- number containing coliforms	25	24	41
- % containing coliforms	0.1	<0.1	0.1
Treatment works with coliforms detected	**18**	**20**	**30**
- % of all works	9	10	14
FAECAL COLIFORMS			
Total number of determinations	22,726	29,293	29,616
- number containing faecal coliforms	2	4	9
- % containing faecal coliforms	<0.1	<0.1	<0.1
Treatment works with faecal coliforms detected	**2**	**3**	**9**
- % of all works	1	1	4

Table 3.19.2 Severn Trent Water Limited
MICROBIOLOGICAL QUALITY OF WATER IN SERVICE RESERVOIRS

	1995	1994	1993
Number of service reservoirs	718	806	679
Service reservoirs with no sampling shortfall	717	803	659
COLIFORMS			
Total number of determinations	35,706	35,897	34,357
- number containing coliforms	50	51	101
- % containing coliforms	0.1	0.1	0.3
Service reservoirs with coliforms detected	47	47	78
Service reservoirs with coliforms detected in more than 5% of samples	**0**	**0**	**8**
- % of all service reservoirs	0.0	0.0	1
FAECAL COLIFORMS			
Total number of determinations	35,710	35,897	34,357
- number containing faecal coliforms	9	4	13
- % containing faecal coliforms	<0.1	<0.1	<0.1
Service reservoirs with faecal coliforms detected	**9**	**4**	**13**
- % of all service reservoirs	1	<1	2

Table 3.19.3 Severn Trent Water Limited
WATER QUALITY IN SUPPLY ZONES

Columns 'CBU' show, for determinations, contraventions covered by undertakings and, for zones, the <u>total</u> number of zones covered by undertakings in 1995. Column 'E' shows the number of zones for which new enforcement action is under consideration as a result of contraventions of the PCV in 1995. **Please refer to the Introduction to Chapter 3 for more detailed explanation of this table.**

| Parameter | DETERMINATIONS in 1995 | | | | ZONES (347 in 1995)* | | | | |
| | Total | Contravening PCV | | | Non-compliant | | | | |
		No.	%	CBU	CBU 1995	E	Number in: 1995	1994	1993
Coliforms	20,595	56	0.3	0	0	0	0	0	1
Faecal coliforms	20,610	3	<0.1	0	0	0	3	6	4
Colour	1,997	0	0.0	0	0	0	0	0	0
Turbidity	2,051	0	0.0	0	347	0	0	4	10
Odour	1,806	20	1.1	0	0	0	14	3	3
Taste	1,432	1	<0.1	0	0	0	1	0	1
Hydrogen ion	2,706	5	0.2	0	0	0	4	20	30
Nitrate	7,799	22	0.3	0	0	0	6	3	3
Nitrite	1,915	6	0.3	0	0	2	3	5	8
Aluminium	2,241	2	<0.1	0	0	0	2	5	11
Iron	4,983	67	1.3	67	347	0	45	72	79
Manganese	2,315	4	0.2	0	2	0	4	11	8
Lead	4,047	137	3.4	137	347	0	90	111	101
PAH	1,913	44	2.3	4	6	0	23	30	5
Trihalomethanes	1,449	11	0.8	7	29	0	6	6	37
Total pesticides	2,025	4	0.2	3	75	0	3	5	24
Atrazine	1,557	3	0.2	0	80	1	1	8	30
Chlorotoluron	697	0	0.0	0	98	0	0	0	8
Clopyralid	1,292	9	0.7	9	75	0	3	0	0
2,4-D	1,283	0	0.0	0	76	0	0	0	4
2,4-Db	1,283	0	0.0	0	76	0	0	0	1
Dichlorprop	1,264	1	<0.1	0	76	0	1	0	0
Diuron	697	0	0.0	0	56	0	0	0	22
Fluroxpyr	1,288	0	0.0	0	75	0	0	1	0
Iprodione	55	0	0.0	0	2	0	0	1	0
Isoproturon	697	14	2.0	14	56	0	4	10	11
MCPA	1,284	3	0.2	1	76	0	2	10	37
MCPB	1,286	0	0.0	0	76	0	0	0	1
Mecoprop	1,283	8	0.6	7	76	0	5	28	75
Simazine	1,557	6	0.4	6	80	0	3	3	7
Other pesticides	14,514	0	0.0	0	81	0	0	0	0
Magnesium	2,637	1	<0.1	0	0	0	1	0	0
Ammonium	1,722	0	0.0	0	0	0	0	1	1
Fluoride	3,675	0	0.0	0	0	0	0	0	1
Mercury	990	0	0.0	0	0	0	0	0	5
Phosphorus	1,027	3	0.3	0	0	0	1	0	0
Sulphate	2,600	2	<0.1	0	0	0	2	0	0
Benzo 3,4 pyrene	1,936	12	0.6	0	0	0	0	1	0
Tetrachloroethene	1,026	1	1.0	0	0	0	1	0	0
All others	76,028	0	0.0	0	0	0	0	0	0
Total	**201,562**	**445**	**0.2**	**255**	-	-	-	-	-

* 374 zones in 1994; 382 zones in 1993.

Inspection

Mr R J Vincent, Principal Inspector, assisted by Mr P L Jiggins, Inspector, carried out an inspection of Severn Trent Water Limited in a series of visits throughout 1995. Mr Vincent concluded that:

(a) satisfactory progress has been made in respect of the matters which were the subject of recommendations made in the 1994 technical audit inspection report;

(b) the Company's arrangements for zone delineation and pesticide monitoring are sound, and sampling is performed satisfactorily;

(c) the Company's designation of sampling points at water treatment works and service reservoirs is generally satisfactory, but that the current arrangements do not meet the requirements of regulation 21(2)(a) in some cases;

(d) the arrangements for sampling and analysis of microbiological parameters are generally satisfactory but would benefit from minor amendments to the quality assurance procedures;

(e) the Company's arrangements for recording compliance sampling, analysis and reporting are generally satisfactory;

(f) the Company has made generally satisfactory progress with respect to its compliance programme and completed a number of major schemes within schedule, however the Company will not complete at least two schemes involving the installation of treatment to deal with plumbo-solvency on schedule;

(g) the water treatment processes audited complied with regulation 23;

(h) there are satisfactory arrangements for the identification and rectification of potential or actual water quality problems arising in the operation of service reservoirs;

(i) the Company's arrangements for mains rehabilitation using epoxy resin relining are generally satisfactory and repaired mains are being sampled and analysed reasonably promptly;

(j) the Company has embarked on a major initiative in respect of quality assurance, but that they will not necessarily accord explicitly with formal systems of accreditation or certification; and

(k) the Company has good arrangements for communications with local authorities which ensure compliance with the relevant parts of regulations 30 and 31.

Enforcement action was considered for the contravention of regulation 21(2)(a) but the Company took prompt action to prevent recurrence and enforcement action was not required. Further enforcement action was initiated for the failure to install and commission on time treatment to reduce lead concentrations, as described below.

In October, Dr A K Hughes, representing the consultants Rofe, Kennard and Lapworth, working under the general direction of Mr Vincent, carried out inspections of selected water treatment works and selected service reservoirs. He concluded that:

(l) the treatment processes complied with Regulation 23;

(m) the use of substances and products satisfied the requirements of Regulation 25;

(n) the Company's policy and arrangements for disinfection at treatment works were satisfactory; and

(o) the Company's arrangements for compliance sampling at treatment works and service reservoirs are generally in accordance with the recommendations of paragraph 2.8 of the Guidance Document and with the requirements of Regulation 21(2)(a).

As a result of these inspections, 18 recommendations were conveyed to the Company for formal response. 50 suggestions on various matters were also made. The Company has already taken action on most of these recommendations and is taking action on others.

Improvement programmes

Six undertakings in respect of improvement programmes accepted by the Secretary of State from the Company were due for full completion or the completion of major steps during 1995 and five of these were completed on schedule. Treatment plant to reduce lead concentrations was installed on time at 26 sites but at six sites the due date was not met. In January 1996 the Secretary of State issued a Notice of Intention to make a Final Enforcement Order in respect of the late installation of treatment plant at six sites to reduce lead concentrations, scheduled for completion by 31 December 1995. The Company completed installation at all six sites by 1 February 1996, therefore the Final Enforcement Order was not made. A new undertaking given by the Company to carry out improvement works to its distribution system, with a completion date of 31 March 2000, is being considered by the Secretary of State.

Incidents

Nine events notified during 1995 by the Company to the Secretary of State under the terms of the Water Undertakers (Information) Direction 1992 are regarded by the Inspectorate as constituting incidents in which drinking water quality demonstrably deteriorated. Five incidents involved bacteriological contamination of the water supply following operational work and repairs to mains. In all cases advice to boil water was issued to the affected consumers whilst remedial action was taken. In April, an incident occurred involving the contamination of the water supply by the pesticide MCPA. The water was abstracted from the River Avon and following treatment at Avon water treatment works was supplied to some 60,000 consumers in the Rugby area. It was concluded that the contamination was of short duration and posed no risk to public health. In May and July, disinfection failures occurred at Eyton and Rodmore water treatment works respectively. At both these borehole sources no deterioration in the bacteriological quality of the water supply was detected. The Company identified deficiencies in control of the chlorination process which have been addressed at these and other works with similar operational controls. One incident involving the contamination of the water supply to Lea Castle estates, Kidderminster has been notified to the Inspectorate and is awaiting assessment.

No other events regarded as constituting incidents came to the attention of the Inspectorate in 1995.

Enforcement action

Table 3.19.4 summarises enforcement action under consideration for the Company as a result of the Inspectorate's work in, or pertaining to, the calendar year 1995.

Table 3.19.4	Severn Trent Water Limited SUMMARY OF ENFORCEMENT ACTION CONSIDERED IN 1995
Regulation	**Reason for enforcement**
3(3)(c)	Contraventions for nitrite in two zones and individual pesticides in respect of atrazine in one zone.
21(2)(a)	Use of inappropriate sampling points at a number of water treatment works and service reservoirs.

SOUTH EAST WATER LIMITED

Introduction

The Company was formed by the merger of Eastbourne Water plc, Mid-Sussex Water plc and West Kent Water plc on 1 April 1994. The Company supplies on average 154 Ml/d of water to a population of approximately 618,000 in Mid Sussex, East Sussex and West Kent between Eastbourne in the south and Sevenoaks in the north. Approximately 60% of the water put into supply is derived from boreholes and springs in chalk, sandstone and greensand aquifers. The remaining 40% of the company's water is from four surface water abstractions with a small import of water from two other water undertakers. The Company operates 36 water treatment works. Treated water is distributed via 114 service reservoirs and 4,678 km of water mains. The supply area is divided into 46 water supply zones.

Overall water quality

At water treatment works and service reservoirs and in water supply zones, the Company carried out a total of 59,906 determinations in 1995. Of these, 99.5% demonstrated compliance with the relevant water quality standards, but 268 showed a PCV to have been contravened.

Coliforms were not detected at 32 (89%) of the Company's 36 water treatment works. At 110 (97%) of the Company's 114 service reservoirs, coliforms were absent from at least 95% of samples. Of the Company's 46 water supply zones in 1995, 43 (94%) complied fully with the relevant water quality standards or had breaches of the standards which were either trivial or were fully covered by undertakings. In the other 3 (6%) of the zones, some breaches could result in enforcement action.

Microbiological quality of water leaving treatment works

Table 3.20.1 shows the Company's performance in 1995, with data for 1994 and 1993 for comparison. The data presented for 1993 represents combined data for the three predecessor companies. Differences between the three years are not considered significant. Had the definition of the coliform parameter not been changed as described in 3.35 above, but remained as it was for 1994 and previous years, the number of treatment works with coliforms detected would have been two and the number of determinations containing coliforms two.

Table 3.20.1 South East Water Limited
MICROBIOLOGICAL QUALITY OF WATER LEAVING TREATMENT WORKS

	1995	1994	1993[a]
Number of water treatment works	36	34	36
Works with no sampling shortfall	31	26	28
COLIFORMS			
Total number of determinations	3,371	4,466	4,231
- number containing coliforms	4	9	14
- % containing coliforms	0.1	0.2	0.3
Treatment works with coliforms detected	**4**	**7**	**10**
- % of all works	11	21	28
FAECAL COLIFORMS			
Total number of determinations	3,371	4,466	4,213
- number containing faecal coliforms	2	2	7
- % containing faecal coliforms	<0.1	<0.1	0.2
Treatment works with faecal coliforms detected	**2**	**2**	**6**
- % of all works	6	6	17

[a] Numbers in this column represent combined data for the predecessor companies.

The Company complied with the sampling frequencies required by regulation 17 at 31 of its 36 treatment works in 1995. Shortfalls at the other five are regarded as trivial.

All contraventions of the standards at works are considered trivial or unlikely to recur.

Microbiological quality of water in service reservoirs

Table 3.20.2 shows the Company's performance in 1995, with data for 1994 and combined data for the three predecessor companies for 1993 for comparison. Differences between the three years are not considered significant. Had the definition of the coliform parameter not been changed as described in 3.35 above, but remained as it was for 1994 and previous years, the number of service reservoirs with coliforms detected in more than 5% of samples would have been two and the number of determinations containing coliforms 20.

Table 3.20.2 South East Water Limited
MICROBIOLOGICAL QUALITY OF WATER IN SERVICE RESERVOIRS

	1995	1994	1993[a]
Number of service reservoirs	114	114	116
Service reservoirs with no sampling shortfall	112	77	104
COLIFORMS			
Total number of determinations	5,860	5,719	5,810
- number containing coliforms	45	29	30
- % containing coliforms	0.8	0.5	0.5
Service reservoirs with coliforms detected	27	19	27
Service reservoirs with coliforms detected in more than 5% of samples	**4**	**1**	**0**
- % of all service reservoirs	4	1	0
FAECAL COLIFORMS			
Total number of determinations	5,860	5,719	5,786
- number containing faecal coliforms	8	7	8
- % containing faecal coliforms	0.1	0.1	0.1
Service reservoirs with faecal coliforms detected	**7**	**5**	**8**
- % of all service reservoirs	6	4	7

[a] Numbers in this column represent combined data for the predecessor companies.

The Company complied with the sampling frequencies required by regulation 18 at 112 of its 114 service reservoirs in 1995. Shortfalls at the other two are regarded as trivial.

Contraventions of the microbiological quality standards at a total of five service reservoirs has resulted in the consideration of enforcement action, as shown in table 3.20.4. All other contraventions of the standards at service reservoirs are considered trivial.

Water quality in water supply zones

The Company failed to comply with the required sampling frequencies for parameters iron, manganese and carbendazim in two zones, however the Company has taken action and the breach of regulation 13 is considered unlikely to recur.

Table 3.20.3 shows the Company's performance in 1995, with data for 1994 and combined data for the three predecessor companies for 1993 for comparison. Several substances have given rise to changing patterns of compliance of zones with the total and individual pesticides parameters; of these changes the decreases in the number of

Table 3.20.3 South East Water Limited
WATER QUALITY IN SUPPLY ZONES

Columns 'CBU' show, for determinations, contraventions covered by undertakings and, for zones, the total number of zones covered by undertakings in 1995. Column 'E' shows the number of zones for which new enforcement action is under consideration as a result of contraventions of the PCV in 1995. **Please refer to the Introduction to Chapter 3 for more detailed explanation of this table.**

| Parameter | DETERMINATIONS in 1995 | | | | ZONES (46 in 1995)* | | | | |
| | Total | Contravening PCV | | | Non-compliant | | | | |
		No.	%	CBU	CBU 1995	E	Number[a] in: 1995	1994	1993
Coliforms	2,345	54	2.3	0	0	1	1	0	0
Faecal coliforms	2,345	3	0.1	0	0	0	3	2	10
Colour	653	0	0.0	0	0	0	0	1	0
Turbidity	653	2	0.3	0	0	0	2	2	1
Odour	487	1	0.2	0	0	0	1	0	0
Taste	486	0	0.0	0	0	0	0	0	0
Hydrogen ion	1,537	0	0.0	0	0	0	0	0	0
Nitrate	470	0	0.0	0	0	0	0	0	0
Nitrite	500	2	0.4	1	1	0	2	1	5
Aluminium	564	1	0.2	0	0	0	1	0	1
Iron	958	39	4.1	39	46	0	14	19	19
Manganese	561	1	0.2	1	46	0	1	1	1
Lead	369	8	2.2	8	46	0	4	7	5
PAH	257	7	2.7	0	0	0	5	4	4
Trihalomethanes	259	12	4.6	11	3	0	0	4	2
Total pesticides	422	7	1.7	7	12	0	2	10	13
Amitrole	216	1	0.5	1	12	0	1	0	0
Atrazine	480	12	2.5	12	12	0	1	7	9
Carbetamide	458	0	0.0	0	12	0	0	2	8
Chlorotoluron	458	11	2.4	9	12	1	4	3	5
2,4-D	432	0	0.0	0	12	0	0	6	2
Dicamba	432	0	0.0	0	12	0	0	0	2
Dichlobenil	291	0	0.0	0	12	0	0	2	0
Diuron	473	0	0.0	0	12	0	0	9	11
EPTC	306	0	0.0	0	12	0	0	0	4
Flutriafol	461	1	0.2	1	12	0	1	0	0
Glyphosate	286	0	0.0	0	12	0	0	1	0
Isoproturon	470	7	1.5	6	12	0	2	10	2
Linuron	458	1	0.2	1	12	0	1	0	8
MCPA	440	0	0.0	0	12	0	0	6	2
Mecoprop	478	17	3.6	17	12	0	2	8	3
Methabenzthiazuron	458	7	1.5	4	12	1	2	6	0
Simazine	455	8	1.8	8	12	0	2	2	2
Trietazine	462	2	0.4	2	12	0	2	0	0
Other pesticides	12,705	0	0.0	0	12	0	0	0	0
Temperature	2,193	1	<0.1	0	0	0	1	0	0
Potassium	121	0	0.0	0	0	0	0	0	1
Mercury	94	1	1.1	0	0	0	1	0	0
Benzo 3,4 pyrene	257	3	1.2	0	0	0	0	0	0
All others	5,694	0	0.0	0	0	0	0	0	0
Total	**41,444**	**209**	**0.5**	**128**	-	-	-	-	-

* 57 zones in 1994; 56 zones in 1993 refers to the total in the predecessor companies.
[a] Numbers in the 1993 column represent combined data for the predecessor companies.

zones failing to comply in respect of total pesticides, atrazine, carbetamide, diuron and linuron are significant. Other differences between the three years are not considered significant. Had the definition of the coliform parameter not been changed as described in 3.35 above, but remained as it was for 1994 and previous years, no zones would have contravened the PCV for coliforms and the number of determinations containing coliforms would have been 23.

Enforcement action is being considered in respect of some contraventions of standards, as shown in tables 3.20.3 and 3.20.4. All other contraventions of the standards in zones are considered trivial or are covered by undertakings.

Inspection

Mr R J Vincent, Principal Inspector assisted by Mr P L Jiggins, Inspector, carried out an inspection of South East Water Limited in a series of visits between 26 September and 14 December 1995. Mr Vincent concluded that:

(a)   the arrangements for sampling are generally carried out competently in the Company;

(b)   the Company's analytical arrangements are generally satisfactory, however regulation 21(2)(d)(iii) has been breached trivially for some parameters;

(c)   the Company's arrangements for recording and reporting compliance data are generally satisfactory;

(d)   the arrangements for dissemination of results and the information on the public record generally satisfied part VII of the Regulations;

(e)   the Company is making satisfactory progress with its compliance programmes;

(f)   the Company's arrangements for water distribution are generally satisfactory but the procedures for epoxy lining of mains would benefit from improvements to recording practice;

(g)   the water treatment processes audited complied with regulation 23;

(h)   the Company's arrangements for rehearsals of emergency procedures are generally satisfactory;

(i)   the Company provides local authorities with the water quality reports required by regulations 30 and 31, but liaison between the Company and local authorities would be strengthened by annual meetings; and

(j)   the Company is committed to an extensive programme of developing quality systems with a view to formal accreditation wherever possible, but that the programme is still in its early stages.

In November, Mr A J Elder, representing consultants Rofe, Kennard and Lapworth, and working under the general direction of Mr Vincent, carried out inspections of selected water treatment works and selected service reservoirs. He concluded that:

(k)   the treatment processes at Hempstead water treatment works complied with the relevant regulations;

(l)   the Company's policy and arrangements for disinfection at Hempstead water treatment works were satisfactory; and

(m)   the Company's arrangements for compliance sampling at Hempstead water treatment works and St Francis service reservoir are generally satisfactory.

As a result of these inspections, 22 recommendations on various matters were conveyed to the Company for formal response, together with 42 suggestions for the Company to consider. The Company is taking action or has already taken action on a number of the recommendations.

Improvement programmes

Four undertakings in respect of improvement programmes accepted by the Secretary of State from the Company were due for full completion or the completion of major steps during 1995 and two of these were completed on schedule. Commissioning of the GAC filtration installed at Pembury in respect of the pesticide undertaking and commissioning of treatment to reduce plumbo-solvency at one of the five works specified in the lead undertaking were slightly delayed for reasons beyond the Company's control. A new undertaking given by the Company to carry out improvement works to its distribution system, with a completion date of 31 March 2000, is being considered by the Secretary of State.

Incidents

No events regarded as constituting incidents in which drinking water quality demonstrably deteriorated came to the attention of the Inspectorate in 1995.

Enforcement action

Table 3.20.4 summarises enforcement action under consideration for the Company as a result of the Inspectorate's work in, or pertaining to, the calendar year 1995.

Table 3.20.4 South East Water Limited
SUMMARY OF ENFORCEMENT ACTION CONSIDERED IN 1995

Regulation	Reason for enforcement
3(3)(c)	Contravention of the standard for two individual pesticides in one zone and coliforms in one zone.
3(7)	Contravention of the coliforms standard at two service reservoirs, the faecal coliforms standard at one other service reservoir and both standards at two further service reservoirs.

SOUTH STAFFORDSHIRE WATER PLC

Introduction

The Company supplies on average 354 Ml/d of water to a population of approximately 1.2 million. The supply area stretches from the edge of Ashbourne (Derbyshire) in the north to Halesowen (Worcestershire) in the south and from Tamworth in the east to the M6 motorway in the west. Water supplies are drawn from two major surface water sources and 27 boreholes. Surface water abstraction currently accounts for 50% of the water put into supply. Several boreholes have high nitrate concentrations and one has a high sodium concentration. As a result, the Company is adopting both blending techniques and nitrate removal technology to meet the requirements of the Regulations. Treated water from 29 water treatment works is distributed via 38 service reservoirs and 5,618 km of mains. The supply area is divided into 38 water supply zones.

Overall water quality

At water treatment works and service reservoirs and in water supply zones, the Company carried out a total of 31,982 determinations in 1995. Of these, 99.8% demonstrated compliance with the relevant water quality standards, but 59 showed a PCV to have been contravened.

Coliforms were not detected at 28 (97%) of the Company's 29 water treatment works. At all of the Company's 38 service reservoirs, coliforms were absent from at least 95% of samples. Of the Company's 38 water supply zones in 1995, 36 (95%) complied fully with the relevant water quality standards or had breaches of the standards which were either trivial or were fully covered by undertakings. In the other two (5%) of the zones, some breaches could result in enforcement action.

Microbiological quality of water leaving treatment works

Table 3.21.1 shows the Company's performance in 1995, with data for 1994 and 1993 for comparison. Differences between the three years are not considered significant.

The Company complied with the sampling frequencies required by regulation 17 at 25 of its 29 treatment works in 1995. Shortfalls at two are regarded as trivial, and at the other two as unlikely to recur.

All contraventions of the standards at works are considered trivial.

Table 3.21.1 South Staffordshire Water Plc MICROBIOLOGICAL QUALITY OF WATER LEAVING TREATMENT WORKS			
	1995	1994	1993
Number of water treatment works	29	29	29
Works with no sampling shortfall	25	28	27
COLIFORMS			
Total number of determinations	2,696	2,718	2,340
- number containing coliforms	1	2	0
- % containing coliforms	<0.1	<0.1	0.0
Treatment works with coliforms detected	**1**	**2**	**0**
- % of all works	3	7	0
FAECAL COLIFORMS			
Total number of determinations	2,696	2,713	2,340
- number containing faecal coliforms	1	2	0
- % containing faecal coliforms	<0.1	<0.1	0.0
Treatment works with faecal coliforms detected	**1**	**2**	**0**
- % of all works	3	7	0

Microbiological quality of water in service reservoirs

Table 3.21.2 shows the Company's performance in 1995, with data for 1994 and 1993 for comparison. Differences between the three years are not considered significant.

The Company complied with the sampling frequencies required by regulation 18 at 34 of its 38 service reservoirs in 1995. Shortfalls at the other four are regarded as trivial.

All contraventions of the standards at service reservoirs are considered trivial.

Table 3.21.2 South Staffordshire Water Plc
MICROBIOLOGICAL QUALITY OF WATER IN SERVICE RESERVOIRS

	1995	1994	1993
Number of service reservoirs	38	38	37
Service reservoirs with no sampling shortfall	34	38	37
COLIFORMS			
Total number of determinations	1,914	1,928	1,776
- number containing coliforms	3	2	4
- % containing coliforms	0.2	0.1	0.2
Service reservoirs with coliforms detected	3	2	2
Service reservoirs with coliforms detected in more than 5% of samples	**0**	**0**	**1**
- % of all service reservoirs	0	0	3
FAECAL COLIFORMS			
Total number of determinations	1,914	1,928	1,776
- number containing faecal coliforms	0	1	2
- % containing faecal coliforms	0	<0.1	0.1
Service reservoirs with faecal coliforms detected	**0**	**1**	**1**
- % of all service reservoirs	0	3	3

Water quality in water supply zones

The Company failed to comply with the required sampling frequencies for parameters total coliforms, faecal coliforms and some other parameters in a number of zones. However the Company has taken action and the breach of regulation 13 is considered not likely to recur.

Table 3.21.3 shows the Company's performance in 1995, with data for 1994 and 1993 for comparison. There has been a significant reduction over the three years in the number of zones failing to comply with the faecal coliform standard. All other differences between the three years are not considered significant.

Enforcement action is being considered in respect of contraventions of the standard for the individual pesticide atrazine, as shown in tables 3.21.3 and 3.21.4. All other contraventions of the standards in zones are covered by undertakings.

Inspection

Mr R J Vincent, Principal Inspector, assisted by Mr P L Jiggins, Inspector, carried out an inspection of South Staffordshire Water Plc in a series of visits between 28 November and 8 December 1995. Mr Vincent concluded that:

(a)   the Company has taken appropriate and satisfactory measures to implement the recommendations made in the 1994 technical audit inspection reports;

**Table 3.21.3 South Staffordshire Water Plc
WATER QUALITY IN SUPPLY ZONES**

*Columns 'CBU' show, for determinations, contraventions covered by undertakings and, for zones, the total number
of zones covered by undertakings in 1995. Column 'E' shows the number of zones for which new enforcement
action is under consideration as a result of contraventions of the PCV in 1995. **Please refer to the Introduction to
Chapter 3 for more detailed explanation of this table.***

| Parameter | DETERMINATIONS in 1995 | | | | ZONES (38 in 1995)* | | | | |
| | Total | Contravening PCV | | | CBU | E | Non-compliant Number in: | | |
		No.	%	CBU	1995		1995	1994	1993
Coliforms	3,200	17	0.5	0	0	0	0	0	0
Faecal coliforms	3,200	0	0.0	0	0	0	0	3	10
Colour	409	0	0.0	0	0	0	0	0	0
Turbidity	696	0	0.0	0	0	0	0	0	1
Odour	462	0	0.0	0	0	0	0	2	1
Taste	462	0	0.0	0	0	0	0	0	0
Hydrogen ion	409	0	0.0	0	0	0	0	0	0
Nitrate	631	1	0.2	1	8	0	1	4	5
Nitrite	631	0	0.0	0	0	0	0	1	1
Aluminium	586	1	0.2	1	38	0	1	1	1
Iron	707	6	0.9	6	38	0	5	4	7
Manganese	696	0	0.0	0	0	0	0	1	0
Lead	457	8	1.8	8	38	0	7	9	7
PAH	47	0	0.0	0	0	0	0	0	0
Trihalomethanes	316	0	0.0	0	0	0	0	0	0
Total pesticides	406	0	0.0	0	4	0	0	0	0
Atrazine	289	21	7.3	16	4	2	5	3	3
Isoproturon	216	0	0.0	0	4	0	0	5	0
Other pesticides	769	0	0.0	0	4	0	0	0	0
Copper	445	0	0.0	0	0	0	0	1	1
All others	7,728	0	0.0	0	0	0	0	0	0
Total	**22,762**	**54**	**0.2**	**32**	-	-	-	-	-

* 38 zones in 1994; 38 zones in 1993.

(b) the Company's arrangements for supply zone delineation and selection of sample points are generally satisfactory but that further review of supply zone delineation and sampling from water treatment works that incorporate blending is required;

(c) the performance characteristics of the chemical analytical methods used in the Company's laboratory are generally satisfactory;

(d) the analytical method for the determination of manganese is satisfactory however the arrangements for the acidification of samples require improvement;

(e) the analytical system for the quantitative assessment of taste and odour is satisfactory;

(f) the arrangements for microbiological parameters are generally satisfactory but could benefit from improvements to the arrangements for confirmatory testing and some aspects of quality assurance;

(g) the Company's procedures for recording compliance sampling, analysis and reporting are generally satisfactory but that some attention to aspects of analytical quality control and documentation would result in further improvement;

(h) the Company has continued to make good general progress on its few remaining compliance programmes;

(i) the Company has satisfactorily installed phosphate dosing plant for plumbosolvency control at seven of its pumping stations;

(j) the Company's arrangements for rehearsals of emergency procedures are satisfactory;

(k) communications between the Company and the Birmingham City Council are generally satisfactory; and

(l) communications between the Company and the Lichfield District Council are fully satisfactory.

In September, Mr R J Kidson, representing consultants Rofe, Kennard & Lapworth and working under the general direction of Mr Vincent, carried out inspections of selected water treatment works and selected service reservoirs. He concluded that:

(m) the treatment processes at Shenstone WTW complied with the requirements of Regulation 23;

(n) the use of substances and products satisfied the requirements of Regulation 25;

(o) the Company's arrangements for compliance sampling at treatment works and service reservoirs are generally in accordance with the recommendations of paragraph 2.8 of the Guidance Document and with the requirements of Regulation 21(2)(a);

(p) arrangements for the management of water quality at source was satisfactory; and

(q) the arrangements for ensuring the security, integrity and inspection/maintenance of service reservoirs were generally satisfactory.

As a result of these inspections, 12 recommendations were conveyed to the Company for a formal response, together with 30 suggestions for the Company to consider. The Company has already taken action on a number of these recommendations and is taking action on others.

Improvement programmes

One undertaking in respect of improvement programmes accepted by the Secretary of State from the Company was due for full completion during 1995. The Company had installed treatment by the due date at only seven of the 16 sources established as supplying zones in which a risk of exceeding the lead standard had been identified. The company sought to demonstrate that some of the works required by the undertaking had not been carried out as they were not necessary. Having considered the evidence presented, and making additional investigations, the Inspectorate concluded that the works were necessary and issued a Notice of Intention to make an Enforcement Order. An Order will be issued after the necessary period for representations or objections has passed. A new undertaking given by the Company to carry out improvement works to its distribution system, with a completion date of 31 March 2000, has been accepted by the Secretary of State.

Relaxations

The Secretary of State had authorised relaxation of a PCV in two individual cases, subject to review by 31 December 1995. These cases involved two parameters in zones supplied from two water treatment works. As a result of the review the Company was given notice of revocation of both relaxations because the Inspectorate concluded, from the data supplied, that non-trivial contraventions of the standard in question were unlikely to occur.

Incidents

One event notified during 1995 by the Company to the Secretary of State under the terms of the Water Undertakers (Information) Direction 1992 is regarded by the Inspectorate as constituting an incident in which drinking water quality demonstrably deteriorated.

In November an incident at Canwell, Tamworth involved the bacteriological contamination of the water supply following the installation of a fire hydrant. Advice to boil water was issued to the consumers in the 16 properties affected. The Inspectorate was critical of the Company's response and made recommendations accordingly. The failure of the Company to notify promptly the local authority and the health authority, and the Inspectorate, of the incident resulted in consideration of enforcement action for contravention of regulation 30(5) and s5(1) of the Water Undertakers (Information) Direction 1992 respectively. The Company subsequently provided satisfactory assurance that it had taken measures to prevent a recurrence of this failing so it was not necessary to proceed with enforcement.

Enforcement action

Table 3.21.4 summarises enforcement action under consideration for the Company as a result of the Inspectorate's work in, or pertaining to, the calendar year 1995.

Table 3.21.4 South Staffordshire Water Plc SUMMARY OF ENFORCEMENT ACTION CONSIDERED IN 1995

Regulation	Reason for enforcement
3(3)(c)	Contravention of the standard for atrazine in two zones.
30(5)	Incident involving the failure to notify the local authority and health authority promptly of an event which gave rise to a significant health risk.
Information Direction	Incident involving the failure to notify the Inspectorate promptly of an event which gave rise to a significant health risk.

SOUTH WEST WATER SERVICES LIMITED

Introduction

The Company supplies on average 508 Ml/d of water to a population of 1.5 million consumers in an area approximating to the counties of Devon and Cornwall. Approximately 90% of the water put into supply comes from surface water sources, the remaining 10% is obtained from groundwater sources. The Company has 48 water treatment works on 45 sites. There are three treatment streams at one site, and two at another. Surface derived water is treated at 40 of these sites, including 25 supplied from direct river abstractions. Treated water is distributed via 368 service reservoirs and over 15,000 km of water mains. The supply area is divided into 82 water supply zones.

Overall water quality

At water treatment works and service reservoirs and in water supply zones, the Company carried out a total of 111,562 determinations in 1995. Of these, 99.6% demonstrated compliance with the relevant water quality standards, but 485 showed a PCV to have been contravened.

Coliforms were not detected at 33 (69%) of the Company's 48 water treatment works. At 359 (91%) of the Company's 368 service reservoirs, coliforms were absent from at least 95% of samples. Of the Company's 82 water supply zones in 1995, 77 (94%) complied fully with the relevant water quality standards or had breaches of the standards which were either trivial or were fully covered by undertakings. In the other five (6%) of the zones, some breaches are regarded as unlikely to recur, but others could result in enforcement action.

Microbiological quality of water leaving treatment works

Table 3.22.1 shows the Company's performance in 1995, with data for 1994 and 1993 for comparison. Differences between the three years are not considered significant. Had the definition of the coliform parameter not been changed as described in 3.35 above, but remained as it was for 1994 and previous years, the number of treatment works with coliforms detected would have been 10 and the number of determinations containing coliforms 14.

Table 3.22.1 South West Water Services Limited
MICROBIOLOGICAL QUALITY OF WATER LEAVING TREATMENT WORKS

	1995	1994	1993
Number of water treatment works	48	46	50
Works with no sampling shortfall	44	43	50
COLIFORMS			
Total number of determinations	8,047	9,040	9,689
- number containing coliforms	23	9	22
- % containing coliforms	0.3	0.1	0.2
Treatment works with coliforms detected	**15**	**7**	**13**
- % of all works	31	15	26
FAECAL COLIFORMS			
Total number of determinations	8,069	9,056	9,691
- number containing faecal coliforms	5	1	3
- % containing faecal coliforms	0.1	<0.1	<0.1
Treatment works with faecal coliforms detected	**5**	**1**	**3**
- % of all works	10	2	6

The Company complied with the sampling frequencies required by regulation 17 at 44 of its 48 treatment works in 1995. Shortfalls at the other four are regarded as trivial.

Contraventions of the microbiological quality standards at one works has resulted in the consideration of enforcement action, as shown in table 3.22.4. All other contraventions of the standards at works are considered trivial or unlikely to recur, or covered by undertakings.

Microbiological quality of water in service reservoirs

Table 3.22.2 shows the Company's performance in 1995, with data for 1994 and 1993 for comparison. Differences between the three years are not considered significant. Had the definition of the coliform parameter not been changed as described in 3.35 above, but remained as it was for 1994 and previous years, the number of service reservoirs with coliforms detected in more than 5% of samples would have been five and the number of determinations containing coliforms 86.

Table 3.22.2 South West Water Services Limited MICROBIOLOGICAL QUALITY OF WATER IN SERVICE RESERVOIRS			
	1995	**1994**	**1993**
Number of service reservoirs	368	373	365
Service reservoirs with no sampling shortfall	365	372	365
COLIFORMS			
Total number of determinations	19,542	19,864	20,576
- number containing coliforms	118	74	75
- % containing coliforms	0.6	0.4	0.4
Service reservoirs with coliforms detected	77	57	57
Service reservoirs with coliforms detected in more than 5% of samples	**9**	**3**	**4**
- % of all service reservoirs	2	1	1
FAECAL COLIFORMS			
Total number of determinations	19,595	19,898	20,577
- number containing faecal coliforms	21	20	11
- % containing faecal coliforms	0.1	0.1	0.1
Service reservoirs with faecal coliforms detected	**18**	**16**	**10**
- % of all service reservoirs	5	4	3

The Company complied with the sampling frequencies required by regulation 18 at 365 of its 368 service reservoirs in 1995. Shortfalls at the other three are regarded as trivial.

Contraventions of the microbiological quality standards at one service reservoir have resulted in the consideration of enforcement action, as shown in table 3.22.4. All other contraventions of the standards at service reservoirs are considered trivial or unlikely to recur, or covered by undertakings.

Water quality in water supply zones

The Company complied with the required sampling frequencies for all parameters in all zones.

Table 3.22.3 shows the Company's performance in 1995, with data for 1994 and 1993 for comparison. Differences between the three years are not considered significant. Had the definition of the coliform parameter not been changed as described in 3.35

**Table 3.22.3 South West Water Services Limited
WATER QUALITY IN SUPPLY ZONES**

Columns 'CBU' show, for determinations, contraventions covered by undertakings and, for zones, the total *number of zones covered by undertakings in 1995. Column 'E' shows the number of zones for which new enforcement action is under consideration as a result of contraventions of the PCV in 1995.* **Please refer to the Introduction to Chapter 3 for more detailed explanation of this table.**

| Parameter | DETERMINATIONS in 1995 | | | | ZONES (82 in 1995)* | | | | |
| | Total | Contravening PCV | | | | | Non-compliant | | |
		No.	%	CBU	CBU 1995	E	Number in: 1995	1994	1993
Coliforms	5,116	35	0.7	7	11	0	0	0	0
Faecal coliforms	5,123	6	0.1	0	0	0	6	5	1
Colour	2,280	0	0	0	0	0	0	1	1
Turbidity	2,280	6	0.3	0	4	0	6	2	7
Odour	870	0	0	0	0	0	0	0	0
Taste	854	1	0.1	0	0	0	1	0	0
Hydrogen ion	2,280	15	0.7	3	3	0	9	7	10
Nitrate	1,097	0	0	0	0	0	0	0	0
Nitrite	1,097	1	0.1	0	0	0	1	0	0
Aluminium	2,274	27	1.2	26	10	0	6	2	4
Iron	2,274	102	4.5	102	82	0	38	30	27
Manganese	2,274	12	0.5	12	82	0	9	6	9
Lead	549	4	0.7	0	0	0	4	7	14
PAH	789	101	12.8	99	36	1	26	29	33
Trihalomethanes	382	2	0.5	0	0	0	1	0	0
Total pesticides	372	0	0	0	0	0	0	0	1
Atrazine	372	0	0	0	0	0	0	0	2
Carbofuran	372	0	0	0	0	0	0	0	1
Other pesticides	13,123	0	0.0	0	0	0	0	0	0
Oxidisability	90	0	0	0	0	0	0	0	1
Cadmium	94	1	1.1	0	0	0	1	0	0
Benzo 3,4 pyrene	789	5	0.6	5	36	0	0	0	5
All others	11,558	0	0.0	0	0	0	0	0	0
Total	**56,309**	**318**	**0.6**	**254**	-	-	-	-	-

* 82 zones in 1994; 82 zones in 1993.

above, but remained as it was for 1994 and previous years, the number of zones contravening the PCV for coliforms would have remained unchanged and the number of determinations containing coliforms would have been 28.

Enforcement action is being considered in respect of one contravention of the standards, as shown in tables 3.22.3 and 3.22.4. All other contraventions of the standards in zones are considered trivial or unlikely to recur, or are covered by undertakings.

Inspection

Mr R J Vincent, Principal Inspector, assisted by Mr P L Jiggins, Inspector, carried out an inspection of South West Water Services Limited during a number of visits throughout 1995.

Mr Vincent concluded that:

(a) satisfactory progress has been made in respect of the majority of the matters which were the subject of recommendations made in the 1994 technical audit inspection report;

(b) the Company's processes of gathering and updating information on pesticide use in the area is not as rigorous as it might be;

(c) provided observations on the sampling run inspected are representative of the practice as a whole, sampling is generally carried out competently in the Company;

(d) the Company's delineation of its water supply zones is consistent with chapter 1 of "Guidance on Safeguarding the Quality of Public Water Supplies";

(e) the performance characteristics of all but two of the chemical analytical methods used in the Exeter laboratory are satisfactory, but further performance testing is required for mercury and an individual pesticide;

(f) the continued use of a method for the determination of individual pesticides with a detection limit of 0.1 µg/l or higher concentration constitutes a contravention of regulation 21(2)(d)(iii);

(g) the analytical method for nitrite at the Exeter laboratory is satisfactory;

(h) the Company's arrangements for sampling and analysis of microbiological parameters are generally satisfactory;

(i) the Company's arrangements for recording compliance sampling, analysis and reporting are generally satisfactory;

(j) the arrangements for the Public Record at the Exeter headquarters generally conform to the requirements of regulations 29 and 30, however the failure to record the results of the determination of sulcofuron constitutes a trivial contravention of regulation 29(1)(f) which is unlikely to recur;

(k) the Company has satisfactorily completed all its compliance programmes at works and service reservoirs which had been due for completion by 31 December 1994;

(l) the compliance programme at Tamar water treatment works and the undertaking for lead were satisfactorily completed by the due dates;

(m) Bovey Cross water treatment works is operated satisfactorily and secures compliance with the aluminium standard in the associated water supply zone, however disinfection may be compromised by the existing lime dosing arrangements;

(n) Newbridge water treatment works is operated satisfactorily and that the robustness of the treatment process has been enhanced by recent modifications to the filter backwash process;

(o) the Company's arrangements for mains rehabilitation using epoxy resin relining are generally satisfactory;

(p) communications between the Company and (i) the Penwith District Council; and (ii) the Torridge District Council are satisfactory; and

(q) the Company is making progress with the implementation of quality assurance systems.

As a result of this inspection the Company was notified that enforcement action was being considered for the contravention of regulation 21(2)(d)(iii). The Company took prompt remedial action and enforcement was not required.

In October, Mr A J Elder representing consultants Rofe, Kennard & Lapworth, working under the general supervision of Mr Vincent, carried out an inspection of a water treatment works and a service reservoir. He concluded that:

(r)   the treatment processes at Dousland water treatment works complied with Regulation 23;

(s)   the use of substances and products at Dousland water treatment works satisfied the requirements of Regulation 25;

(t)   the Company's policy and arrangements for disinfection at Dousland water treatment works were satisfactory;

(u)   the Company's arrangements for compliance sampling at Dousland water treatment works and Halwell service reservoir are generally in accordance with the recommendations of paragraph 2.8 of the Guidance Document and with the requirements of regulation 21(2)(a); and

(v)   Halwell Service Reservoir is being utilised and maintained to a satisfactory standard.

As a result of these inspections, 35 recommendations were conveyed to the Company for a formal response. The inspectors also made a total of 41 suggestions for the Company to consider. The Company has already taken action on most of these recommendations, and is taking action on others. It has also taken action on a number of suggestions.

Improvement programmes

Three undertakings in respect of improvement programmes accepted by the Secretary of State from the Company were due for full completion or the completion of major steps during 1995 and two of these were completed on schedule. The remaining scheme at Beacon Hill service reservoir was delayed for reasons beyond the Company's control and has now been completed. A new undertaking given by the Company to carry out improvement works to its distribution system, with a completion date of 31 March 2000, is being considered by the Secretary of State.

Incidents

Five events notified during 1995 by the Company to the Secretary of State under the terms of the Water Undertakers (Information) Direction 1992 are regarded by the Inspectorate as constituting incidents in which drinking water quality demonstrably deteriorated.

One incident involved the microbiological contamination of supplies from a service reservoir. Consumers living in 30 properties near St Cleer, Cornwall were advised to boil water until the contamination was eliminated. The incident was probably caused by the poor condition of a main supplying water to the reservoir. The main has been replaced.

A second incident involved the contamination of supplies by hydrocarbons. This incident was associated with mains rehabilitation work and affected supplies to 27 properties in Bideford, Devon. It has not been possible to establish the route of contamination.

A third incident related to significant adverse publicity resulting from the discolouration of water supplies caused by abnormally high demand for water during the summer. The affected area, Kings Nympton, is included in the new distribution system undertaking.

Two incidents arising in 1995, involving the contamination of supplies by hydrocarbons in the Falmouth area and an outbreak of cryptosporidiosis in the Torbay area, are still under consideration by the Inspectorate.

No other events regarded as constituting incidents came to the attention of the Inspectorate in 1995.

Enforcement action

Table 3.22.4 summarises enforcement action under consideration for the Company as a result of the Inspectorate's work in, or pertaining to, the calendar year 1995.

Table 3.22.4 South West Water Services Limited
SUMMARY OF ENFORCEMENT ACTION CONSIDERED IN 1995

Regulation	Reason for enforcement
3(3)(c)	Contravention of the standard for PAH in one zone.
3(3)(c)	Contravention of the lead standard in previous years in three zones. (An undertaking has subsequently been accepted and completed)
3(7)	Contravention of the coliforms standard at one water treatment works.
3(7)	Contravention of the coliforms standard at one service reservoir.
21(2)(d)(iii)	Inadequate limit of detection for analytical systems for three individual pesticides. (Remedial action taken by the Company)

SOUTHERN WATER SERVICES LIMITED

Introduction

The Company supplies on average 655 Ml/d of water to a resident population of approximately 2.19 million people in an area covering the Isle of Wight and parts of the counties of Hampshire, Kent and Sussex.

Approximately 71% of the Company's water resources are derived from groundwater sources, mainly from high quality chalk aquifers. The remainder is obtained from surface water sources or combined surface and groundwater sources. About 19% of surface water is drawn from storage reservoirs.

The Company operates 100 water supply works. The treated water is distributed via 212 service reservoirs and some 12,987 km of water mains. The supply area is divided into 119 water supply zones.

Overall water quality

At water treatment works and service reservoirs and in water supply zones, the Company carried out a total of 114,345 determinations in 1995. Of these, 99.7% demonstrated compliance with the relevant water quality standards, but 297 showed a PCV to have been contravened.

Coliforms were not detected at 91 (91%) of the Company's 100 water treatment works. At all of the Company's 212 service reservoirs, coliforms were absent from at least 95% of samples. Of the Company's 119 water supply zones in 1995, 118 (99%) complied fully with the relevant water quality standards or had breaches of the standards which were either trivial or were fully covered by undertakings or will be covered by the new distribution undertaking. In the other zone (1%) breaches are regarded as unlikely to recur.

Microbiological quality of water leaving treatment works

Table 3.23.1 shows the Company's performance in 1995, with data for 1994 and 1993 for comparison. Differences between the three years are not considered significant.

Table 3.23.1   Southern Water Services Limited
MICROBIOLOGICAL QUALITY OF WATER LEAVING TREATMENT WORKS

	1995	1994	1993
Number of water treatment works	100	99	101
Works with no sampling shortfall	100	99	87
COLIFORMS			
Total number of determinations	13,424	16,350	16,890
- number containing coliforms	9	9	18
- % containing coliforms	<0.1	<0.1	0.1
Treatment works with coliforms detected	**9**	**8**	**15**
- % of all works	9	8	15
FAECAL COLIFORMS			
Total number of determinations	13,426	16,349	16,912
- number containing faecal coliforms	1	1	8
- % containing faecal coliforms	<0.1	<0.1	<0.1
Treatment works with faecal coliforms detected	**1**	**1**	**8**
- % of all works	1	1	8

The Company complied with the sampling frequencies required by regulation 17 at all its treatment works in 1995. All contraventions of the standards at works are considered trivial.

Microbiological quality of water in service reservoirs

Table 3.23.2 shows the Company's performance in 1995, with data for 1994 and 1993 for comparison. Differences between the three years are not considered significant.

Table 3.23.2 Southern Water Services Limited MICROBIOLOGICAL QUALITY OF WATER IN SERVICE RESERVOIRS

	1995	1994	1993
Number of service reservoirs	212	216	217
Service reservoirs with no sampling shortfall	211	216	217
COLIFORMS			
Total number of determinations	10,875	10,912	10,978
- number containing coliforms	11	12	18
- % containing coliforms	0.1	0.1	0.2
Service reservoirs with coliforms detected	11	12	18
Service reservoirs with coliforms detected in more than 5% of samples	**0**	**0**	**0**
- % of all service reservoirs	0	0	0
FAECAL COLIFORMS			
Total number of determinations	10,875	10,912	10,994
- number containing faecal coliforms	3	0	4
- % containing faecal coliforms	<0.1	0.0	<0.1
Service reservoirs with faecal coliforms detected	**3**	**0**	**4**
- % of all service reservoirs	1	0	2

The Company complied with the sampling frequencies required by regulation 18 at 211 of its 212 service reservoirs in 1995. The shortfall at the single service reservoir is regarded as trivial.

Contraventions of the microbiological quality standards at one service reservoir has resulted in the consideration of enforcement action, as shown in table 3.23.4. All other contraventions of the standards at service reservoirs are considered trivial.

Water quality in water supply zones

The Company failed to comply with the required sampling frequencies for parameters coliforms, faecal coliforms, taste, odour, surfactants and phosphorus in six zones, however the Company has taken action and the breach of regulation 13 is considered not likely to recur.

Table 3.23.3 shows the Company's performance in 1995, with data 1994 and 1993 for comparison. Several substances have given rise to changing patterns of compliance of zones with the individual pesticides standard; of these changes the decrease over the three years in the number of zones failing to comply in respect of diuron, mecoprop and simazine and the increase in respect of 2,4D and flutriafol are significant. Other differences between the three years are not considered significant.

All contraventions of the standards in zones are considered trivial or are covered by undertakings or will be covered by the new distribution undertaking.

Table 3.23.3 Southern Water Services Limited
WATER QUALITY IN SUPPLY ZONES

Columns 'CBU' show, for determinations, contraventions covered by undertakings and, for zones, the <u>total</u> number of zones covered by undertakings in 1995. Column 'E' shows the number of zones for which new enforcement action is under consideration as a result of contraventions of the PCV in 1995. **Please refer to the Introduction to Chapter 3 for more detailed explanation of this table.**

| Parameter | DETERMINATIONS in 1995 | | | | ZONES (119 in 1995)* | | | | |
| | Total | Contravening PCV | | | | | Non-compliant | | |
		No.	%	CBU	CBU 1995	E 1995	Number in: 1995	1994	1993
Coliforms	6,171	21	0.3	0	0	0	0	0	0
Faecal coliforms	6,171	1	<0.1	0	0	0	1	0	3
Colour	853	0	0.0	0	0	0	0	0	0
Turbidity	853	0	0.0	0	0	0	0	0	0
Odour	547	0	0.0	0	0	0	0	2	0
Taste	478	0	0.0	0	0	0	0	0	0
Hydrogen ion	856	0	0.0	0	0	0	0	0	0
Nitrate	993	2	0.2	0	0	0	2	3	1
Nitrite	862	3	0.3	3	1	0	1	1	1
Aluminium	894	1	0.1	0	0	0	1	0	0
Iron	1,553	14	0.9	14	119	0	11	12	14
Manganese	889	1	0.1	0	0	0	1	0	2
Lead	736	14	1.9	9	25	0	8	16	17
PAH	990	90	9.1	49	0	0	47	39	37
Trihalomethanes	542	9	1.7	8	1	0	1	1	1
Total pesticides	1282	15	1.5	15	63	0	5	13	15
Atrazine	1,002	13	1.3	13	63	0	11	13	23
Chlorotoluron	941	8	0.9	6	63	0	5	13	9
2,4 D	832	8	1.0	8	63	0	7	1	0
Dichlorprop	832	0	0.0	0	63	0	0	1	0
Diuron	941	2	0.2	1	63	0	2	3	15
Flutriafol	72	38	52.8	38	63	0	5	0	0
Isoproturon	941	8	0.9	8	63	0	3	13	0
Linuron	941	0	0.0	0	63	0	0	1	1
MCPA	826	3	0.4	2	63	0	3	6	0
Mecoprop	832	9	1.1	9	63	0	3	16	12
Methabenzthiazuron	933	1	0.1	1	63	0	1	0	0
Simazine	1,002	5	0.5	4	63	0	4	7	16
Other pesticides	17,173	0	0.0	0	63	0	0	0	0
Copper	484	0	0.0	0	0	0	0	0	1
Zinc	519	0	0.0	0	0	0	0	0	1
Benzo 3,4 pyrene	990	7	0.7	0	0	0	0	0	1
All others	11,814	0	0.0	0	0	0	0	0	0
Total	**65,745**	**273**	**0.4**	**188**	-	-	-	-	-

* 128 zones in 1994; 131 zones in 1993.

Inspection

The 1995 inspection of Southern Water Services Limited was carried out by Mr D Drury, Principal Inspector, assisted by Dr P Marsden, Inspector. Mr Drury concluded that:

(a) the Company made a very positive response to the recommendations to the 1994 inspection;

(b) on the basis of inspection of a limited number of items, the Company continues to have sound arrangements for sampling that satisfy the requirements of parts IV and V of the Regulations and generally accord with the recommendations in the Guidance Document;

(c) on the basis of detailed audit trails of thirty randomly selected samples and of other specific items, the Company is generally meeting the requirements of regulation 21(2) but a number of discrepancies and deviations from procedures and good practice by its analytical contractor were noted and a recommendation is made in respect of those relating to analytical quality control;

(d) the audit trails showed that arrangements for reporting compliance data are generally satisfactory and secure and that the Company is taking appropriate action in respect of contraventions of standards;

(e) the Company generally fulfilled its obligations given in undertakings linked to improvement programmes at 33 sites in respect of the lead and pesticides parameters;

(f) at treatment works utilising on site electrolytic chlorination, the Company is monitoring chlorate and able to demonstrate that the approval conditions for this process have been met;

(g) the Company had breached a requirement of regulation 25(1) in respect of the epoxy relining work undertaken by its contractor between 11 September 1995 and 19 October 1995. However, this breach was neither intentional nor as a result of negligence, there was no concern over the integrity of the work carried out during this period and therefore the breach was considered trivial;

(h) based on an audit of its Falmer Control Room, the Company was not keeping fully adequate records of its response to water quality alarms and procedures could not ensure that its response was always wholly adequate or timely although there was no evidence to suggest that the Company was not taking appropriate action. However, the urgent remedial action taken by the Company should address the problem;

(i) the Company did not report one water quality incident to the Inspectorate in contravention of the requirements of the Information Direction and a recommendation is made on improving procedures;

(j) the Company has sound arrangements for dealing with emergencies and incidents and is keeping these under review by means of regular rehearsals; and

(k) the Company has good procedures for liaising with local authorities and district health authorities.

Also in September, Mr R M Walls, representing consultants Rofe, Kennard and Lapworth, and working under the general direction of Mr Drury, carried out inspection of selected water treatment works and selected service reservoirs. He concluded that:

(l) the treatment processes at the three works inspected complied with the requirements of Regulation 23;

(m) the use of substances and products satisfied the requirements of Regulation 25;

(n) the Company's policy and arrangements for disinfection at treatment works were satisfactory; and

(o) the Company's arrangements for compliance sampling at treatment works and service reservoirs are generally in accordance with the recommendations of paragraph 2.8 of the Guidance Document and with the requirements of Regulation 21(2)(a).

As a result of these inspections, 17 recommendations mainly relating to water treatment were conveyed to the Company for formal response, along with 23 suggestions on various matters for the Company to consider. The Company is taking action or has already taken action on all of the recommendations.

Improvement programmes

11 undertakings in respect of improvement programmes accepted by the Secretary of State from the Company were due for full completion or the completion of major steps during 1995 and six of these were completed on schedule. Four schemes involving the installation and commissioning of treatment to remove pesticides at Hardham, Northbrook, Falmer and Lewes Road were subject to delays which were beyond the Company's control. At Hardham compliance was achieved by the introduction of temporary treatment and at Northbrook the works has been taken out of supply until the new treatment plant has been commissioned. At Falmer and Lewes Road commissioning of the installations was slightly delayed. The remaining undertaking involved the installation and commissioning of treatment to reduce lead plumbosolvency. The Inspectorate confirmed that treatment had been installed by the due date, but that the reliability of dosing was not satisfactory. The Company has since taken steps to improve the reliability of dosing and the Inspectorate will assess the outcome of further monitoring data. A new undertaking given by the Company to carry out improvement works to its distribution system, with a completion date of 31 March 2000, is being considered by the Secretary of State.

Incidents

No events notified during 1995 by the Company to the Secretary of State under the terms of the Water Undertakers (Information) Direction 1992 are regarded by the Inspectorate as constituting incidents in which drinking water quality demonstrably deteriorated.

The Inspectorate was informed by a local authority of an event which the Inspectorate regards as constituting an incident in which drinking water quality demonstrably deteriorated. The incident involved the discolouration of the water supply to the Langley Green area of Crawley and attracted significant local publicity. The incident remains under consideration by the Inspectorate.

No other events regarded as constituting incidents came to the attention of the Inspectorate in 1995.

Enforcement action

Table 3.23.4 summarises enforcement action under consideration for the Company as a result of the Inspectorate's work in, or pertaining to, the calendar year 1995.

Table 3.23.4	Southern Water Services Limited SUMMARY OF ENFORCEMENT ACTION CONSIDERED IN 1995
Regulation	**Reason for enforcement**
3(7)	Contravention of the faecal coliforms standard at one service reservoir.

THE SUTTON DISTRICT WATER PLC

Introduction

The Company supplies on average approximately 64 Ml/d to a population of some 280,000 in the London Boroughs of Sutton, Croydon and Merton and parts of Surrey. All water is derived from chalk ground water sources and is treated at two water treatment works. Bulk supplies of treated water are available from Thames Water Utilities at Epsom and Merton as emergency sources.

Treated water is distributed by pumping and gravity through 11 service reservoirs and some 1,040 km of water mains. The Company has seven designated water supply zones.

Overall water quality

At water treatment works and service reservoirs and in water supply zones, the Company carried out a total of 10,920 determinations in 1995. Of these, 99.1% demonstrated compliance with the relevant water quality standards, but 100 showed a PCV to have been contravened.

Coliforms were not detected at either of the Company's two water treatment works. At all of the Company's 11 service reservoirs, coliforms were absent from at least 95% of samples. Of the Company's seven water supply zones in 1995, five (71%) complied fully with the relevant water quality standards or had breaches of the standards which were either trivial or were fully covered by undertakings. In the other two zones, breaches are regarded as unlikely to recur.

Microbiological quality of water leaving treatment works

Table 3.24.1 shows the Company's performance in 1995, with data for 1994 and 1993 for comparison.

The Company complied with the sampling frequencies required by regulation 17 at both of its treatment works in 1995. There were no contraventions of the microbiological standards at either of the Company's water treatment works in 1995.

Table 3.24.1 The Sutton District Water Plc
MICROBIOLOGICAL QUALITY OF WATER LEAVING TREATMENT WORKS

	1995	1994	1993
Number of water treatment works	2	2	2
Works with no sampling shortfall	2	2	2
COLIFORMS			
Total number of determinations	730	729	730
- number containing coliforms	0	0	0
- % containing coliforms	0.0	0.0	0.0
Treatment works with coliforms detected	**0**	**0**	**0**
FAECAL COLIFORMS			
Total number of determinations	730	729	730
- number containing faecal coliforms	0	0	0
- % containing faecal coliforms	0.0	0.0	0.0
Treatment works with faecal coliforms detected	**0**	**0**	**0**

Microbiological quality of water in service reservoirs

Table 3.24.2 shows the Company's performance in 1995, with data for 1994 and 1993 for comparison. Differences between the three years are not regarded as significant.

The Company complied with the sampling frequencies required by regulation 18 at 10 of its 11 service reservoirs in 1995. The shortfall at one reservoir is regarded as trivial. There were no contraventions of the microbiological standards at any of the Company's service reservoirs in 1995.

Table 3.24.2 The Sutton District Water Plc
MICROBIOLOGICAL QUALITY OF WATER IN SERVICE RESERVOIRS

	1995	1994	1993
Number of service reservoirs	11	11	11
Service reservoirs with no sampling shortfall	10	10	11
COLIFORMS			
Total number of determinations	571	546	529
- number containing coliforms	0	2	0
- % containing coliforms	0.0	0.4	0.0
Service reservoirs with coliforms detected	0	2	0
Service reservoirs with coliforms detected in more than 5% of samples	**0**	**0**	**0**
- % of all service reservoirs	0	0	0
FAECAL COLIFORMS			
Total number of determinations	571	546	529
- number containing faecal coliforms	0	0	0
- % containing faecal coliforms	0.0	0.0	0.0
Service reservoirs with faecal coliforms detected	**0**	**0**	**0**
- % of all service reservoirs	0	0	0

Water quality in water supply zones

The Company failed to comply with the required sampling frequencies for the aluminium and cyanide parameters in one zone, the iron parameter in one zone and the nitrite parameter in two zones. The shortfalls are regarded as trivial or unlikely to recur.

Table 3.24.3 shows the Company's performance in 1995, with data for 1994 and 1993 for comparison. Differences between the three years are not regarded as significant.

All contraventions of the standards in zones are considered trivial or unlikely to recur, or are covered by undertakings.

Inspection

Miss C Y Hill, Inspector, carried out part of the inspection of Sutton District Water Plc during a visit in September 1995. Dr Gray, Principal Inspector, assisted by Miss Hill carried out an inspection of the Company's contract laboratory in July 1995. Dr Gray and Miss Hill concluded that:

(a) appropriate and satisfactory measures have been taken or are being taken to implement the recommendations made in the 1994 technical audit inspection report;

(b) the Company's analytical arrangements satisfied the requirements of regulation 21(2)(d)(iii);

(c) the Company's arrangements for reporting compliance data were satisfactory and secure;

Table 3.24.3   The Sutton District Water Plc
WATER QUALITY IN SUPPLY ZONES

Columns 'CBU' show, for determinations, contraventions covered by undertakings and, for zones, the total *number of zones covered by undertakings in 1995. Column 'E' shows the number of zones for which new enforcement action is under consideration as a result of contraventions of the PCV in 1995.* **Please refer to the Introduction to Chapter 3 for more detailed explanation of this table.**

| Parameter | DETERMINATIONS in 1995 | | | | ZONES (7 in 1995)* | | | | |
| | Total | Contravening PCV | | | | | Non-compliant | | |
		No.	%	CBU	CBU 1995	E	1995	Number in: 1994	1993
Coliforms	815	0	0.0	0	0	0	0	0	0
Faecal coliforms	815	0	0.0	0	0	0	0	0	1
Colour	82	0	0.0	0	0	0	0	0	0
Turbidity	83	0	0.0	0	7	0	0	0	0
Odour	121	0	0.0	0	0	0	0	1	0
Taste	121	0	0.0	0	0	0	0	0	0
Hydrogen ion	430	0	0.0	0	0	0	0	0	0
Nitrate	83	0	0.0	0	0	0	0	0	0
Nitrite	170	8	4.7	0	0	0	3	1	1
Aluminium	152	8	5.3	0	0	0	1	1	1
Iron	115	1	0.7	0	0	0	1	0	1
Manganese	83	0	0.0	0	0	0	0	0	0
Lead	28	0	0.0	0	0	0	0	0	0
PAH	28	0	0.0	0	0	0	0	0	0
Trihalomethanes	28	0	0.0	0	0	0	0	0	0
Total pesticides	218	0	0.0	0	7	0	0	0	0
Atrazine	218	83	38.1	85	7	0	7	7	7
Other pesticides	4,229	0	0.0	0	7	0	0	0	0
All others	499	0	0.0	0	0	0	0	0	0
Total	**8,318**	**100**	**1.2**	**83**	-	-	-	-	-

* 7 zones in 1994; 7 zones in 1993.

(d)   the arrangements for the dissemination of water quality data both within the Company and to members of the public were satisfactory and the public record satisfies the requirements of regulation 29;

(e)   from the information provided, the Company is on target to meet key stages of its compliance programmes by the due dates although the completion of the work at Cheam may be slightly delayed;

(f)   the Company is aware of the advice provided in the document "Civil Emergencies involving Radioactive Substances: The Department's Role and Arrangements" published June 1995 and its role in the event of a radioactive release to the environment; and

(g)   the Company has a satisfactory system for liaising with and reporting to local authorities and is meeting the requirements of regulations 30(4), 30(5) and 31.

There were no recommendations arising from these inspections. Ten suggestions on various matters were made.

Improvement programmes

Two undertakings in respect of improvement programmes accepted by the Secretary of State from the Company were due for full completion during 1995 and one of these was completed on schedule. The remaining scheme at Cheam treatment works was delayed for reasons beyond the Company's control but was completed early in 1996.

Incidents

No events regarded as constituting incidents in which drinking water quality demonstrably deteriorated came to the attention of the Inspectorate in 1995.

Enforcement action

No enforcement action needed to be considered for the Company as a result of the Inspectorate's work in, or pertaining to, the calendar year 1995.

TENDRING HUNDRED WATER SERVICES LIMITED

Introduction

The Company supplies on average 34.5 Ml/d of water to a resident population of some 140,000 in the mainly rural Tendring peninsula of Essex. The demand can rise to approximately 50 Ml/d during peak summer periods.

Approximately 80% of the Company's water is abstracted from boreholes in the chalk aquifer and is treated at a single treatment works at Horsley Cross. The remaining 20% of the demand is met by the Ardleigh water treatment works which treats surface water abstracted from the River Colne and stored in Ardleigh Reservoir. The reservoir and treatment works are jointly owned and managed by the Company and Anglian Water Services Limited and the output is shared between them.

Treated water is distributed by pumping via seven service reservoirs and some 946 km of water mains. The supply area is divided into four water supply zones.

Overall water quality

At water treatment works and service reservoirs and in water supply zones, the Company carried out a total of 6,044 determinations in 1995. Of these, 99.6% demonstrated compliance with the relevant water quality standards, but 25 showed a PCV to have been contravened.

Coliforms were detected at one of the Company's water treatment works. At all of the Company's service reservoirs, coliforms were absent from at least 95% of samples. All the Company's four water supply zones complied fully with the relevant water quality standards or had breaches of the standards which were either trivial or were fully covered by undertakings.

Microbiological quality of water leaving treatment works

Table 3.25.1 shows the Company's performance in 1995, with data for 1994 and 1993 for comparison. Differences between the three years are not considered significant.

The Company complied with the sampling frequencies required by regulation 17 at one of its two treatment works in 1995. The shortfall at the other works has been regarded as trivial.

Table 3.25.1 Tendring Hundred Water Services Limited
MICROBIOLOGICAL QUALITY OF WATER LEAVING TREATMENT WORKS

	1995	1994	1993
Number of water treatment works	2	2	[a]6
Works with no sampling shortfall	1	2	5
COLIFORMS			
Total number of determinations	728	730	713
- number containing coliforms	1	2	0
- % containing coliforms	0.1	0.3	0.0
Treatment works with coliforms detected	**1**	**1**	**0**
- % of all works	50	50	0
FAECAL COLIFORMS			
Total number of determinations	728	730	716
- number containing faecal coliforms	1	1	0
- % containing faecal coliforms	0.1	0.1	0.0
Treatment works with faecal coliforms detected	**1**	**1**	**0**
- % of all works	50	50	0

[a] Five works were replaced by a single new works in April 1993.

The single contraventions of the coliform and faecal coliform standards at one treatment works are regarded as trivial.

Microbiological quality of water in service reservoirs

Table 3.25.2 shows the Company's performance in 1995, with data for 1994 and 1993 for comparison. Differences between the three years are not considered significant.

The Company complied with the required sampling frequencies at all of its 7 service reservoirs in 1995.

There were no contraventions of the coliform standard at any of the Company's service reservoirs. The single contravention of the faecal coliform standard at one service reservoir has been regarded as trivial.

Table 3.25.2   Tendring Hundred Water Services Limited MICROBIOLOGICAL QUALITY OF WATER IN SERVICE RESERVOIRS

	1995	1994	1993
Number of service reservoirs	7	10	11
Service reservoirs with no sampling shortfall	7	10	11
COLIFORMS			
Total number of determinations	371	572	625
- number containing coliforms	1	0	0
- % containing coliforms	0.3	0.0	0.0
Service reservoirs with coliforms detected	1	0	0
Service reservoirs with coliforms detected in more than 5% of samples	**0**	**0**	**0**
- % of all service reservoirs	0	0	0
FAECAL COLIFORMS			
Total number of determinations	371	572	627
- number containing faecal coliforms	1	0	0
- % containing faecal coliforms	0.3	0.0	0.0
Service reservoirs with faecal coliforms detected	**1**	**0**	**0**
- % of all service reservoirs	14	0	0

Water quality in water supply zones

The Company failed to comply with the required sampling frequencies for quantitative taste and odour and a number of individual pesticides in all four zones. The shortfalls were due to problems with sample programming. These problems have been addressed and the shortfalls are considered unlikely to recur.

Table 3.25.3 shows the Company's performance in 1995 with data for 1994 and 1993 for comparison. Differences between the three years are not considered significant.

All contraventions in 1995 of the standards in zones are considered trivial or unlikely to recur or are covered by undertakings.

Inspection

The inspection of the Company was carried out in October 1995 by Dr J Gray, Principal Inspector, assisted by Miss C Y Hill, Inspector. Dr Gray concluded that:

(a)   appropriate and satisfactory measures have been taken or are being taken to implement the recommendations made in the 1994 technical audit inspection report;

Table 3.25.3   Tendring Hundred Water Services Limited
WATER QUALITY IN SUPPLY ZONES

*Columns 'CBU' show, for determinations, contraventions covered by undertakings and, for zones, the total number of zones covered by undertakings in 1995. Column 'E' shows the number of zones for which new enforcement action is under consideration as a result of contraventions of the PCV in 1995. **Please refer to the Introduction to Chapter 3 for more detailed explanation of this table.***

| Parameter | DETERMINATIONS in 1995 | | | | ZONES (4 in 1995)* | | | | |
| | Total | Contravening PCV | | | Non-compliant | | | | |
		No.	%	CBU	CBU 1995	E 1995	Number in: 1995	1994	1993
Coliforms	387	4	1.0	0	0	0	0	0	1
Faecal coliforms	387	3	0.8	0	0	0	3	1	1
Colour	40	0	0.0	0	0	0	0	0	0
Turbidity	55	0	0.0	0	0	0	0	0	0
Odour	23	0	0.0	0	0	0	0	0	0
Taste	23	0	0.0	0	0	0	0	0	0
Hydrogen ion	195	0	0.0	0	0	0	0	0	0
Nitrate	41	0	0.0	0	0	0	0	0	0
Nitrite	198	13	6.6	13	4	0	2	3	1
Aluminium	42	0	0.0	0	0	0	0	0	0
Iron	195	1	0.5	1	4	0	1	1	1
Manganese	41	0	0.0	0	0	0	0	0	0
Lead	25	0	0.0	0	0	0	0	0	0
PAH	26	0	0.0	0	0	0	0	0	0
Trihalomethanes	64	0	0.0	0	0	0	0	0	0
Total pesticides	64	0	0.0	0	2	0	0	0	0
Individual pesticides	1175	0	0.0	0	2	0	0	0	0
All others	865	0	0.0	0	0	0	0	0	0
Total	**3,846**	**21**	**0.6**	**14**	-	-	-	-	-

* 4 zones in 1993; 4 zones in 1992.

(b)   the arrangements for sampling as audited generally satisfied parts IV and V of the Regulations and accorded with the recommendations of the Guidance Document;

(c)   the Company's analytical arrangements satisfied the requirements of regulation 21(2)(d)(iii) although in respect of microbiological parameters, there were some deficiencies in quality control systems;

(d)   the Company is aware of the contents of the most recent issue of Report 71 and, in general, action has been taken or is being taken to implement changes where appropriate;

(e)   the Company has an adequate system for reporting compliance information although some deficiencies were identified with regards to recording of analytical results;

(f)   the public record satisfies the requirements of regulation 29;

(g)   from the information provided, the Company is on target to meet all key stages of its compliance programmes;

(h)   the Company has a satisfactory approach to handling complaints on water quality;

(i)   the Company's interpretation of the criteria for notification of events that have affected or could affect water quality is not wholly satisfactory;

(j)   the Company is aware of the advice provided in the document "Civil Emergencies involving Radioactive Substances: The Department's Role and Arrangements" published June 1995 and its role in the event of a radioactive release to the environment; and

(k)   the Company has a satisfactory system for liaising with and reporting to local authorities and is meeting the requirements of regulations 30(4), 30(5) and 31.

As a result of the inspection, five recommendations were conveyed to the Company for formal response mainly concerning analytical arrangements at its microbiological laboratory. Nine suggestions on various matters were also made for the Company to consider.

Since the inspection, the Company has closed the microbiology laboratory and made alternative arrangements for analysis of samples for microbiological determinands.

Improvement programmes

Two undertakings in respect of improvement programmes were due for full completion or completion of major steps during 1995 and both of these were completed on schedule. However, the Company is concerned that the treatment installed at Horsley Cross to meet its undertaking for nitrite is causing consumer taste and odour complaints. A new undertaking has been submitted which is currently under consideration. A new undertaking given by the Company to carry out improvement works to its distribution system, with a completion date of 31 March 2000, is being considered by the Secretary of State.

Incidents/Events

No events regarded as constituting incidents in which drinking water quality demonstrably deteriorated came to the attention of the Inspectorate in 1995.

Enforcement action

No enforcement action needed to be considered for the Company as a result of the Inspectorate's work in, or pertaining to, the calendar year 1995.

THAMES WATER UTILITIES LIMITED

Introduction

The Company supplies an average of 2,900 Ml/d to some 7.3 million people. The supply area includes London and a large proportion of central southern England. Approximately three quarters of the Company's water supplies are derived from surface water sources, principally the Rivers Thames and Lee. The remainder is drawn from groundwater sources. Water from these sources is treated at 99 water treatment works. Treated water is distributed through 364 service reservoirs and almost 31,000 km of mains. The supply area is divided into 232 water supply zones.

Overall water quality

At water treatment works and service reservoirs and in water supply zones, the Company carried out a total of 480,832 determinations in 1995. Of these, 98.9% demonstrated compliance with the relevant water quality standards, but 5,353 showed a PCV to have been contravened.

Coliforms were not detected at 86 (87%) of the Company's 99 water treatment works. At 346 (95%) of the Company's 364 service reservoirs, coliforms were absent from at least 95% of samples. Of the Company's 232 water supply zones in 1995, 224 (97%) complied fully with the relevant water quality standards or had breaches of the standards which were either trivial or were fully covered by undertakings. In the other eight (3%) zones, two breaches are regarded as unlikely to recur, but the other six could result in enforcement action.

Microbiological quality of water leaving treatment works

Table 3.26.1 shows the Company's performance in 1995, with data for 1994 and 1993 for comparison. Differences between the three years are not considered significant.

The Company complied with the sampling frequencies required by regulation 17 at all its treatment works in 1995.

All contraventions of the standards at works are considered trivial or unlikely to recur, or are covered by undertakings.

Table 3.26.1 Thames Water Utilities Limited
MICROBIOLOGICAL QUALITY OF WATER LEAVING TREATMENT WORKS

	1995	1994	1993
Number of water treatment works	99	100	101
Works with no sampling shortfall	99	100	99
COLIFORMS			
Total number of determinations	18,748	18,403	18,124
- number containing coliforms	14	29	19
- % containing coliforms	0.1	0.2	0.1
Treatment works with coliforms detected	**13**	**22**	**17**
- % of all works	13	22	17
FAECAL COLIFORMS			
Total number of determinations	18,748	18,403	18,124
- number containing faecal coliforms	2	3	2
- % containing faecal coliforms	<0.1	<0.1	<0.1
Treatment works with faecal coliforms detected	**2**	**3**	**2**
- % of all works	2	3	2

Microbiological quality of water in service reservoirs

Table 3.26.2 shows the Company's performance in 1995, with data for 1994 and 1993 for comparison. Differences between the three years are not considered significant.

The Company complied with the sampling frequencies required by regulation 18 at all its service reservoirs in 1995.

Contraventions of the microbiological quality standards at a total of seven service reservoirs have resulted in the consideration of enforcement action, as shown in table 3.26.4. All other contraventions of the standards at service reservoirs are considered trivial or unlikely to recur, or are covered by undertakings.

Table 3.26.2 Thames Water Utilities Limited
MICROBIOLOGICAL QUALITY OF WATER IN SERVICE RESERVOIRS

	1995	1994	1993
Number of service reservoirs	364	368	353
Service reservoirs with no sampling shortfall	364	368	353
COLIFORMS			
Total number of determinations	18,226	18,171	17,268
- number containing coliforms	164	136	140
- % containing coliforms	0.9	0.7	0.8
Service reservoirs with coliforms detected	68	83	84
Service reservoirs with coliforms detected in more than 5% of samples	**18**	**14**	**20**
- % of all service reservoirs	5	4	6
FAECAL COLIFORMS			
Total number of determinations	18,226	18,171	17,268
- number containing faecal coliforms	5	4	13
- % containing faecal coliforms	<0.1	<0.1	<0.1
Service reservoirs with faecal coliforms detected	**5**	**4**	**12**
- % of all service reservoirs	1	1	3

Water quality in water supply zones

The Company complied with the required sampling frequencies required by regulation 13 in all of its supply zones in 1995

Table 3.26.3 shows the Company's performance in 1995, with data for 1994 and 1993 for comparison. Several substances have given rise to changing patterns of compliance of zones with the individual pesticides standard; of these changes the decreases in the number of zones failing to comply in respect of atrazine, simazine and mecoprop are significant.

Enforcement action is being considered in respect of some contraventions of standards, as shown in tables 3.26.3 and 3.26.4. All other contraventions of the standards in zones are considered trivial or unlikely to recur, or are covered by undertakings or will be covered by the new distribution undertaking.

Inspection

Mr M J Purcell, Principal Inspector, assisted by Mr R F Millar, Inspector, Mr B S Bell, Inspector, and Mr P Jiggins, Inspector, carried out an inspection of Thames Water Utilities Limited in a series of visits between 18 August and 15 November 1995. Mr Purcell concluded that:

Table 3.26.3 **Thames Water Utilities Limited**
WATER QUALITY IN SUPPLY ZONES

*Columns 'CBU' show, for determinations, contraventions covered by undertakings and, for zones, the <u>total</u> number of zones covered by undertakings in 1995. Column 'E' shows the number of zones for which new enforcement action is under consideration as a result of contraventions of the PCV in 1995. **Please refer to the Introduction to Chapter 3 for more detailed explanation of this table.***

| Parameter | DETERMINATIONS in 1995 | | | | ZONES (232 in 1995)* | | | | |
| | Total | Contravening PCV | | | | | Non-compliant | | |
		No.	%	CBU	CBU 1995	E	Number in: 1995	1994	1993
Coliforms	19,393	293	1.5	98	58	4	6	4	9
Faecal coliforms	19,393	20	0.1	1	7	1	18	38	31
Colour	1,250	0	0.0	0	0	0	0	0	0
Turbidity	2,162	0	0.0	0	232	0	0	1	0
Odour	1,127	0	0.0	0	0	0	0	0	0
Taste	1,125	1	<0.1	0	0	0	1	0	1
Hydrogen ion	1,345	0	0.0	0	0	0	0	0	0
Nitrate	2,324	33	1.4	32	5	0	5	7	4
Nitrite	7,159	1,070	14.9	1,063	135	1	115	111	100
Aluminium	1,322	2	0.2	1	24	0	2	2	3
Iron	2,536	25	1.0	25	232	0	14	11	15
Manganese	1,233	0	0.0	0	0	0	0	2	1
Lead	1,056	2	0.2	0	0	0	2	4	3
PAH	934	18	1.9	8	80	0	12	14	19
Trihalomethanes	726	0	0.0	0	2	0	0	0	0
Total pesticides	16,437	534	3.2	534	157	0	123	128	138
Atrazine	15,788	51	0.3	47	157	0	15	126	179
Chlorotoluron	15,660	170	1.1	170	157	0	78	129	39
Diuron	15,769	106	0.7	106	157	0	103	126	136
Isoproturon	15,813	2,716	17.2	2,716	157	0	138	139	145
MCPA	9,303	0	0.0	0	157	0	0	0	2
Mecoprop	9,303	0	0.0	0	157	0	0	0	31
Simazine	15,769	117	0.7	117	157	0	43	50	138
Terbutryn	15,624	0	0.0	0	157	0	0	1	0
Other pesticides	174,030	0	0.0	0	157	0	0	0	0
Temperature	19,508	4	<0.1	0	0	0	2	2	3
Ammonium	1,251	0	0.0	0	0	0	0	0	1
Copper	1,054	0	0.0	0	0	0	0	2	1
Zinc	1,054	0	0.0	0	0	0	0	0	1
Phosphorus	293	0	0.0	0	0	0	0	1	0
Antimony	259	0	0.0	0	0	0	0	2	0
Conductivity	8,665	1	<0.1	0	0	0	0	0	0
Benzo 3,4 pyrene	964	4	0.4	1	80	0	0	0	0
Trichloroethene	727	1	0.1	0	0	0	0	0	0
All others	6,528	0	0.0	0	0	0	0	0	0
Total	**406,884**	**5,168**	**1.3**	**4,919**	-	-	-	-	-

* 233 zones in 1994; 229 zones in 1993.

(a)   a review of the Company's arrangements for water supply confirmed that data provided was an accurate record of the Company's current water supply arrangements;

(b)   the Company had made significant progress in addressing the recommendations made by the Inspectors and consultants in the 1994 inspection report;

(c)   there had been an overall improvement with respect to laboratory practice and document control since the 1994 inspection; audits carried out by the Inspectors identified some areas which required attention, most of which have since been satisfactorily addressed;

(d)   the Company's arrangements for monitoring the quality of water supplied to consumers through the Thames Water Ring Main are generally satisfactory; some areas that were identified as requiring attention have been addressed by the Company;

(e)   the Company needs to review its emergency procedures relating to radioactive releases into the environment;

(f)   the Company arrangements for the analysis of microbiological parameters were not satisfactory;

(g)   arrangements were in hand to incorporate the recommendations of the new Report 71, but some minor areas required attention;

(h)   the Company is continuing to develop its internal quality assurance initiatives and has achieved third party accreditation for some of the Company functions;

(i)   the Company has in place satisfactory arrangements for liaison with local authorities on issues concerning water quality;

(j)   progress with capital schemes related to undertakings, including mains rehabilitation, was satisfactory; and

(k)   the water treatment processes and records reviewed on a reinspection of Farmoor water treatment works were generally maintained and operated satisfactorily.

Mr Millar recommended that the Inspectorate considers the making of an Enforcement Order to secure compliance with the requirements of regulation 21(2)(d)(iii), in respect of the use by the Company of the Colilert method for analysis of microbiology parameters. The Company has taken steps to satisfactorily address most areas of concern. However, one of the conditions of approval, i.e. that the Company should have DWTS accreditation for the method, has not been met; consideration of an Enforcement Order has been delayed to enable the position on this issue to be clarified. Mr Millar was also concerned that the Company should put in place procedures to ensure that any new methodologies used by its laboratories in the future comply fully with the requirements of the Regulations before they are introduced.

In December 1995 Mr R M Walls, representing the consultants Rofe, Kennard & Lapworth and working under Mr Purcell's general direction, carried out inspection of selected water treatment works and service reservoirs. He concluded that:

(l)   the treatment processes complied with Regulation 23;

(m)   the use of substances and products satisfied the requirements of regulation 25;

(n)   the Company's policy and arrangements for disinfection at treatment works were satisfactory; and

(o)   the Company's arrangements for compliance sampling at treatment works and service reservoirs are generally in accordance with the recommendations of paragraph 2.8 of the Guidance Document and with the requirements of regulation 21(2)(a).

As a result of these inspections, 20 recommendations were made to the Company, mainly in respect of water treatment, laboratory procedures and arrangements for the Thames Water Ring Main, together with 50 suggestions on various matters.

Improvement programmes

Thirty-four undertakings in respect of improvement programmes accepted by the Secretary of State from the Company were due for full completion or the completion of major steps during 1995 and all of these were completed on schedule. A new undertaking given by the Company to carry out improvement works to its distribution system, with a completion date of 31 March 2000, is being considered by the Secretary of State.

Incidents

One event notified during 1995 by the Company to the Secretary of State under the terms of the Water Undertakers (Information) Direction 1992 is regarded by the Inspectorate as constituting an incident in which drinking water quality demonstrably deteriorated. The incident occurred following emergency work on the distribution system by the Company. Consumers in the village of Eastbury in Berkshire experienced taste and odour problems with their supply. The incident remains under consideration by the Inspectorate.

No other events regarded as constituting incidents came to the attention of the Inspectorate in 1995.

Enforcement action

Table 3.26.4 summarises enforcement action under consideration for the Company as a result of the Inspectorate's work in, or pertaining to, the calendar year 1995.

Prosecution

In October 1994 consumers in parts of south west London were affected by an incident which led to complaints of discoloured water following work carried out on trunk mains in the area by Company personnel. Following investigation by the Inspectorate, the Secretary of State for the Environment instituted legal proceedings against the Company for allegedly supplying water unfit for human consumption. The prosecution is being brought under the provisions of section 70 of the Water Industry Act 1991.

Table 3.26.4	Thames Water Utilities Limited SUMMARY OF ENFORCEMENT ACTION CONSIDERED IN 1995
Regulation	**Reason for enforcement**
3(3)(c)	Contravention of the standards for total coliforms in four zones, faecal coliforms in one zone and nitrite in one zone.
3(7)	Contravention of the total coliform standard at seven service reservoirs.

THREE VALLEYS WATER PLC

Introduction

Three Valleys Water Plc was formed by the merger of Lee Valley Water Limited, Colne Valley Water Limited and Rickmansworth Water Limited on 31 March 1994. The Company supplies an average of 735.2 Ml/day to a population of some 2.3 million customers in parts of Bedfordshire, Berkshire, Buckinghamshire, Essex and several London Boroughs. Approximately two thirds of the Company's water resources are derived from 100 ground water sources in chalk aquifers which are treated at 80 water treatment works. The remainder is surface water derived from the River Thames and treated at Iver water treatment works and a bulk supply of treated water provided by Anglian Water Services from Grafham works.

Treated water is distributed by gravity via 126 service reservoirs through approximately 11,000 km of mains. The area is divided into 94 water supply zones.

Overall water quality

At water treatment works and service reservoirs and in water supply zones, the Company carried out a total of 97,048 determinations in 1995. Of these, 99.5% demonstrated compliance with the relevant water quality standards, but 476 showed a PCV to have been contravened.

Coliforms were not detected at 75 (93%) of the Company's 81 water treatment works. At 125 (99.2%) of the Company's 126 service reservoirs, coliforms were absent from at least 95% of samples. Of the Company's 94 water supply zones in 1995, 89 (94.7%) complied fully with the relevant water quality standards or had breaches of the standards which were either trivial or were fully covered by undertakings. In the other five (5.3%) of the zones, breaches are regarded as unlikely to recur.

Microbiological quality of water leaving treatment works

Table 3.27.1 shows the Company's performance in 1995, with data for 1994 and combined data for the three predecessor companies for 1993 for comparison. Differences between the three years are not regarded as significant.

Table 3.27.1 Three Valleys Water Plc MICROBIOLOGICAL QUALITY OF WATER LEAVING TREATMENT WORKS	1995	1994	1993[a]
Number of water treatment works	81	79	81
Works with no sampling shortfall	79	78	75
COLIFORMS			
Total number of determinations	8,712	8,779	8,050
- number containing coliforms	6	6	4
- % containing coliforms	<0.1	<0.1	<0.1
Treatment works with coliforms detected	**6**	**6**	**4**
- % of all works	7	8	5
FAECAL COLIFORMS			
Total number of determinations	8,712	8,779	8,068
- number containing faecal coliforms	0	1	1
- % containing faecal coliforms	0	<0.1	<0.1
Treatment works with faecal coliforms detected	**0**	**1**	**1**
- % of all works	0	1	1

[a] Numbers in this column represent combined data for the predecessor companies.

The Company complied with the sampling frequencies required by regulation 17 at 79 of its 81 treatment works in 1995. Shortfalls at the other works are regarded as trivial or unlikely to recur.

All contraventions of the microbiological standards at works are considered trivial.

Microbiological quality of water in service reservoirs

Table 3.27.2 shows the Company's performance in 1995, with data for 1994 and combined data for the three predecessor companies for 1993 for comparison. Differences between the three years are not regarded as significant.

The Company complied with the sampling frequencies required by regulation 18 at 124 of its 126 service reservoirs in 1995. Shortfalls at the other two are regarded as trivial. All contraventions of the microbiological standards at service reservoirs are considered trivial or unlikely to recur.

Table 3.27.2   Three Valleys Water Plc
MICROBIOLOGICAL QUALITY OF WATER IN SERVICE RESERVOIRS

	1995	1994	1993[a]
Number of service reservoirs	126	127	128
Service reservoirs with no sampling shortfall	124	127	119
COLIFORMS			
Total number of determinations	6,623	6,454	6,307
- number containing coliforms	12	8	16
- % containing coliforms	0.2	0.1	0.3
Service reservoirs with coliforms detected	9	7	15
Service reservoirs with coliforms detected in more than 5% of samples	**1**	**0**	**0**
- % of all service reservoir	<1	0	0
FAECAL COLIFORMS			
Total number of determinations	6,623	6,454	6,331
- number containing faecal coliforms	5	2	5
- % containing faecal coliforms	<0.1	<0.1	<0.1
Service reservoirs with faecal coliforms detected	**4**	**2**	**4**
- % of all service reservoirs	3	2	3

[a] Numbers in this column represent combined data for the predecessor companies.

Water quality in water supply zones

The Company complied with the required sampling frequencies for all parameters in all of its zones.

Table 3.27.3 shows the Company's performance in 1995, with data for 1994 and combined data for the three predecessor companies for 1993 for comparison. Several substances have given rise to changing patterns of compliance of zones with the individual pesticides standard; of these changes the decrease over the three years in the number of zones failing to comply in respect of total pesticides is significant.

Enforcement action is being considered for contraventions of the nitrite standard in two zones. All other contraventions of the standards in zones are considered trivial or unlikely to recur, or are covered by undertakings.

Table 3.27.3   Three Valleys Water Plc
WATER QUALITY IN SUPPLY ZONES

Columns 'CBU' show, for determinations, contraventions covered by undertakings and, for zones, the total number of zones covered by undertakings in 1995. Column 'E' shows the number of zones for which new enforcement action is under consideration as a result of contraventions of the PCV in 1995. **Please refer to the Introduction to Chapter 3 for more detailed explanation of this table.**

Parameter	DETERMINATIONS in 1995				ZONES (94 in 1995)*				
	Total	Contravening PCV			CBU	E	Non-compliant		
		No.	%	CBU	1995		Number(a) in:		
							1995	1994	1993
Coliforms	6,405	39	0.6	0	0	0	0	3	0
Faecal coliforms	6,405	4	<0.1	0	0	0	4	2	4
Colour	624	0	0.0	0	0	0	0	0	0
Turbidity	3,448	0	0.0	0	44	0	0	3	4
Odour	736	0	0.0	0	0	0	0	0	0
Taste	736	0	0.0	0	0	0	0	0	0
Hydrogen ion	3,448	0	0.0	0	0	0	0	0	0
Nitrate	728	0	0.0	0	2	0	0	0	1
Nitrite	942	30	3.2	0	0	2	9	11	7
Aluminium	639	1	0.2	1	21	0	1	0	1
Iron	1,170	19	1.6	18	94	0	12	12	21
Manganese	537	0	0.0	0	0	0	0	0	1
Lead	552	8	1.4	8	94	0	6	8	14
PAH	590	16	2.7	5	4	0	10	13	10
Trihalomethanes	382	0	0.0	0	0	0	0	0	0
Total pesticides	1,340	9	0.7	9	60	0	8	15	22
Atrazine	889	206	23.2	206	60	0	28	37	45
Chlorotoluron	752	1	0.1	0	60	0	1	1	0
Cyanazine	884	0	0.0	0	60	0	0	2	0
Dichlobenil	387	0	0.0	0	60	0	0	1	0
Diuron	752	96	12.8	94	60	0	18	27	28
Flutriafol	377	0	0.0	0	60	0	0	0	1
Iprodione	377	0	0.0	0	60	0	0	0	10
Isoproturon	753	6	0.8	6	60	0	3	8	1
Linuron	752	0	0.0	0	60	0	0	1	0
MCPA	388	0	0.0	0	60	0	0	1	1
MCPP (Mecoprop)	388	0	0.0	0	60	0	0	1	3
Methabenzthiazuron	751	0	0.0	0	60	0	0	1	0
Simazine	889	17	1.9	17	60	0	13	8	36
2, 4-D	388	0	0.0	0	60	0	0	1	3
Other pesticides	14,248	0	0.0	0	60	0	0	0	0
Benzo 3,4 pyrene	590	1	0.2	0	4	0	0	0	1
Potassium	107	0	0.0	0	0	0	0	0	1
All others	14,024	0	0.0	0	0	0	0	0	0
Total	**66,378**	**453**	**0.7**	**364**	-	-	-	-	-

* 103 zones in 1993; 103 zones in 1992 - both numbers refer to the total in the predecessor companies.
(a) Numbers in the 1993 column represent combined data for the predecessor companies.

Inspection

Dr M J Gray, Principal Inspector, assisted by Miss C Y Hill, Inspector carried out an inspection of Three Valleys Water Plc in October 1995. Dr Gray concluded that:

(a)   the Company had taken appropriate and satisfactory measures to implement the recommendations made in the 1994 technical audit inspection report;

(b)   the general arrangements for sampling satisfied parts IV and V of the Regulations and accorded with the recommendations of the Guidance Document;

(c)   the Company's arrangements for reporting compliance data were generally satisfactory and secure although there were some deficiencies in the integrity of the compliance data in some of the laboratories in which analysis was carried out on behalf of the Company;

(d)   the arrangements for the dissemination of water quality data both within the Company and to members of the public were satisfactory and the public record satisfies the requirements of regulation 29;

(e)   the Company is on target to meet all key stages of its compliance programmes by the due dates;

(f)   the management arrangements for incidents and emergencies are satisfactory;

(g)   the arrangements for liaising with the NRA are satisfactory;

(h)   the Company is aware of the advice provided in the document "Civil Emergencies involving Radioactive Substances: The Department's Role and Arrangements" published in June 1995 and the actions to take in the event of radioactive release to the environment;

(i)   the Company has a satisfactory approach to dealing with complaints on water quality; and

(j)   the Company arrangements for liaising with and reporting to local authorities satisfies the requirements of regulations 30(4), 30(5) and 31(3).

Also, in September, Mr P S Durrant, representing consultants Rofe, Kennard and Lapworth and working under the general direction of Dr Gray, carried out inspection of selected water treatment works and selected service reservoirs. He concluded that:

(k)   the treatment processes in operation at Ickenham and Fulling Mill treatment works complied with regulation 23;

(l)   the Company's policy and arrangements for disinfection at Ickenham and Fulling Mill treatment works treatment works were generally satisfactory; and

(m)   the Company's arrangements for compliance sampling at Ickenham and Fulling Mill treatment works are generally in accordance with the recommendations of paragraph 2.8 of the Guidance Document and with the requirements of regulation 21(2)(a); however, there were some deficiencies with compliance sampling arrangements at Arkley and Bushey Heath service reservoirs.

As a result of these inspections, nine recommendations were conveyed to the Company for formal response most of which were related to reporting arrangements. 25 suggestions on various matters were also made. Following the inspection, the Company took immediate action to address most of the recommendations.

Improvement programmes

Five undertakings in respect of improvement programmes accepted by the Secretary of State from the Company were completed during 1995. A new undertaking given by the Company to carry out improvement works to its distribution system, with a completion date of 31 March 2000, is being considered by the Secretary of State.

Incidents

Two events notified during 1995 by the Company to the Secretary of State under the terms of the Water Undertakers (Information) Direction 1992 are regarded by the Inspectorate as constituting incidents in which drinking water quality demonstrably deteriorated.

In May, water containing elevated levels of chlorine was supplied from Clay Lane treatment works. At the time, the works was undergoing extensive reconstruction as part of a pesticide improvement programme. The increase in chlorine levels arose when a 24 inch inlet main had been isolated to install a new valve. Although the sodium hypochlorite pumps had been switched off, they were not isolated. This allowed hypochlorite to seep into the main which, when recharged and returned to service, passed out into supply. Since the incident, the Company has taken action to ensure such a problem does not recur.

In September, low numbers of coliform organisms were detected in the water supplied to parts of Ware and Tonwell, Hertfordshire. Advice to boil water was issued to approximately 3,000 properties as a precautionary measure. The contamination was considered to have occurred as a result of biofilm disturbance in the distribution system following increased flows through the mains.

No other events regarded as constituting incidents came to the attention of the Inspectorate in 1995.

Enforcement action

Table 3.27.4 summarises enforcement action under consideration for the Company as a result of the Inspectorate's work in, or pertaining to, the calendar year 1995.

Table 3.27.4	Three Valleys Water Plc SUMMARY OF ENFORCEMENT ACTION CONSIDERED IN 1995
Regulation	**Reason for enforcement**
3(3)(c)	Contravention of the standard for nitrite in two zones.

WESSEX WATER SERVICES LIMITED

Introduction

The Company supplies on average some 419 Ml/d of water to a resident population of approximately 1.1 million in an area including most of the counties of Dorset and Somerset, and parts of Avon, Wiltshire and Hampshire. The Company's water resources consist of:

(a) groundwater sources from boreholes and springs, mainly in the central and eastern regions of the supply area (approximately 77% of supply);

(b) surface water sources either as impoundments or lowland pumped storage reservoirs (approximately 22% of supply); and

(c) bulk supplies of treated water imported from other water companies (less than 1% of supply).

The Company has 111 source works at 103 sites. The Central Area Link Main enabled the Company to maximise its resources during the 1995 drought period, with supplies being transferred from Wiltshire into the central Somerset area to meet demand. The treated water is distributed by pumping and gravity through 337 service reservoirs and some 10,800 kilometres of water mains. The supply area is divided into 114 designated water supply zones.

Overall water quality

At water treatment works and service reservoirs and in water supply zones, the Company carried out a total of 123,530 determinations in 1995. Of these, 99.7% demonstrated compliance with the relevant water quality standards, but 325 showed a PCV to have been contravened.

Coliforms were not detected at 79 (71%) of the Company's 111 water treatment works. At 334 (99%) of the Company's 337 service reservoirs, coliforms were absent from at least 95% of samples. Of the Company's 114 water supply zones in 1995, 111 (97%) complied fully with the relevant water quality standards or had breaches of the standards which were either trivial or were fully covered by undertakings or are included in the new distribution undertaking. In the other three (3%) of the zones, some breaches could result in enforcement action.

Microbiological quality of water leaving treatment works

Table 3.28.1 shows the Company's performance in 1995, with data for 1994 and 1993 for comparison. There has been a significant decrease over the three years in the number of works contravening the faecal coliform standard.

Had the definition of the coliform parameter not been changed as described in 3.35 above, but remained as it was for 1994 and previous years, the number of treatment works with coliforms detected would have been 19 and the number of determinations containing coliforms 28.

The Company complied with the sampling frequencies required by regulation 17 at 109 of its 111 treatment works in 1995. The Company has identified the reasons for the sampling shortfalls at the other two treatment works and these are regarded as trivial and unlikely to recur.

The contraventions of the microbiological standards at ten water treatment works were not trivial but the Company has taken remedial action to prevent further recurrences. The Inspectorate will assess the results of further monitoring during the first six months of 1996 before deciding on the need for enforcement action at eight of these works. A similar assessment will be carried out at the other two works when refurbishment has been completed. All other contraventions of the standards at works are considered trivial or unlikely to recur.

Table 3.28.1 Wessex Water Services Limited
MICROBIOLOGICAL QUALITY OF WATER LEAVING
TREATMENT WORKS

	1995	1994	1993
Number of water treatment works	111	113	116
Works with no sampling shortfall	109	107	116
COLIFORMS			
Total number of determinations	11,987	12,835	13,389
- number containing coliforms	32	29	42
- % containing coliforms	0.3	0.2	0.3
Treatment works with coliforms detected	**21**	**22**	**32**
- % of all works	19	19	28
FAECAL COLIFORMS			
Total number of determinations	11,994	12,869	13,390
- number containing faecal coliforms	3	12	21
- % containing faecal coliforms	<0.1	<0.1	0.2
Treatment works with faecal coliforms detected	**3**	**10**	**16**
- % of all works	3	9	14

Microbiological quality of water in service reservoirs

Table 3.28.2 shows the Company's performance in 1995, with data for 1994 and 1993 for comparison. Differences between the three years are not regarded as significant.

Had the definition of the coliform parameter not been changed as described in 3.35 above, but remained as it was for 1994 and previous years, the number of service reservoirs with coliforms detected in more than 5% of samples would have been two and the number of determinations containing coliforms would have been 61.

Table 3.28.2 Wessex Water Services Limited
MICROBIOLOGICAL QUALITY OF WATER IN SERVICE
RESERVOIRS

	1995	1994	1993
Number of service reservoirs	337	336	345
Service reservoirs with no sampling shortfall	336	336	345
COLIFORMS			
Total number of determinations	17,695	18,198	18,895
- number containing coliforms	67	50	97
- % containing coliforms	0.4	0.3	0.5
Service reservoirs with coliforms detected	54	43	66
Service reservoirs with coliforms detected in more than 5% of samples	**3**	**2**	**9**
- % of all service reservoirs	<1	<1	3
FAECAL COLIFORMS			
Total number of determinations	17,709	18,244	18,896
- number containing faecal coliforms	9	8	15
- % containing faecal coliforms	<0.1	<0.1	<0.1
Service reservoirs with faecal coliforms detected	**7**	**8**	**13**
- % of all service reservoirs	2	2	4

The Company complied with the sampling frequencies required by regulation 18 at 336 of its 337 service reservoirs in 1995. The Company has identified the reason for the sampling shortfall at the other service reservoir and this is regarded as trivial and unlikely to recur.

Contraventions of the microbiological standards at three service reservoirs were not trivial but the Company has taken remedial action to prevent further recurrences. The Inspectorate will assess the results of further monitoring during the first six months of 1996 before deciding on the need for enforcement action. All other contraventions of the standards at service reservoirs are considered trivial.

Water quality in water supply zones

The Company complied fully with the required sampling frequencies in all zones.

Table 3.28.3 shows the Company's performance in 1995, with data for 1994 and 1993 for comparison. Differences between the three years are not regarded as significant.

Had the definition of the coliform parameter not been changed as described in 3.35 above, but remained as it was for 1994 and previous years, the number of determinations containing coliforms would have been 41.

Enforcement action is being considered in respect of some contraventions of standards, as shown in tables 3.28.3 and 3.28.4. All other contraventions of the standards in zones are considered trivial or unlikely to recur, or were covered by undertakings, or are covered by the new distribution undertaking.

Inspection

Mr A Hallas, Principal Inspector, assisted by Miss C R Jackson, Inspector, carried out an inspection of Wessex Water Services Limited between 27 and 30 November 1995. Mr Hallas concluded that:

(a) the Company had taken appropriate and satisfactory measures to implement the eight recommendations made in the 1994 technical audit inspection report;

(b) the general arrangements for sampling satisfied parts IV and V of the Regulations and accorded with the recommendations of the Guidance Document;

(c) the Company's sampling procedures, as audited, met the requirements of regulation 21(2)(a)(b) and (c);

(d) the Company had taken into account most, but not all, the recommendations on sampling given in the new edition of report 71;

(e) the Company's arrangement for analytical services were generally satisfactory and the laboratory was well run;

(f) the Company's responses to contraventions of prescribed standards were satisfactory;

(g) the Company's progress with capital schemes related to undertakings was generally satisfactory;

(h) the Company continued to take a positive approach in respect of its water treatment policies and the Company's procedures for disinfection of water supplies, as audited, were satisfactory;

(i) the Company's operational procedures to ensure adequate turnover of water in service reservoirs were satisfactory;

(j) the Company had systems in place for seeking advice in the event of a radioactive release into the environment;

(k) the Company's procedures and arrangements for communications and liaison with the local authorities in its area of supply were satisfactory; and

Table 3.28.3 Wessex Water Services Limited
WATER QUALITY IN SUPPLY ZONES

Columns 'CBU' show, for determinations, contraventions covered by undertakings and, for zones, the total number of zones covered by undertakings in 1995. Column 'E' shows the number of zones for which new enforcement action is under consideration as a result of contraventions of the PCV in 1995. **Please refer to the Introduction to Chapter 3 for more detailed explanation of this table.**

| Parameter | DETERMINATIONS in 1995 | | | | ZONES (114 in 1995)* | | | | |
| | Total | Contravening PCV | | | | | Non-compliant | | |
		No.	%	CBU	CBU 1995	E	Number in: 1995	1994	1993
Coliforms	5,255	42	0.8	0	0	0	0	1	1
Faecal coliforms	5,257	2	<0.1	0	0	0	2	9	6
Colour	1,777	0	0.0	0	1	0	0	0	0
Turbidity	5,241	1	<0.1	0	0	0	1	3	1
Odour	280	0	0.0	0	0	0	0	0	1
Taste	281	0	0.0	0	0	0	0	0	1
Hydrogen ion	5,242	0	0.0	0	0	0	0	3	1
Nitrate	1,586	1	<0.1	0	0	0	1	2	0
Nitrite	1,605	0	0.0	0	0	0	0	0	0
Aluminium	1,488	0	0.0	0	1	0	0	0	4
Iron	1,640	19	1.2	9	29	0	15	12	12
Manganese	1,598	6	0.4	0	0	1	5	3	3
Lead	931	10	1.1	6	12	0	9	8	11
PAH	1,073	116	10.7	27	13	0	43	41	36
Trihalomethanes	573	1	0.2	0	0	0	0	0	0
Total pesticides	871	0	0.0	0	10	0	0	1	0
Atrazine	612	11	1.8	11	10	0	3	4	3
Ioxynil	260	0	0.0	0	10	0	0	1	3
Mecoprop	246	0	0.0	0	10	0	0	0	1
Simazine	610	0	0.0	0	10	0	0	0	1
Other pesticides	4,385	0	0.0	0	10	0	0	0	0
Temperature	5,345	1	<0.1	0	0	0	1	0	0
Benzo 3,4, pyrene	1,073	4	0.4	0	0	0	0	1	0
All others	16,918	0	0.0	0	0	0	0	0	0
Total	**64,147**	**214**	**0.3**	**53**	-	-	-	-	-

* 119 zones in 1994; 119 zones in 1993.

(l)   the Company was continuing to make good progress in becoming a quality organisation.

In December 1995, Mr R Kidson, representing consultants Rofe, Kennard and Lapworth, and working under the general direction of Mr Hallas, carried out inspection of selected water treatment works and selected service reservoirs. He concluded for the sites that he inspected that:

(m)   the treatment processes complied with Regulation 23;

(n)   the use of substances and products satisfied the requirements of Regulation 25;

(o)   the Company's policy and arrangements for disinfection at water treatment works were satisfactory; and

(p)   the Company's arrangements for compliance sampling at treatment works and service reservoirs are generally in accordance with the recommendations of paragraph 2.8 of the Guidance Document and with the requirements of regulation 21(2)(a).

Mr Hallas and Miss Jackson also visited two water treatment works on 12 and 13 July 1995, to review the action being taken by the Company following disinfection failures at the works.

As a result of these inspections, nine recommendations were conveyed to the Company for formal response, mainly relating to water treatment functions. Twenty six suggestions on various matters were also made. The Company is taking action or has already taken action on the recommendations

Improvement programmes

Thirteen undertakings in respect of improvement programmes accepted by the Secretary of State from the Company were due for full completion during 1995. All of these were completed on or ahead of schedule. The Company was relieved of its obligations in respect of a further undertaking. A new undertaking given by the Company to carry out improvement works to its distribution system, with a completion date of 31 March 2000, has been accepted by the Secretary of State.

Incidents

There were no events notified during 1995 by the Company to the Secretary of State under the terms of the Water Undertakers (Information) Direction 1992 which were regarded by the Inspectorate as constituting incidents in which drinking water quality demonstrably deteriorated.

However, two events were notified under the terms of the Water Undertakers (Information) Direction 1992 which constituted incidents because they involved disinfection failures at water treatment works. The first occurred in May at Pitcombe water treatment works and resulted in undisinfected or partially disinfected water being supplied to some 2,400 consumers in the area of Wincanton for several hours. Regulation 23(1) was contravened but enforcement action was not required as the Company identified the cause of the failure and took appropriate remedial action to prevent recurrence. The second occurred at the end of December at Traphole water treatment works and remains under consideration by the Inspectorate.

No other events regarded as constituting incidents came to the attention of the Inspectorate in 1995.

Enforcement action

Table 3.28.4 summarises enforcement action under consideration for the Company as a result of the Inspectorate's work in, or pertaining to, the calendar year 1995.

Formal caution

On 16 November 1995 the Company received a formal caution, which will remain on the files, having admitted to an offence under regulation 28 of the Water Supply (Water Quality) Regulations 1989. The offence related to the Company's failure to observe the conditions of approval for the use of an epoxy material used to reline internally some 1.5 km of water mains near Porlock, Somerset, in early 1993.

Table 3.28.4	Wessex Water Services Limited SUMMARY OF ENFORCEMENT ACTION CONSIDERED IN 1995
Regulation	**Reason for enforcement**
3(3)(c)	Contravention of the standard for manganese in one zone.
3(7)	Contravention of the coliforms standard at one water treatment works.

WREXHAM WATER PLC

Introduction

The Company supplies on average 44 Ml/d of water to some 150,000 people in the Wrexham area. The Company's water resources consist of an intake on the River Dee which provides some 60% of total requirements, nine upland impounding reservoirs, one borehole and one spring. These sources are treated at seven treatment works. Treated water is distributed via 27 service reservoirs and some 1,350 km of mains. The supply area is divided into 13 water supply zones.

Overall water quality

At water treatment works and service reservoirs and in water supply zones, the Company carried out a total of 12,191 determinations in 1995. Of these, 99.8% demonstrated compliance with the relevant water quality standards, but 26 showed a PCV to have been contravened.

Coliforms were not detected at any of the Company's seven water treatment works. At all the Company's 27 service reservoirs, coliforms were absent from at least 95% of samples. All of the Company's 13 zones complied fully with the relevant water quality standards or had breaches of the standards which were trivial or were fully covered by undertakings.

Microbiological quality of water leaving treatment works

Table 3.29.1 shows the Company's performance in 1995, with data for 1994 and 1993 for comparison. The small differences between the three years are not considered significant.

The Company complied with the sampling frequencies required by regulation 17 at all its treatment works in 1995. There were no contraventions of the microbiological standards at any of the Company's water treatment works in 1995.

Table 3.29.1 Wrexham Water Plc
MICROBIOLOGICAL QUALITY OF WATER LEAVING TREATMENT WORKS

	1995	1994	1993
Number of water treatment works	7	7	9
Works with no sampling shortfall	7	7	9
COLIFORMS			
Total number of determinations	1,086	938	1,010
- number containing coliforms	0	0	0
- % containing coliforms	0.0	0.0	0.0
Treatment works with coliforms detected	**0**	**0**	**0**
FAECAL COLIFORMS			
Total number of determinations	1,086	938	1,010
- number containing faecal coliforms	0	0	0
- % containing faecal coliforms	0.0	0.0	0.0
Treatment works with faecal coliforms detected	**0**	**0**	**0**
FAECAL STREPTOCOCCI			
Total number of determinations	1,086	938	1,010
- number containing faecal streptococci	0	0	0
- % containing faecal streptococci	0.0	0.0	0.0
Treatment works with faecal streptococci detected	**0**	**0**	**0**

Microbiological quality of water in service reservoirs

Table 3.29.2 shows the Company's performance in 1995, with data for 1994 and 1993 for comparison. Differences between the three years are not considered significant.

The Company complied with the sampling frequencies required by regulation 18 at all its service reservoirs in 1995. Contraventions of the microbiological standards at two service reservoirs have resulted in the consideration of enforcement action, as shown in 3.29.4. All other contraventions of the standards at service reservoirs are considered trivial or unlikely to recur.

Table 3.29.2 Wrexham Water Plc
MICROBIOLOGICAL QUALITY OF WATER IN SERVICE RESERVOIRS

	1995	1994	1993
Number of service reservoirs	27	27	30
Service reservoirs with no sampling shortfall	27	27	30
COLIFORMS			
Total number of determinations	1,397	1,373	1,447
- number containing coliforms	11	5	5
- % containing coliforms	0.8	0.4	0.4
Service reservoirs with coliforms detected	10	4	5
Service reservoirs with coliforms detected in more than 5% of samples	**0**	**0**	**0**
- % of all service reservoirs	0	0	0
FAECAL COLIFORMS			
Total number of determinations	1,397	1,373	1,447
- number containing faecal coliforms	4	4	2
- % containing faecal coliforms	0.3	0.3	0.1
Service reservoirs with faecal coliforms detected	**4**	**3**	**2**
- % of all service reservoirs	15	11	7
FAECAL STREPTOCOCCI			
Total number of determinations	1,397	1,373	1,447
- number containing faecal streptococci	3	5	3
- % containing faecal streptococci	0.2	0.4	0.2
Service reservoirs with faecal streptococci detected	**3**	**5**	**3**
- % of all service reservoirs	11	19	10

Water quality in water supply zones

Table 3.29.3 shows the Company's performance in 1995, with data for 1994 and 1993 for comparison. Differences between the three years are not considered significant.

Inspection

Dr P K Marsden, Inspector, carried out an inspection of Wrexham Water Plc in November 1995. Dr Marsden concluded that:

(a) the Company has implemented or intends to implement most of the recommendations of the 1994 inspection;

(b) the Company's records were adequate to allow full audit trails to be followed;

Table 3.29.3   Wrexham Water Plc
WATER QUALITY IN SUPPLY ZONES

Columns 'CBU' show, for determinations, contraventions covered by undertakings and, for zones, the total number of zones covered by undertakings in 1995. Column 'E' shows the number of zones for which new enforcement action is under consideration as a result of contraventions of the PCV in 1995. **Please refer to the Introduction to Chapter 3 for more detailed explanation of this table.**

| Parameter | DETERMINATIONS in 1995 | | | | ZONES (13 in 1995)* | | | | |
| | Total | Contravening PCV | | | | | Non-compliant | | |
		No.	%	CBU	CBU 1995	E	Number in: 1995	1994	1993
Coliforms	499	3	0.6	0	0	0	0	0	1
Faecal coliforms	499	1	0.2	0	0	0	1	0	1
Colour	70	0	0.0	0	13	0	0	0	1
Turbidity	70	0	0.0	0	13	0	0	0	0
Odour	70	0	0.0	0	0	0	0	0	0
Taste	70	0	0.0	0	0	0	0	0	0
Hydrogen ion	334	0	0.0	0	13	0	0	0	0
Nitrate	70	0	0.0	0	0	0	0	0	0
Nitrite	70	0	0.0	0	0	0	0	0	0
Aluminium	84	2	2.4	2	13	0	1	1	1
Iron	70	0	0.0	0	13	0	0	0	0
Manganese	84	1	1.2	1	13	0	1	0	0
Lead	52	0	0.0	0	13	0	0	0	0
PAH	52	0	0.0	0	0	0	0	0	0
Trihalomethanes	52	0	0.0	0	0	0	0	0	0
Total pesticides	156	0	0.0	0	0	0	0	0	0
Simazine	52	1	1.9	0	0	0	1	0	0
Other pesticides	624	0	0.0	0	0	0	0	0	0
Faecal streptococci	499	0	0.0	0	0	0	0	0	0
All others	1,265	0	0.0	0	0	0	0	0	0
Total	**4,742**	**8**	**0.2**	**3**	**-**	**-**	**-**	**-**	**-**

* 13 zones in 1994; 13 zones in 1993.

(c)   at the time of inspection, the Company had not completed its lead undertaking and it needs to gather further evidence to demonstrate that the steps it proposes to take will be effective;

(d)   the records of epoxy relining generally met the conditions of approval; and

(e)   the records of water quality alarms were generally sufficient to allow responses to be audited.

Subsequent to the inspection the Company reported that it completed the steps that it proposed to take under its lead undertaking by the due date.

In October, Mr K Bamford, a consultant from Rofe, Kennard and Lapworth, working under the general direction of Mr Drury, Principal Inspector, carried out inspection of two treatment works (Llwyn-On and Tregeiriog) and two service reservoirs (Upper Garth and Rhewl). Mr Bamford concluded that:

(f)   the treatment processes complied with Regulation 23;

(g)   the use of substances and products satisfied the requirements of Regulation 25;

(h) the Company's policy and arrangements for disinfection at the treatment works were satisfactory; and

(i) the Company's arrangements for compliance sampling at treatment works and service reservoirs are generally in accordance with the recommendations of paragraph 2.8 of the Guidance Document and with the requirements of Regulation 21(2)(a).

As a result of these inspections, five recommendations were conveyed to the Company for formal response. Thirteen suggestions on various matters were also made.

Improvement programmes

One undertaking in respect of an improvement programme accepted by the Secretary of State from the Company was due for full completion by the end of 1995. This was the undertaking in respect of minimising the risk of breaching the lead standard at consumers' taps. The Company reported that the scheme was completed by the due date. The Inspectorate is awaiting further data to confirm the effectiveness of the steps taken. A new undertaking given by the Company to carry out improvement works to its distribution system, with a completion date of 31 March 2000, is being considered by the Secretary of State.

Incidents

No events regarded as constituting incidents in which drinking water quality demonstrably deteriorated came to the attention of the Inspectorate in 1995.

Enforcement action

Table 3.29.4 summarises enforcement action under consideration for the Company as a result of the Inspectorate's work in, or pertaining to, the year 1995.

Table 3.29.4 Wrexham Water Plc
SUMMARY OF ENFORCEMENT ACTION CONSIDERED IN 1995

Regulation	Reason for enforcement
3(7)	Contravention of the standard for faecal coliforms at two service reservoirs.

THE YORK WATERWORKS PLC

Introduction

The Company supplies on average approximately 47 Ml/d to a population of some 177,000 in the City of York and the surrounding districts. The Company's water resources are derived almost entirely from the River Ouse, abstracted immediately upstream of York and treated at Acomb Landing Water Treatment Works. The Company also imports treated water from Yorkshire Water Services to supply 17 properties in the Escrick area. The Company has an arrangement to obtain a supply of treated water from an alternative source in the event of an emergency. The treated water is distributed by pumping and gravity through six service reservoirs and some 957 km of water mains. The supply area is divided into five water supply zones.

Overall water quality

At water treatment works and service reservoirs and in water supply zones, the Company carried out a total of 8,051 determinations in 1995. Of these, 99.4% demonstrated compliance with the relevant water quality standards, but 52 showed a PCV to have been contravened.

Coliforms were detected at the Company's only water treatment works. Coliforms were absent from at least 95% of samples taken at all the Company's six service reservoirs. Of the Company's five water supply zones in 1995, all complied fully with the relevant water quality standards or had breaches of the standards which were either trivial or were fully covered by undertakings.

Microbiological quality of water leaving treatment works

Table 3.30.1 shows the Company's performance in 1995, with data for 1994 and 1993 for comparison. Differences between the three years are not regarded as significant.

The Company complied with the sampling frequency required by regulation 17 at its treatment works in 1995.

The Company has identified the probable cause of the contraventions of the standard for total coliforms at its water treatment works as being sample contamination and has taken appropriate action to prevent a recurrence. Enforcement action is not being considered.

Table 3.30.1 The York Waterworks Plc
MICROBIOLOGICAL QUALITY OF WATER LEAVING TREATMENT WORKS

	1995	1994	1993
Number of water treatment works	1	1	1
Works with no sampling shortfall	1	1	1
COLIFORMS			
Total number of determinations	365	365	365
- number containing coliforms	2	0	1
- % containing coliforms	0.5	0.0	0.3
Treatment works with coliforms detected	**1**	**0**	**1**
- % of all works	100	0	100
FAECAL COLIFORMS			
Total number of determinations	365	365	365
- number containing faecal coliforms	0	0	0
- % containing faecal coliforms	0.0	0.0	0.0
Treatment works with faecal coliforms detected	**0**	**0**	**0**
- % of all works	0	0	0

Microbiological quality of water in service reservoirs

Table 3.30.2 shows the Company's performance in 1995, with data for 1994 and 1993 for comparison. Had the definition of the coliform parameter not been changed as described in paragraph 3.34 above, but remained as it was for 1994 and previous years, only a single sample from a service reservoir would have been reported as containing coliforms. Differences between the three years are not regarded as significant.

The Company complied with the sampling frequencies required by regulation 18 at all its service reservoirs in 1995.

The contravention of the microbiological standards at one service reservoir is considered trivial.

Table 3.30.2 The York Waterworks Plc
MICROBIOLOGICAL QUALITY OF WATER IN SERVICE RESERVOIRS

	1995	1994	1993
Number of service reservoirs	6	6	6
Service reservoirs with no sampling shortfall	6	6	6
COLIFORMS			
Total number of determinations	302	296	312
- number containing coliforms	2	1	4
- % containing coliforms	0.7	0.3	1.3
Service reservoirs with coliforms detected	2	1	3
Service reservoirs with coliforms detected in more than 5% of samples	**0**	**0**	**0**
FAECAL COLIFORMS			
Total number of determinations	302	296	312
- number containing faecal coliforms	1	0	2
- % containing faecal coliforms	0.3	0.0	0.6
Service reservoirs with faecal coliforms detected	**1**	**0**	**2**
- % of all service reservoirs	17	0	33

Water quality in water supply zones

The Company complied fully with the required sampling frequencies in all zones.

Table 3.30.3 shows the Company's performance in 1995, with data for 1994 and 1993 for comparison. Had the definition of the coliform parameter not been changed as described in paragraph 3.34 above, but remained as it was for 1994 and previous years, the number of determinations containing coliforms would have been two. Differences between the three years are not regarded as significant.

All contraventions of the standards in zones are considered trivial or are covered by an undertaking.

Inspection

Miss C Jackson, Inspector, carried out an inspection of the York Waterworks Plc in September 1995. Miss Jackson concluded that:

(a)   the Company had taken appropriate and satisfactory measures to implement the ten recommendations made in the 1994 Inspection Report;

(b)   the Company's method of defining water supply zones met the requirements of the Regulations and accorded with the recommendations given in the Guidance Document;

Table 3.30.3   The York Waterworks Plc
WATER QUALITY IN SUPPLY ZONES

*Columns 'CBU' show, for determinations, contraventions covered by undertakings and, for zones, the <u>total</u> number of zones covered by undertakings in 1995 Column 'E' shows the number of zones for which new enforcement action is under consideration as a result of contraventions of the PCV in 1995. **Please refer to the Introduction to Chapter 3 for more detailed explanation of this table.***

Parameter	DETERMINATIONS in 1995				ZONES (5 in 1995)*				
	Total	Contravening PCV			CBU	E	Non-compliant		
		No.	%	CBU	1995		Number in:		
							1995	1994	1993
Coliforms	504	4	0.8	0	0	0	0	0	0
Faecal coliforms	504	0	0.0	0	0	0	0	0	0
Colour	161	0	0.0	0	0	0	0	0	0
Turbidity	504	1	0.2	1	4	0	1	0	0
Odour	40	0	0.0	0	0	0	0	0	0
Taste	40	0	0.0	0	0	0	0	0	0
Hydrogen ion	504	0	0.0	0	0	0	0	0	0
Nitrate	52	0	0.0	0	0	0	0	0	0
Nitrite	52	0	0.0	0	0	0	0	0	0
Aluminium	98	0	0.0	0	0	0	0	0	1
Iron	220	3	1.4	3	4	0	3	2	0
Manganese	62	1	1.6	0	0	0	1	0	0
Lead	114	2	1.8	0	0	0	2	0	3
PAH	16	0	0.0	0	0	0	0	0	0
Trihalomethanes	16	0	0.0	0	0	0	0	0	0
Total pesticides	100	4	4.0	4	4	0	4	4	0
Diuron	100	4	4.0	4	4	0	4	4	0
Isoproturon	100	20	20.0	20	4	0	4	4	4
Mecoprop	68	8	11.8	8	4	0	4	0	0
Other pesticides	2,048	0	0.0	0	4	0	0	0	0
Oxidizability	15	0	0.0	0	0	0	0	1	0
All others	1,399	0	0.0	0	0	0	0	0	0
Total	**6,717**	**47**	**0.7**	**40**	-	-	-	-	-

* 5 zones in 1994; 5 zones in 1993.

(c)   the general arrangements for sampling satisfied parts IV and V of the Regulations and accorded with the recommendations of the Guidance Document;

(d)   the Company's laboratory at Acomb Landing continued to be well run and most of the consequential changes in the new edition of Report 71 had been incorporated into existing laboratory procedures;

(e)   the Company's contractual arrangements for outside analytical services continued to be satisfactory;

(f)   the Company was on target to meet the key stages of its compliance programme by the due dates, although the timescale was tight;

(g)   the Company had done all that was reasonably practicable to reduce the concentration of lead in the water at consumers' taps;

(h)   the Company's procedures for disinfection of the water supplied, as audited, were satisfactory;

(i)   the Company's operational procedures to ensure adequate turn over of water in its service reservoirs were satisfactory;

(j)   the Company had systems in place for seeking advice in the event of a radioactive release into the environment; and

(k)   the Company's procedures and arrangements for communications and liaison with the local authorities in its area of supply were satisfactory.

As a result of this inspection, four recommendations were conveyed to the Company for formal response. Twelve suggestions on various matters were also made. The Company is taking action or has already taken action on the recommendations.

Improvement programmes

One undertaking in respect of improvement programmes accepted by the Secretary of State from the Company was due for the completion of a major step during 1995 and this was completed on schedule.

Incidents

No events regarded as constituting incidents in which drinking water quality demonstrably deteriorated came to the attention of the Inspectorate in 1995.

Enforcement action

No enforcement action needed to be considered for the Company as a result of the Inspectorate's work in, or pertaining to, the calendar year 1995.

YORKSHIRE WATER SERVICES LIMITED

Introduction

The Company supplies on average approximately 1,460 Ml/d of water to a resident population of more than 4.4 million in an area covering broadly the counties of North, West and South Yorkshire and part of Humberside.

The Company's water resources consist of:

(a) surface waters impounded in upland storage reservoirs (approximately 50% of supply);

(b) direct river abstractions and lowland pumped storage reservoirs (approximately 28% of supply); and

(c) groundwater sources from boreholes and springs (approximately 22% of supply).

The raw water is treated at 138 water treatment works. The large conurbations in the west and south of the Company's supply area are supplied mainly from the impounding reservoirs in the Pennines. The eastern and northern parts of the supply area are supplied mainly from the groundwater sources and from the direct river abstractions. The Company also has a regional grid network which enables treated water from the major sources to be pumped long distances across the supply area. The Company resorted to a number of emergency measures to maintain supplies during the drought period, including returning a small number of previously abandoned works to service and tankering raw water to various works for treatment.

The treated water is distributed by pumping and gravity through 395 service reservoirs and some 27,600 km of water mains. The supply area is divided into 204 designated water supply zones.

Overall water quality

At water treatment works and service reservoirs and in water supply zones, the Company carried out a total of 310,083 determinations in 1995. Of these, 99.7% demonstrated compliance with the relevant water quality standards, but 834 showed a PCV to have been contravened.

Coliforms were not detected at 124 (90%) of the Company's 138 water treatment works. At 391 (99%) of the Company's 395 service reservoirs, coliforms were absent from at least 95% of samples. Of the Company's 204 water supply zones in 1995, 183 (90%) complied fully with the relevant water quality standards or had breaches of the standards which were either trivial or were fully covered by undertakings or are to be included in the new distribution undertaking. In the other 21 (10%) of the zones, some breaches are regarded as unlikely to recur, but others could result, or have already resulted, in enforcement action.

Microbiological quality of water leaving treatment works

Table 3.31.1 shows the Company's performance in 1995, with data for 1994 and 1993 for comparison. Differences between the three years are not considered significant.

The Company complied with the sampling frequencies required by regulation 17 at 129 of its 138 treatment works in 1995. The single shortfalls at the other nine works were a deliberate decision on the part of the Company and enforcement action is being considered.

Contraventions of the microbiological quality standards at one works has resulted in the consideration of enforcement action, as shown in table 3.31.4. The Inspectorate will assess the results of further monitoring for the first six months of 1996 at one works before deciding on the need for enforcement action. All other contraventions of the standards at works are considered trivial or unlikely to recur.

Table 3.31.1 Yorkshire Water Services Limited
MICROBIOLOGICAL QUALITY OF WATER LEAVING
TREATMENT WORKS

	1995	1994	1993
Number of water treatment works	138	135	139
Works with no sampling shortfall	129	115	114
COLIFORMS			
Total number of determinations	16,762	18,470	19,242
- number containing coliforms	16	37	30
- % containing coliforms	0.1	0.2	0.1
Treatment works with coliforms detected	**14**	**23**	**22**
- % of all works	10	17	14
FAECAL COLIFORMS			
Total number of determinations	16,762	18,472	19,229
- number containing faecal coliforms	4	10	13
- % containing faecal coliforms	<0.1	<0.1	<0.1
Treatment works with faecal coliforms detected	**4**	**8**	**11**
- % of all works	3	6	7

Microbiological quality of water in service reservoirs

Table 3.31.2 shows the Company's performance in 1995, with data for 1994 and 1993 for comparison. There has been a significant reduction in the number of service reservoirs in which faecal coliforms have been detected. All other differences between the three years are not considered significant.

Table 3.31.2 Yorkshire Water Services Limited
MICROBIOLOGICAL QUALITY OF WATER IN SERVICE
RESERVOIRS

	1995	1994	1993
Number of service reservoirs	395	403	405
Service reservoirs with no sampling shortfall	388	387	330
COLIFORMS			
Total number of determinations	20,243	20,836	20,817
- number containing coliforms	54	68	93
- % containing coliforms	0.3	0.3	0.4
Service reservoirs with coliforms detected	41	50	68
Service reservoirs with coliforms detected in more than 5% of samples	**4**	**4**	**5**
- % of all service reservoirs	1	1	1
FAECAL COLIFORMS			
Total number of determinations	20,243	20,857	20,817
- number containing faecal coliforms	7	24	25
- % containing faecal coliforms	<0.1	0.1	0.1
Service reservoirs with faecal coliforms detected	**6**	**18**	**22**
- % of all service reservoirs	2	4	5

The Company complied with the sampling frequencies required by regulation 18 at 388 of its 395 service reservoirs in 1995. Shortfalls at the other seven were due to circumstances beyond the Company's control and are regarded as trivial.

Contraventions of the microbiological quality standards at one service reservoir has resulted in the consideration of enforcement action, as shown in table 3.31.4. The Inspectorate will assess the results of further monitoring for the first six months of 1996 at four service reservoirs before deciding on the need for enforcement action. All other contraventions of the standards at service reservoirs are considered trivial.

Water quality in water supply zones

Although the Company has made significant improvements in the management of its sampling programme, it still failed to comply with the required sampling frequencies for five parameters in three zones and failed to ensure that a sample taken for one parameter in one zone was analysed. The sampling shortfalls could have been avoided and enforcement action is under consideration in respect of these breaches of regulations 10 and 13.

Table 3.31.3 shows the Company's performance in 1995, with data for 1994 and 1993 for comparison. There have been significant reductions over the three years in the number of zones contravening the standards for trihalomethanes, total pesticides and the individual pesticides MCPA and MCPP. All other differences between the three years are not considered significant.

Enforcement action was initiated during 1995 in respect of some contraventions of standards and is being considered in respect of further contraventions of standards, as shown in tables 3.31.3 and 3.31.4. The Inspectorate will assess the results of further monitoring for the first six months of 1996 for total coliforms in one zone, oxidisability in one zone, aluminium in one zone, iron in one zone, nitrite in two zones and trihalomethanes in two zones before deciding on the need for enforcement action. All other contraventions of the standards in zones are considered trivial or unlikely to recur, or are covered by undertakings or will be covered by the new distribution undertaking.

Inspection

Mr A Hallas, Principal Inspector, assisted by Miss C R Jackson, Inspector, carried out an inspection of Yorkshire Water Services Ltd in two visits between 31 July and 3 August and 6 to 10 November 1995. Mr M D Wright, as a Temporary Technical Assessor, also assisted in the first part of the inspection. Mr Hallas concluded that:

(a) the Company had generally taken appropriate and satisfactory measures to implement most of the recommendations made in the 1994 technical audit inspection report;

(b) the Company's method of defining water supply zones met the requirements of the Regulations and accorded with the recommendations given the Guidance Document;

(c) the general arrangements for sampling satisfied parts IV and V of the Regulations and accorded with the recommendations of the Guidance Document;

(d) the Company's general arrangements for the analysis of samples continued to be satisfactory and the contractual arrangements for analytical services with Labservices were well managed;

(e) the public record as audited at the Company's Sheffield offices did not comply fully with regulations 30(1) and 30(2); enforcement action was not initiated as the offices were due to close;

(f) the Company's arrangements for reporting compliance data were generally satisfactory although the audit trails revealed a number of deficiencies which needed to be addressed;

Table 3.31.3 Yorkshire Water Services Limited
WATER QUALITY IN SUPPLY ZONES

*Columns 'CBU' show, for determinations, contraventions covered by undertakings and, for zones, the total number of zones covered by undertakings in 1995. Column 'E' shows the number of zones for which new enforcement action is under consideration as a result of contraventions of the PCV in 1995. **Please refer to the Introduction to Chapter 3 for more detailed explanation of this table.***

| Parameter | DETERMINATIONS in 1995 | | | | ZONES (204 in 1995)* | | | | |
| | Total | Contravening PCV | | | CBU | E | Non-compliant Number in: | | |
		No.	%	CBU	1995		1995	1994	1993
Coliforms	12,483	90	0.7	0	46	0	1	1	3
Faecal coliforms	12,482	11	0.1	0	2	0	11	7	21
Colour	12,474	1	<0.1	0	0	0	1	6	6
Turbidity	12,475	45	0.4	0	0	5	35	36	28
Odour	1,989	0	0.0	0	0	0	0	1	2
Taste	2,004	0	0.0	0	0	0	0	1	4
Hydrogen ion	12,474	19	0.2	4	6	2	17	24	25
Nitrate	2,100	14	0.7	1	1	0	5	2	7
Nitrite	2,239	5	0.2	0	0	0	3	4	6
Aluminium	6,601	18	0.3	10	71	0	15	16	21
Iron	6,619	184	2.8	163	141	2	84	81	96
Manganese	6,600	71	1.1	63	93	2	46	30	44
Lead	2,411	85	3.5	85	204	0	56	60	66
PAH	1,110	34	3.1	3	3	0	12	14	14
Trihalomethanes	1,564	48	3.1	37	14	0	6	10	25
Total pesticides	2,196	2	0.1	2	65	0	2	22	17
2,4-D	1,740	0	0.0	0	65	0	0	12	3
Atrazine	1,379	0	0.0	0	65	0	0	1	1
Bentazone	1,732	0	0.0	0	65	0	0	1	0
Carbendazim	1,135	0	0.0	0	65	0	0	0	1
Chlorotoluron	1,647	0	0.0	0	65	0	0	13	0
pp DDE	1,043	1	0.1	0	65	0	1	0	0
Diuron	1,648	1	0.1	1	65	0	1	12	4
Fluroxpyr	1,732	0	0.0	0	65	0	0	0	11
Imazapyr	1,726	0	0.0	0	65	0	0	3	0
Isoproturon	1,650	87	5.3	70	65	3	31	28	25
Linuron	1,647	0	0.0	0	65	0	0	2	0
MCPA	1,741	3	0.2	2	65	0	3	19	17
MCPB	1,740	0	0.0	0	65	0	0	1	0
MCPP	1,741	26	1.5	26	65	0	15	25	42
Simazine	1,378	0	0.0	0	65	0	0	0	4
Other pesticides	84,029	0	0.0	0	65	0	0	0	0
Ammonium	1,941	1	<0.1	0	0	0	1	1	1
Benzo 3,4, pyrene	1,110	4	0.4	0	3	0	0	0	1
Mercury	289	0	0.0	0	0	0	0	4	2
Nickel	249	0	0.0	0	0	0	0	0	2
Oxidizability	355	3	0.8	0	0	0	2	8	6
Temperature	1,890	0	0.0	0	0	0	0	1	0
All others	24,710	0	0.0	0	0	0	0	0	0
Total	**236,073**	**753**	**0.3**	**467**	-	-	-	-	-

* 210 zones in 1994; 214 zones in 1993.

(g) two of the Company's undertakings and remedial work associated with a Regulation 4 relaxation had not been completed by the due dates; however, the Company was on target to meet most of the key stages of its current compliance programme by the due dates, although the timescales for some schemes are very tight;

(h) the Company had been dilatory in complying with the terms of its lead undertaking and it was possible that the undertaking would not be completed by the due date (this was subsequently achieved with the installation of temporary treatment plant at a number of sites);

(i) the Company's procedures for disinfection of the water supplied, as audited, were satisfactory and a working party had been set up to examine disinfection failures within the Company's water supply area;

(j) the Company's arrangements for monitoring the level of chlorate in the treated water at sites where on site generation of chlorine is practised, were satisfactory and a positive approach was being taken on backflow prevention;

(k) the Company's operational procedures to ensure adequate turn over of water in its service reservoirs were satisfactory, as were the procedures and systems for operating large scale transfers of treated water within the supply area;

(l) the Company procedures and systems for epoxy lining of the distribution system as inspected were satisfactory;

(m) the general arrangements for the chlorination of new mains by Yorkshire Pipeline Services were generally satisfactory, as audited, although some of the practices observed on site were less so;

(n) the Company's procedures for dealing with consumer complaints were generally satisfactory, although some of the advice given particularly in respect of dirty water complaints was questionable;

(o) the Company has systems in place for sampling and seeking advice in the event of a radioactive release;

(p) the Company's liaison with local authorities in its area was adequate but further improvements could be made in respect of more open dialogue at local level; and

(q) the Company was taking a positive response to the introduction of quality systems particularly at water treatment sites which has culminated in the Water Production Department attaining ISO 9002.

Mr Hallas found contraventions of regulation 21(2)(d)(iii) in respect of one parameter and of regulation 17(1) and enforcement action was considered.

Also in November, Mr P Durrant, representing consultants Rofe, Kennard and Lapworth, and working under the general direction of Mr Hallas, carried out inspection of selected water treatment works and selected service reservoirs. He concluded that:

(r) the Company's treatment processes complied with Regulation 23;

(s) the Company's use of substances and products satisfied the requirements of Regulation 25;

(t) the Company's policy and arrangements for disinfection at treatment works were generally satisfactory; and

(u) the Company's arrangements for compliance sampling at treatment works and service reservoirs are generally in accordance with the recommendations of paragraph 2.8 of the Guidance Document and with the requirements of Regulation 21(2)(a).

Miss Jackson and Mr Hallas also visited Marton water treatment works on 8 February as part of their investigations into an incident involving the supply of coloured water. On 28 and 29 June, they visited Irton water treatment works, Snainton service reservoir, Norwood service reservoir and Hurlfield service reservoirs to review the action taken by the Company in respect of contraventions of standards identified in 1994. They also visited the new Loxley water treatment works to assess progress on remedial work associated with regulation 4 relaxations.

As a result of these inspections, 12 recommendations were conveyed to the Company for formal response, mainly relating to deficiencies identified in the detailed audits of compliance results and to water treatment practices. Forty-six suggestions on various matters were also made.

Mr Hallas is satisfied that the Company has made satisfactory progress in implementing the recommendations made in the first part of his inspection and is likewise taking action on the recommendations in the other reports.

On 21 and 22 November, Miss Jackson visited five of the sites involved in the raw water tankering operations to review the water quality aspects of the operation and the degree of checking being carried out. She was generally satisfied with her findings.

Improvement programmes

Fourteen undertakings in respect of improvement programmes accepted by the Secretary of State from the Company were due for full completion or the completion of major steps during 1995. Twelve of these were completed on or ahead of schedule. The scheme for total coliforms at Edge Mount service reservoir was delayed due to poor internal planning and co-ordination. The Inspectorate considered the issue of a Notice of Intention to make a Final Order but the Company subsequently completed the necessary works and a Notice was not required. The scheme for total and faecal coliforms in respect of some concessionary supplies has been delayed due to reasons beyond the Company's control. A new undertaking given by the Company to carry out improvement works to its distribution system, with a completion date of 31 March 2000, is being considered by the Secretary of State.

Relaxations

Eleven authorised relaxations involving four parameters in zones supplied from three water treatment works had been granted to the Company by the Secretary of State, conditional upon remedial action being completed during 1995. Action was completed ahead of schedule in respect of one of these schemes. Progress with the schemes at March Ghyll and Mickley was delayed because of the drought but the Company gave assurances that these schemes would be completed by early 1996.

The Company was also granted authorised relaxations for four parameters conditional on a new water treatment works being constructed to replace the one at Bradfield by 31 December 1994. The scheme was initially delayed by bad weather and then progressively delayed by contractual arguments over the design of one of the components. The Inspectorate considered the issue of a Notice of Intention to make a Final Order for the continuing contraventions of the standard for manganese in the zones supplied but the Company subsequently completed the necessary work and a Notice was not required.

Incidents

Four events notified during 1995 by the Company to the Secretary of State under the terms of the Water Undertakers (Information) Direction 1992 are regarded by the Inspectorate as constituting incidents in which drinking water quality demonstrably deteriorated. In February, one of the borehole sites supplying Marton water treatment works was flooded by river water and this resulted in turbid and possibly inadequately disinfected water entering supply. The Company took appropriate action, including issuing advice to boil water to the consumers affected. In August, coliforms were detected in a service reservoir following the use of a non-sterile hose to transfer treated water during the drought. The Inspectorate was critical of the Company for its lack of procedures for monitoring the transfer arrangements. The others incidents involved the detection of cryptosporidium oocsyts in the treated water leaving one works and the occurrence of a chlorophenolic taste in the water supplied from one works and these remain under consideration by the Inspectorate.

Four further events were notified under the terms of the Water Undertakers (Information) Direction 1992 which constituted incidents because they involved disinfection failures or partial disinfection failures at three water treatment works. The first occurred in July at a small spring source which has subsequently been abandoned. Of the other three, one occurred at an abandoned works which had been brought back into service to augment supplies during the drought and two occurred at the same works within a week. These remain under consideration by the Inspectorate.

The Company omitted to notify the Inspectorate as soon as maybe of an incident involving the loss of water supplies to a large part of Halifax in July 1995 and enforcement action was initiated.

No other events regarded as constituting incidents came to the attention of the Inspectorate in 1995.

Enforcement action

Table 3.31.4 summarises enforcement action under consideration for the Company as a result of the Inspectorate's work in, or pertaining to, the calendar year 1995.

**Table 3.31.4 Yorkshire Water Services Limited
SUMMARY OF ENFORCEMENT ACTION CONSIDERED IN 1995**

Regulation	Reason for enforcement
3(3)(c)	Contravention of the standard for hydrogen ion in two zones; individual pesticides in three zones; iron in two zones; manganese in two zones; and turbidity in five zones.
3(7)	Contravention of the coliforms standard at one water treatment works.
3(7)	Contravention of the faecal coliforms standard at one service reservoir.
10	Failure to have a sample taken under Part IV of the Regulations analysed.
13	Sampling shortfalls in three water supply zones.
17	Sampling shortfalls at nine water treatment works.
21(2)(d)(iii)	Analytical systems not shown to be suitable in respect of one parameter.
Information Direction	
5(1)(a)	Failure to notify the Secretary of State as soon as maybe of an event which was likely to attract significant local publicity.

Chapter 4   Overview of Water Quality in England and Wales

> **KEY POINTS:**
>
> • **further improvements in 1995 in the quality of water at treatment works, slight deterioration at service reservoirs;**
>
> • **more zones than previously complied with standards for 13 key parameters;**
>
> • **increased number of zones not complying with manganese and PAH standards;**
>
> • **reductions in numbers of zones not complying with the pesticides standards; and**
>
> • **new enforcement action under consideration for 2.2% of all zones in respect of nitrite, but for no more than 0.4% for any other parameter.**

Introduction

4.1 In 1995, the 31 water companies supplied on average approximately 16,800 Ml/d of water to about 50 million people. These water supplies are derived in approximately equal amounts from ground waters, upland surface waters and lowland river abstractions, although there are wide variations in the proportions of these sources used within individual companies. In 1995, water from these sources was treated at 1,589 treatment works before distribution, partly by gravity and partly by pumping, through service reservoirs which in 1995 had 5,053 sampling points (the majority corresponding to single reservoir sites) and approximately 315,000 km of mains. There were 2,471 water supply zones in England and Wales in 1995.

4.2 The Inspectorate depends on the data submitted by water companies being on time, comprehensive and in the correct format in order to produce the Annual Report. In previous years reference has been made to the difficulties caused to the Inspectorate by deficiencies in the arrangements of some companies for data provision. Once again the data provided by some companies has been deficient and has necessitated extra work by the Inspectorate to correct deficiencies before the data could be processed.   It should be stressed that this is not a reflection of the quality of the water and due to the efforts of the Inspectors, the compliance data is wholly valid.

4.3 Whilst the data submitted by many companies caused few problems if any, the quality of the initial data submissions from some companies was less satisfactory and in some cases was such as to cause significant problems for the Inspectorate. In previous reports reference was made to the future naming of those companies not achieving sufficiently high standards of data handling and transmission if deficiencies were not eliminated. The adequacy of data provision by the various companies is categorised as follows:

No significant difficulties	Some difficulties	Significant difficulties
Bournemouth and W Hampshire	Bristol	Anglian
Cambridge	Chester	East Surrey
Cholderton	Dŵr Cymru (Welsh Water)	Essex and Suffolk
Hartlepool	Mid Kent	Folkestone and Dover
North West	Mid Southern	South East
Thames	North East	South Staffordshire
Wessex	North Surrey	Southern
Wrexham	Northumbrian	Tendring Hundred[a]
	Portsmouth	Yorkshire
	Severn Trent	
	South West	
	Sutton	
	Three Valleys	
	York	

[a] The data submitted by Tendring Hundred Water for 1995 was deficient but the Inspectorate recognises that there were mitigating circumstances and previous returns by the Company have been satisfactory.

Overall water quality

4.4 Individual water companies complied with the water quality standards of the Regulations for the majority of parameters for most or all of the year. At water treatment works and service reservoirs and in water supply zones, the companies carried out a total of 3,154,249 determinations in 1995. Of these, 99.5% demonstrated compliance with the relevant water quality standards. This confirms that drinking water is of a very high quality.

4.5 Coliforms were not detected at 1,351 (85.0%) of the companies' 1,589 water treatment works. At 4,997 (98.9%) of the 5,053 sampling points at service reservoirs, coliforms were absent from at least 95% of samples. Of the 2,471 water supply zones in England and Wales in 1995, 2,229 (90.0%) complied fully with the relevant water quality standards or had breaches of the standards which were either trivial or were being remedied through legally enforceable undertakings given by companies to carry out improvements. In the other 242 (10.0%) of the zones, some breaches are regarded as unlikely to recur, but others could result in enforcement action.

4.6 As in previous Reports, it is informative to examine the overall total of determinations by categories, as set out in the following table, with the corresponding figures for 1994 and 1993 for comparison:

	1995	1994	1993
Water treatment works:			
Total number of determinations	410,922	438,492	452,443
- number exceeding PCV	424	419	573
- % exceeding PCV	0.1	<0.1	0.1
Service reservoirs:			
Total number of determinations	519,380	525,665	522,597
- number exceeding PCV	1098	949	1,449
- % exceeding PCV	0.2	0.2	0.3
Supply zones:			
Total pesticides			
Total number of determinations	44,256	59,821	56,351
- number exceeding PCV	1,419	2,790	4,067
- % exceeding PCV	3.2	4.7	7.2
Individual pesticides			
Total number of determinations	925,666	1,112,269	1,006,458
- number exceeding PCV	7,291	12,875	21,464
- % exceeding PCV	0.8	1.2	2.1
"Key parameters"[a] excluding pesticides			
Total number of determinations	809,934	895,299	974,267
- number exceeding PCV	7,051	7,993	9,076
- % exceeding PCV	0.9	0.9	0.9
"Other parameters"[b]			
Total number of determinations	444,093	451,395	492,409
- number exceeding PCV	130	145	177
- % exceeding PCV	<0.1	<0.1	<0.1
All parameters			
Total number of determinations	2,223,949	2,518,784	2,529,485
- number exceeding PCV	15,819	23,803	34,784
- % exceeding PCV	0.7	0.9	1.4
ALL SAMPLES:			
Total number of determinations	3,154,249	3,482,941	3,504,525
- number exceeding PCV	17,341	25,171	36,806
- % exceeding PCV	0.5	0.7	1.1

[a] the key parameters listed in paragraph 3.24 and appearing in all tables in Chapter 3.
[b] all parameters with a PCV except the key parameters listed in paragraph 3.24.

4.7 The table shows that the overall number of determinations contravening a PCV has decreased in 1995 by 53% in comparison with 1993. This decrease is mainly due to reductions in the number of contraventions of the pesticides standards. Pesticide monitoring strategies remain focused on those substances likely to be present in water supplies and the decrease in contraventions of those standards provides significant evidence of an improvement in compliance.

4.8 Reductions in the numbers of other determinations carried out on samples from water supply zones when comparing the three years reflect further moves from increased to standard sampling frequencies as contraventions in previous years are shown to have been remedied and, in some cases, moves from standard to reduced sampling frequency where the criteria in regulation 13 apply. The Inspectorate is satisfied that, with the few exceptions noted in the individual company sections in the previous chapter, companies are complying with the minimum sampling frequencies prescribed by the Regulations.

Microbiological quality of water leaving treatment works

4.9 Table 4.1 shows the companies' performance in 1995, with data for 1994 and 1993 for comparison. It shows that, overall, there have been significant improvements in all respects over the three years. In particular, there has been a 22% reduction in the number of works at which coliforms were detected in the water entering supply and a 52% reduction in the corresponding number for faecal coliforms. Compared with 1991, in which year coliforms were detected at 445 treatment works and faecal coliforms at 173, the reductions are 47% and 68% respectively. The small increase in the number of determinations containing coliforms in 1995 compared with 1994 may be attributable to the change in the definition of the coliform parameter referred to in 3.35 above. The charts at the end of this Chapter illustrate the improvements over the four years.

Table 4.1 Summary of water quality in England and Wales
MICROBIOLOGICAL QUALITY OF WATER LEAVING TREATMENT WORKS

	1995	1994	1993
Number of water treatment works	1,588	1,603	1,657
COLIFORMS			
Total number of determinations	204,895	218,770	225,705
- number containing coliforms	355	336	438
- % containing coliforms	0.2	0.2	0.2
Treatment works with coliforms detected	**238**	**242**	**306**
- % of all works	15	15	18
FAECAL COLIFORMS			
Total number of determinations	204,939	218,784	225,728
- number containing faecal coliforms	69	83	135
- % containing faecal coliforms	<0.1	<0.1	<0.1
Treatment works with faecal coliforms detected	**56**	**72**	**117**
- % of all works	4	4	7

4.10 In 1995, 56 (4%) of the 1,588 treatment works in England and Wales had contraventions of the standard in respect of faecal coliforms. The majority of these contraventions are considered trivial. Where necessary, companies have given undertakings to carry out improvement programmes to achieve compliance with the standard as soon as possible; Chapter 5 of this Report shows that contraventions in 1995 were considered to warrant new enforcement action in respect of only one of the 1,588 treatment works. The coliforms standard was contravened at 238 (15%) of the treatment works and new enforcement action is under consideration in respect of 10 of these works.

Microbiological quality of water in service reservoirs

4.11 Table 4.2 shows the companies' performance in 1995, with data for 1994 and 1993 for comparison. There has been a 24% reduction compared with 1993 in the number of service reservoirs contravening the coliforms standard, such that 56 (1%) of the 5,053 service reservoir sampling points in England and Wales did not comply with the standard in 1995. The reduction from 1991, in which year 164 service reservoirs would not have complied with the present standard, is 66%. The 22% increase in the number of determinations containing coliforms, and the 30% increase in the number of service reservoirs not complying with the standard, in 1995 compared with 1994 may be in some part attributable to the change in the definition of the coliform parameter referred to in 3.35 above. The extremely dry conditions in 1995 may also have contributed through soil shrinkage and movement affecting the integrity of service reservoirs. New enforcement action is under consideration in respect of contraventions at 17 service reservoirs.

**Table 4.2 Summary of water quality in England and Wales
MICROBIOLOGICAL QUALITY OF WATER IN SERVICE
RESERVOIRS**

	1995	1994	1993
Number of service reservoirs	5,053	5,186	5,068
COLIFORMS			
Total number of determinations	258,950	262,109	260,575
- number containing coliforms	933	767	1,191
- % containing coliforms	0.4	0.3	0.5
Service reservoirs with coliforms detected	670	590	882
Service reservoirs with coliforms detected in more than 5% of samples	**56**	**43**	**75**
- % of all service reservoirs	1	<1	1
FAECAL COLIFORMS			
Total number of determinations	259,033	262,183	260,575
- number containing faecal coliforms	162	177	255
- % containing faecal coliforms	0.1	<0.1	<0.1
Service reservoirs with faecal coliforms detected	**148**	**147**	**223**
- % of all service reservoirs	3	3	4

4.12 The number of service reservoirs with faecal coliforms detected decreased in 1995 by 33% compared with 1993 and by 57% in comparison with 1991 in which year faecal coliforms were detected in 345 service reservoirs (see the charts at the end of this Chapter). New enforcement action is under consideration in respect of contraventions at 11 of the service reservoirs.

Water quality in water supply zones

4.13 Table 4.3 gives a summary of water quality in respect of the "key parameters" (see paragraph 3.25) for water supply zones in 1995, with data for 1994 and 1993 for comparison. Charts at the end of the Chapter provide further illustration of the last five years covered by these Reports.

Table 4.3 Summary of water quality in England and Wales
WATER QUALITY IN SUPPLY ZONES

Columns 'CBU' show, for determinations, contraventions covered by undertakings and, for zones, the <u>total</u> number of zones covered by undertakings in 1995. Column 'E' shows the number of zones for which new enforcement action is under consideration as a result of contraventions of the PCV in 1995. **Please refer to the Introduction to Chapter 3 for more detailed explanation of this table.**

| Parameter | DETERMINATIONS in 1995 | | | | ZONES (2,471 in 1995)* | | | | |
| | Total | Contravening PCV | | | | | Non-compliant | | |
		No.	%	CBU	CBU 1995	E	Number in: 1995	1994	1993
Coliforms	156,661	1,134	0.7	105	139	8	16	14	29
Faecal coliforms	156,306	111	<0.1	4	15	3	102	125	166
Colour	48,160	6	<0.1	4	544	0	6	16	18
Turbidity	60,117	104	0.2	38	1,239	5	90	91	100
Odour	23,507	30	<0.1	0	0	0	23	18	19
Taste	23,370	38	0.2	0	0	0	23	32	29
Hydrogen ion	70,773	93	0.1	13	246	2	71	100	147
Nitrate	33,607	142	0.4	93	28	0	28	45	52
Nitrite	35,124	1,705	4.9	1,289	217	55	251	250	245
Aluminium	40,968	150	0.4	56	280	0	92	74	140
Iron	55,415	1,237	2.2	1,156	2,083	2	618	614	671
Manganese	44,362	299	0.7	259	928	3	203	145	178
Lead	32,632	1,111	3.4	1,032	1,449	0	463	506	538
PAH	14,307	699	4.9	237	166	2	315	306	261
Trihalomethanes	14,625	192	1.3	123	98	0	37	58	116
Total pesticides	44,256	1,419	3.2	1,389	710	0	243	278	307
Individual pesticides	925,666	7,219	0.78	7,008	8,025	8	515	605	719
"Other parameters"[a]	445,990	130	<0.1	6	130	0	45	49	71
Total	**2,223,949**	**15,819**	**0.7**	**12,812**	-	-	-	-	-

* 2,552 zones in 1994; 2,576 zones in 1993.
[a] all parameters with a PCV except the key parameters listed in paragraph 3.24.

4.14 Comparing 1995 with 1993, there have been reductions in the number of zones not complying with the standards in respect of 13 of the 17 key parameters, as listed below with the percentage reductions, or if in square brackets the percentage increase, in each case. Also shown are the percentage reductions from the highest number of zones not complying with each parameter, with the year for which that was recorded shown in brackets:

Parameter	% Reduction from 1993	% Reduction from highest number non-compliant (year)
Coliforms	45	93 (1990)
Faecal coliforms	39	68 (1990)
Colour	67	85 (1990)
Turbidity	10	39 (1991)
Odour	[21]	72 (1990)
Taste	21	71 (1990)
Hydrogen ion	52	66 (1990)
Nitrate	46	70 (1991)
Nitrite	[2]	20 (1991)
Aluminium	34	64 (1990)
Iron	8	18 (1992)
Manganese	[14]	24 (1991)
Lead	14	30 (1991)
PAH	[21]	[3](1994)
Trihalomethanes	68	73 (1992)
Total pesticides	21	35 (1991)
Individual pesticides	28	35 (1991)

4.15 The reductions from the highest numbers illustrated above are statistically significant in all cases. The major exceptions to the general improvement in compliance over the period are in respect of PAH, for which the number of zones failing to comply with the standard has increased each year since 1990, and manganese for which the downward trend apparent from 1991 to 1994 has been reversed. The change in the number of zones failing to comply with the standard for odour since 1993 is not significant, the percentage increase appearing high due to the small numbers of zones affected in each year. The slight increase in respect of nitrite is not significant.

4.16 Table 4.4 shows the number of zones not complying with each standard as a percentage of all zones for each of the four years. This provides further illustration of the changes, and also highlights, for most of the parameters, the small percentage of zones which is non-compliant. Those parameters for which more than 10% of zones were non-compliant with the standard in 1994 - iron, lead, nitrite, PAH, and individual pesticides - and those showing an increase in the number of zones not complying with the standard, are discussed more fully later in this chapter.

Table 4.4 Summary of water quality in England and Wales
WATER QUALITY IN SUPPLY ZONES, 1991 - 1995

Percentage of zones not complying at all times with prescribed concentrations or values (see also the charts at the end of this chapter).

Parameter	Percentage of zones not complying in:				
	1995	1994	1993	1992	1991
Coliforms	0.6	0.5	1.1	3.3	5.2
Faecal coliforms	4.2	4.9	6.4	10.0	10.7
Colour	0.2	0.6	0.7	0.9	1.4
Turbidity	3.6	3.6	3.9	4.8	5.7
Odour	0.9	0.7	0.7	1.0	2.0
Taste	0.9	1.3	1.1	1.5	2.2
Hydrogen ion	2.9	3.9	5.7	6.7	7.6
Nitrate	1.1	1.8	2.0	3.6	3.6
Nitrite	10.2	9.8	9.5	10.3	12.3
Aluminium	3.7	2.9	5.4	6.3	8.7
Iron	24.8	24.1	26.0	30.9	31.0
Manganese	8.3	5.7	6.9	8.4	10.4
Lead	18.7	19.8	20.9	21.1	25.6
PAH	12.7	12.0	10.1	8.6	6.8
Trihalomethanes	0.6	2.3	4.5	5.2	4.9
Total pesticides	8.8	10.9	11.9	13.3	14.6
Individual pesticides	20.8	23.7	27.9	29.8	30.6
"Other parameters"[a]	2.1	1.9	2.8	5.1	6.1

[a] all parameters with a PCV except the key parameters listed in paragraph 3.24.

The meaning of 'non-compliant zones'

4.17 In all cases, the meaning of the term 'non-compliant' needs to be borne in mind when considering Tables 4.3 and 4.4 and the charts at the end of the Chapter. In many cases, a zone may have become non-compliant because of a single result showing a standard to have been marginally contravened. Such contraventions have been regarded as trivial in the compliance assessment and do not indicate a serious problem with water quality. In other cases the contraventions, although not trivial, are being remedied through undertakings given by the companies concerned to carry out improvement programmes to eradicate the problem. Consideration of the circumstances of some of the remaining contraventions has led the Inspectorate to conclude that they are unlikely to recur.

4.18 Only in a minority of cases has the contravention of water quality standards in zones been such as to lead to the consideration of new enforcement action. Full details of this enforcement action are given in Chapter 5 and particularly in Table 5.4. The largest number of zones for which enforcement action is under consideration - 55, in respect of the nitrite parameter - represents 2.3% of the total number of water supply zones in England and Wales. The other 11 parameters in respect of which enforcement is under consideration concern a total of only 33 zones.

Microbiological quality in water supply zones

4.19 Table 4.4 shows that the considerable improvement in the microbiological quality of water over the previous four years has been substantially maintained in 1995 despite the impact of the change in definition of the coliform parameter described in 3.35 above. The comparative data provided by eight companies on the effect of the change in definition shows an average increase of 36% in the number of coliform determinations judged against the new definition. The lowest increase for any company was 8% and the highest 129%. This latter figure significantly raised the overall percentage figure, which for all other companies together was 26%, and no other Company experienced an increase greater than 50%. It is clear that but for the change in definition of the coliform parameter there would have been a further significant improvement in the microbiological quality of water in supply zones in 1995. The very slight increase in the percentage of zones not complying in 1995 is not significant. The general trend of improvement can probably be attributed in part to the improvement in the quality of water in service reservoirs and possibly also, in the earlier years, to improvement in sampling procedures which have been made - often on the Inspectorate's recommendation - since the commencement of the regulatory regime.

4.20 Regulation 11(2) requires that at least 50% of samples taken from zones for monitoring compliance with the coliforms and faecal coliforms standards be taken from randomly-selected consumers' taps. Contraventions of the standards in samples taken from consumers' taps can be caused solely by the condition of consumers' plumbing; therefore the information presented in Tables 4.3 and 4.4 does not necessarily reflect the microbiological quality of water supplied by companies. However, companies are expected to take appropriate action in the event of any failure of the microbiological standards. The Inspectorate requires evidence from repeat sampling and sampling from related points before accepting the condition of a consumer's plumbing as responsible for a contravention. DWI Information Letter 3/95, dated 25 April 1995, provides further guidance on this matter.

Iron

4.21 There has been no significant change in 1995 in the number of zones not complying with the iron standard. In most cases, contraventions of the iron standard arise as a result of localised problems with iron mains in companies' distribution systems. Some cases have been associated with inadequate removal by treatment of high concentrations of iron present in the raw water, although this cause has largely been eradicated over the five years with the completion of improvement programmes at many of the water treatment works involved. The prolonged drought in 1995 and associated periods of very high demand for water, coupled with the need in many cases to change flow patterns in distribution systems, would have tended to lead to disturbance of deposits within mains and consequential breaches of the standards for iron, manganese, aluminium, turbidity and possibly PAH. But for the drought conditions it is likely that a further reduction in the number of zones not complying with the iron standard would have been observed.

4.22 There is no health risk from these contraventions of the iron standard, but the effects upon the appearance and taste of the water are well known and a cause for concern. Nearly all the contraventions are being remedied through undertakings to carry out improvements in the distribution system or at treatment works. Further details of these undertakings are given in Chapter 5 of this report.

Manganese

4.23 The steady decrease in the number of zones not complying with the standard for manganese since 1991 has been reversed in 1995 with an increase of 16%. This is most likely a consequence of the drought conditions as explained in the commentary on iron in 4.21 above, and it is to be expected that the downward trend will resume in 1996.

Lead

4.24 There has been a significant decrease since 1991 in the number of zones not complying with the lead standard. This largely reflects the modifications to treatment processes which companies have carried out at some water treatment works under the terms of their undertakings in respect of lead. Some of these schemes were completed in earlier years but most were completed during 1995, and compliance data for the year 1996 should demonstrate the full effect of these improvements.

4.25 In considering contraventions of the lead standard, it is particularly important to bear in mind that the nature and condition of the pipework at sampling locations will greatly influence the outcome. A zone which is at first sight non-compliant with the lead standard is not necessarily so because the water is generally plumbosolvent. It is certainly not because the water entering supply itself contains significant concentrations of lead. Rather, a highly localised problem with pipework may have given rise to the contravention.

Odour

4.26 The number of zones not complying with the standard for odour rose from 18 in 1994 to 23 in 1995. This increase is not statistically significant but could be attributable to the growth of algae in impoundment reservoirs and the need to abstract from severely depleted reservoir stocks during the drought.

Polycyclic aromatic hydrocarbons

4.27 The number of zones not complying with the standard for PAH has risen steadily from 176 zones in 1991 to 313 in 1995, an increase of 78%. The increase in earlier years may in part have been due to improvements over the years in analytical systems; reliable detection and quantification of the six individual substances at the very low concentrations of regulatory interest is a particularly exacting task. The factors affecting leaching of PAH from coal tar linings on the internal surfaces of water mains are not yet fully understood but it is likely that disturbance and cleaning of the distribution mains can expose the old coal tar linings which are the source of PAH and give rise to breaches of the standard. The short term remedial measures taken by water companies to alleviate acute water quality problems such as discolouration associated with deposits in water mains may give rise to contraventions of the PAH standard.

4.28 PAH is derived from the distribution system and contravention of the standard in a zone does not mean that the entire supply in that zone is non-compliant - only a highly localised part of the zone which the randomised compliance sampling programme has chanced upon for the first time may be of concern. As the coverage achieved by the sampling programme increases over the years, so may the number of zones in which contraventions are found even though the underlying water quality position has not significantly changed. The distribution undertakings described in Chapter 5 require companies to take account of non-trivial contraventions of the PAH standard when assessing priorities for mains renovation.

4.29 Although these contraventions are of concern because the water cannot be regarded as wholesome according to the definition of regulation 3, detailed examination of the results shows that, in nearly all cases, the contravention of the standard has been caused by only one of the six substances - fluoranthene - being present at concentrations significantly in excess of the combined concentrations of the other five. The concentrations of fluoranthene and the other five PAH were very substantially lower than those known to be harmful.

Pesticides

4.30 Overall, 32 pesticides were reported during 1995 as detected at concentrations above the PCV of 0.1 µg/l in compliance samples. In every instance, the concentrations corresponded to exposures many times (sometimes millions) lower than those known to be harmful or likely to affect health. For 24 of the 32, health-based recommendations on maximum advisable concentrations or exposures have been issued variously by the World Health Organisation (WHO), the UK Scientific Committee on Pesticides, and the US Environmental Protection Agency (USEPA). In all but three cases, trichloroacetic acid (TCA), chlorotoluron and DDT and metabolites, the highest reported concentrations and corresponding exposures were within the ranges considered acceptable by these authorities.

4.31 TCA was detected at concentrations up to 190 µg/l, which is greater than the WHO provisional Guideline Value (GV) of 100 µg/l, but lower than the concentration of 300 µg/l deemed by the USEPA to be protective of adverse human health effects and with an adequate margin of safety. Although TCA is a pesticide, its presence in drinking water usually results from its incidental formation during disinfection by chlorination.

4.32 Chlorotoluron was detected on one occasion at a concentration of 70µg/l, which is greater than the WHO GV of 30µg/l which assumes lifetime exposure, but over four thousand times lower than the dose producing no effects in the study on which the WHO GV was based, in which mice were dosed with chlorotoluron for two years. The detection of 70µg/l was an exceptional occurrence and a resample taken shortly afterwards showed a concentration close to the PCV, confirming that the contamination was transient.

4.33 Five isomers and metabolites of DDT, individually were detected on one occasion at concentrations of 6.6µg/l and as a total of 12.2µg/l. These are greater than the WHO GV of 2µg/l for DDT (total isomers), which assumes a lifetime of exposure, but 50 to 100 times lower than the WHO Acceptable Daily Intake of 0.02mg/kg, which for a 60kg adult equates to a daily intake of 1.2mg. A resample taken shortly afterwards did not detect any DDT or metabolites and laboratory contamination is suspected.

4.34 Comparing 1995 with the previous years, there have been further significant reductions in the numbers of zones not complying with the pesticides standards. These reductions most probably reflect the completion or partial commissioning of more of the improvement programmes in which companies are engaged to deal with pesticides although changes in pesticide usage may also be reflected in some of these reductions. Table 4.3 shows that 7,161 (97.4%) of the 7,351 tests which demonstrated contravention of the standard in 1994 were in the 705 zones covered by legally enforceable undertakings, and that new enforcement action is under consideration in respect of contraventions in a further eight zones.

Nitrite

4.35 The decrease over five years in the number of zones not complying with the nitrite standard has been smaller than for all other key parameters except PAH. Indeed, there was one more zone non-compliant in 1995 than in 1994 although this small increase is not statistically significant. Many of the determinations - 1,289 of 1,705 - showing contravention in 1995 were covered by undertakings which apply to 224 zones and were for the most part due for completion by the end of 1995. However a total of 66 zones were covered by undertakings which expired at the end of 1994 and although the companies had taken all the required steps it is apparent that contraventions of the nitrite standard were still occurring in those zones in 1995 albeit in reduced numbers.

4.36 Nitrite is formed as a consequence of the oxidation of ammonia used to convert residual free chlorine into chloramine after disinfection, a process called chloramination which is used by companies with long distribution systems to provide a more stable chlorine residual. This process is also effective at minimising the production of THM and avoids the need for relatively high concentrations of free chlorine which may be unacceptable to consumers. If companies were to have to abandon chloramination and revert to the use of free chlorine it is likely that this would give rise to a number of water quality problems, including chlorinous taste, and be unacceptable to consumers.

4.37 The Inspectorate commissioned a report from WRc on Nitrite in Drinking Water with a view to identifying what additional steps could be taken by water companies to ensure compliance with the standard for nitrite and this report was circulated to water companies in May 1996. Enforcement action is being initiated for non-trivial contraventions of the nitrite standard in 55 zones not covered by a current undertaking, some of which have been the subject of remedial works which have not been completely effective. In considering any undertakings submitted by companies the Inspectorate will require them to have regard to the conclusions and recommendations of the WRc report

Other parameters

4.38 In 1995, all zones complied with the regulations in respect of 25 of the 55 parameters with prescribed concentrations or values. Another five parameters contravened regulation 3(3)(d) in only a single zone. The regulations were contravened for 10 other parameters in fewer than 12 (0.5% of the total) zones. These contraventions are shown in the tables in the individual company sections in Chapter 3. Each contravention has been examined by the Inspectorate and no enforcement action is being considered in relation to contraventions of the standards for any other than key parameters.

Overall compliance with standards in water supply zones

4.39 Compliance with every one of the 55 standards to be met in each of the water supply zones does not necessarily require every one of the 2.5 million tests carried out annually to give results below the numerical standard because compliance for a few parameters (notably coliforms and trihalomethanes) is assessed on a percentage or an average basis of all results. So a position may be reached where every zone complies but, because of the way compliance is assessed, a very small percentage of the total of all the tests carried out may legitimately show the numerical standard to have been breached.

4.40 The overall position in respect of zone compliance in 1995 is represented in Figure 4.4. Seventeen of the 18 radii represent the percentage of zones complying with the standard for one of the 17 key parameters and the 18th represents the percentage of zones complying with all the other standards. The percentages run linearly from zero at the circumference to 100% at the centre. Ideally, all 18 points should coincide at the centre. Comparison of the analogous Figures 4.5, 4.6 and 4.7, drawn on identical scales, for 1994, 1993 and 1992 shows the improvements which have already been made towards that ideal.

Fig 4.1 Water treatment works not complying with standards

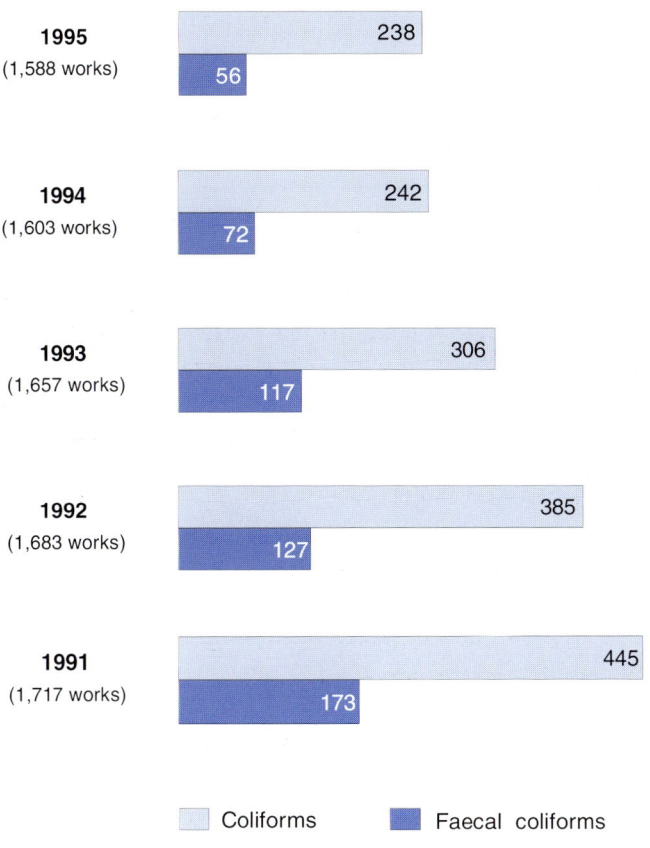

1995
(1,588 works)
238
56

1994
(1,603 works)
242
72

1993
(1,657 works)
306
117

1992
(1,683 works)
385
127

1991
(1,717 works)
445
173

☐ Coliforms   ■ Faecal coliforms

Fig 4.2 Service reservoirs not complying with present standards

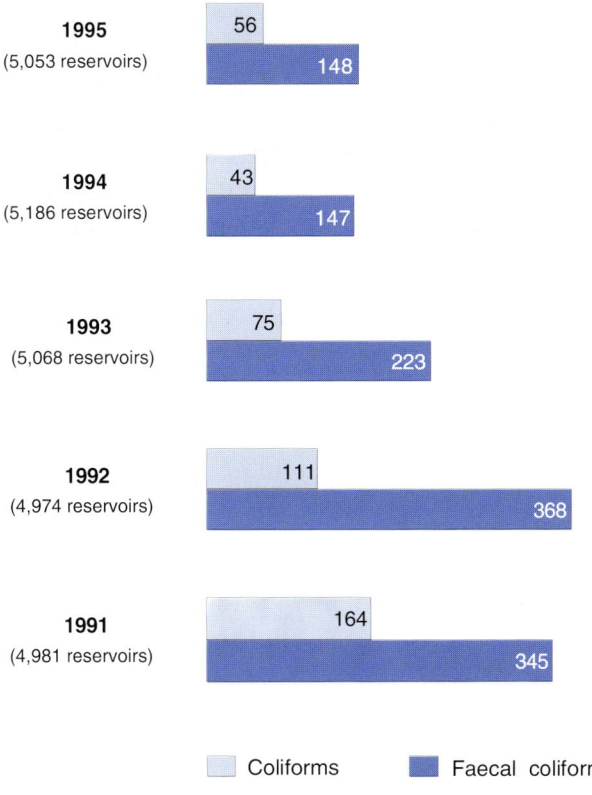

1995
(5,053 reservoirs)
56
148

1994
(5,186 reservoirs)
43
147

1993
(5,068 reservoirs)
75
223

1992
(4,974 reservoirs)
111
368

1991
(4,981 reservoirs)
164
345

☐ Coliforms   ■ Faecal coliforms

Fig 4.3 Water supply zones complying with standards

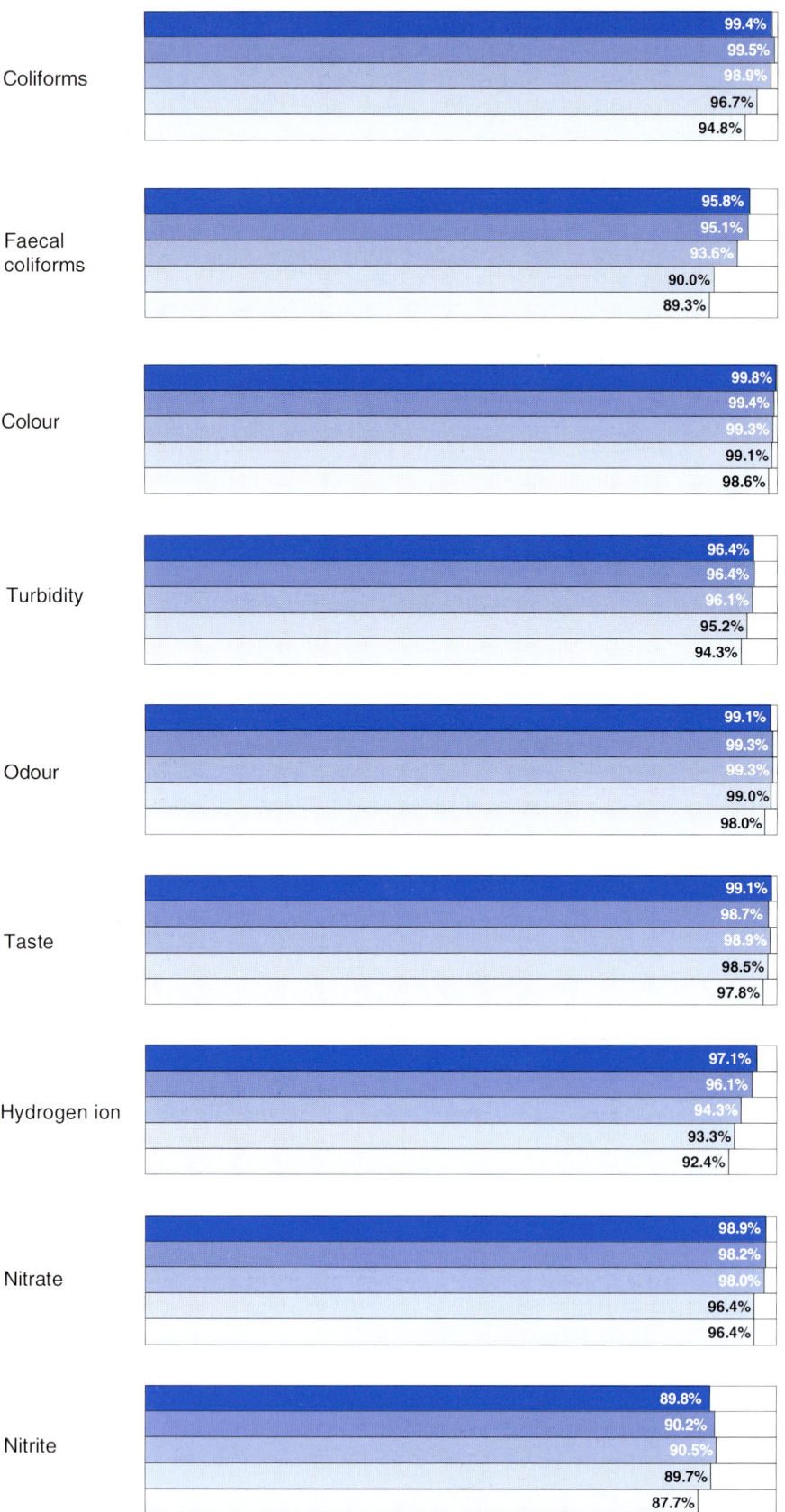

Coliforms	
	99.4%
	99.5%
	98.9%
	96.7%
	94.8%

Faecal coliforms	
	95.8%
	95.1%
	93.6%
	90.0%
	89.3%

Colour	
	99.8%
	99.4%
	99.3%
	99.1%
	98.6%

Turbidity	
	96.4%
	96.4%
	96.1%
	95.2%
	94.3%

Odour	
	99.1%
	99.3%
	99.3%
	99.0%
	98.0%

Taste	
	99.1%
	98.7%
	98.9%
	98.5%
	97.8%

Hydrogen ion	
	97.1%
	96.1%
	94.3%
	93.3%
	92.4%

Nitrate	
	98.9%
	98.2%
	98.0%
	96.4%
	96.4%

Nitrite	
	89.8%
	90.2%
	90.5%
	89.7%
	87.7%

Fig 4.3 (continued)

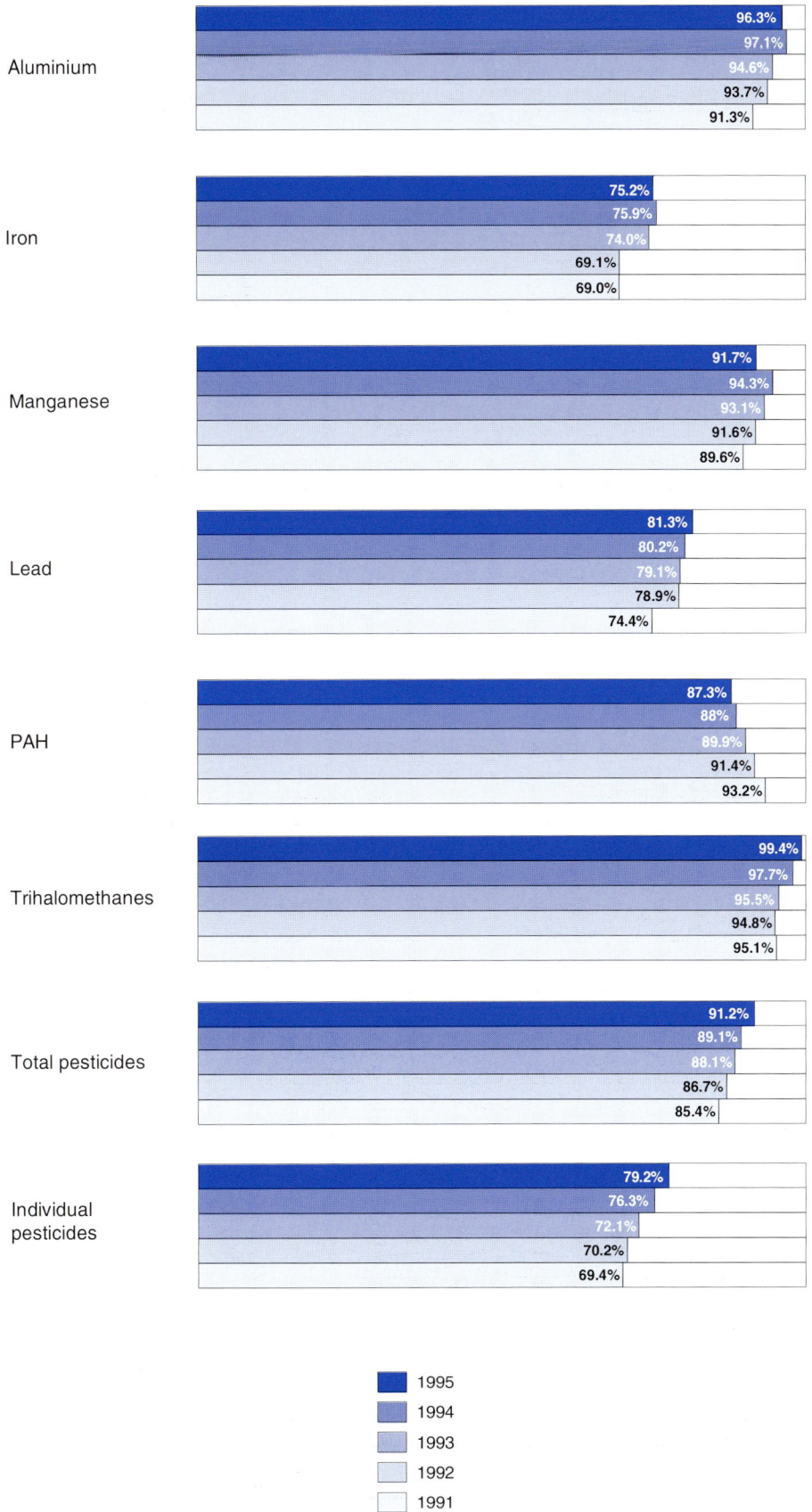

	1995
	1994
	1993
	1992
	1991

Fig 4.4 Water supply zones complying with standards

PERCENTAGES IN 1995 (see paragraph 4.40)

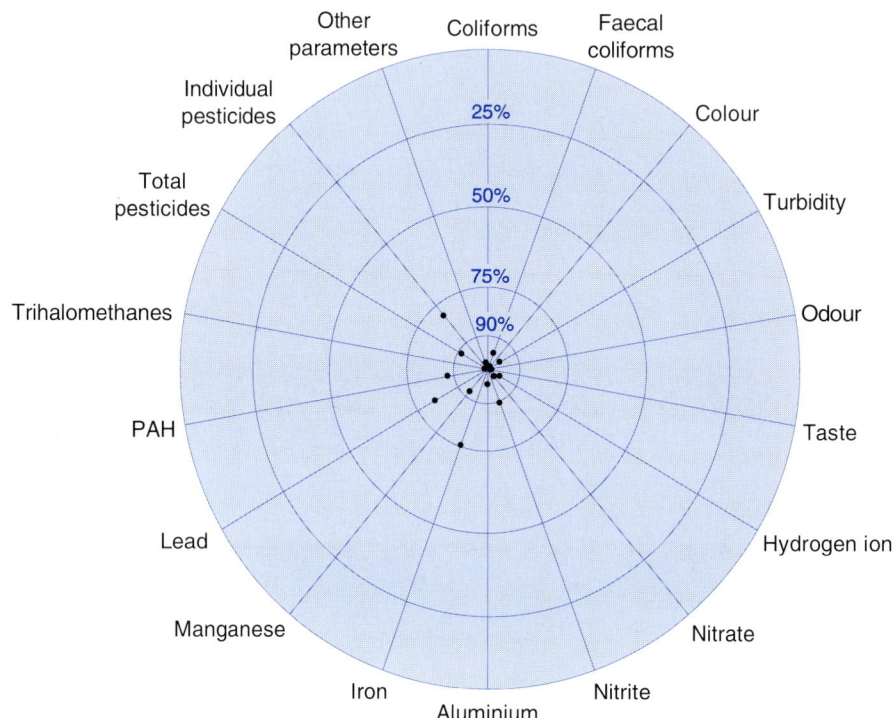

Fig 4.5 Water supply zones complying with standards

PERCENTAGES IN 1994 (see paragraph 4.40)

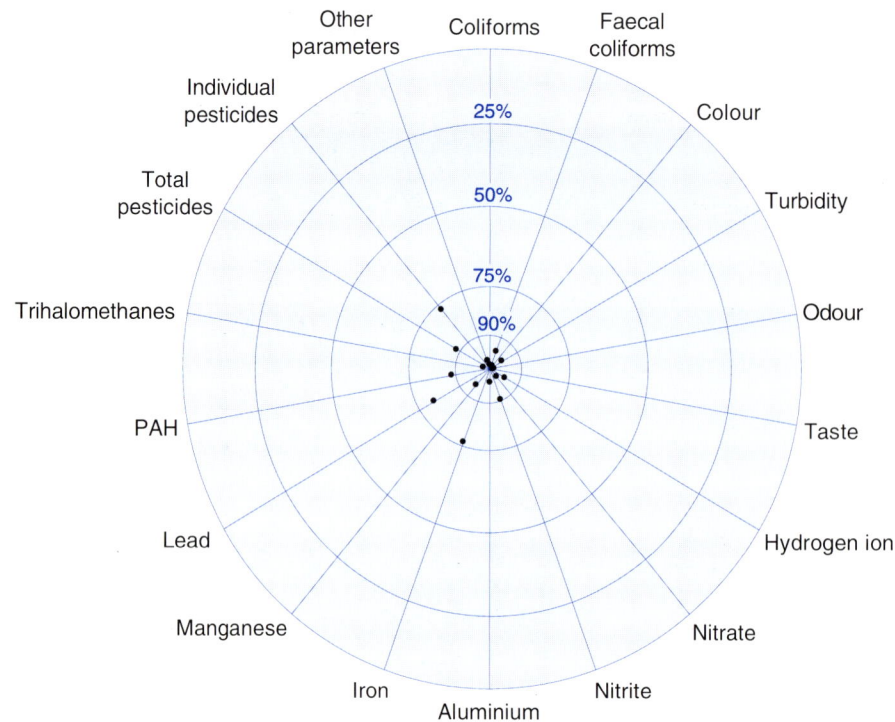

Fig 4.6 Water supply zones complying with standards

PERCENTAGES IN 1993 (see paragraph 4.40)

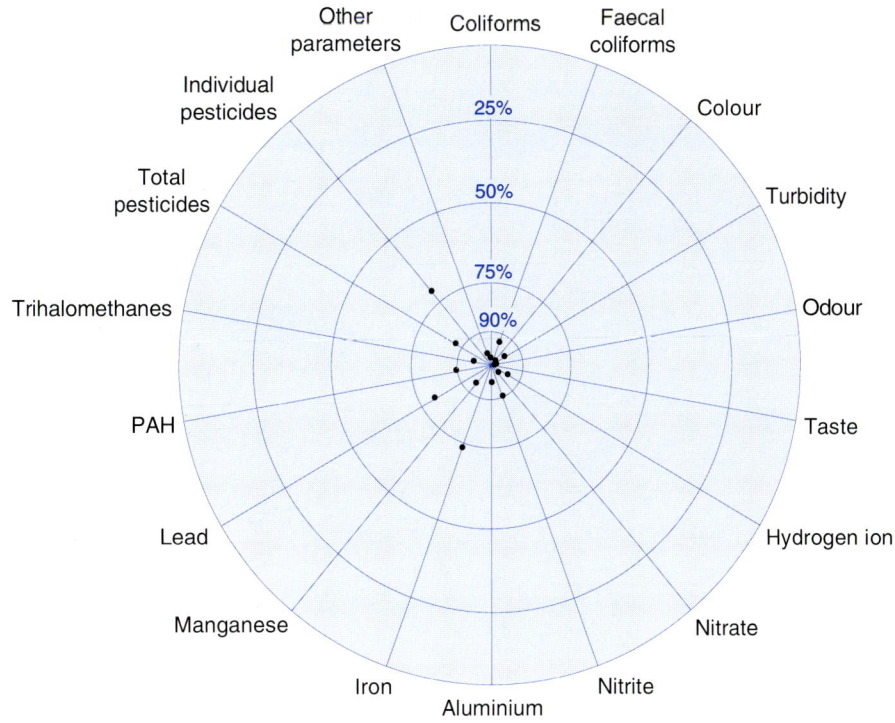

Fig 4.7 Water supply zones complying with standards

PERCENTAGES IN 1992 (see paragraph 4.40)

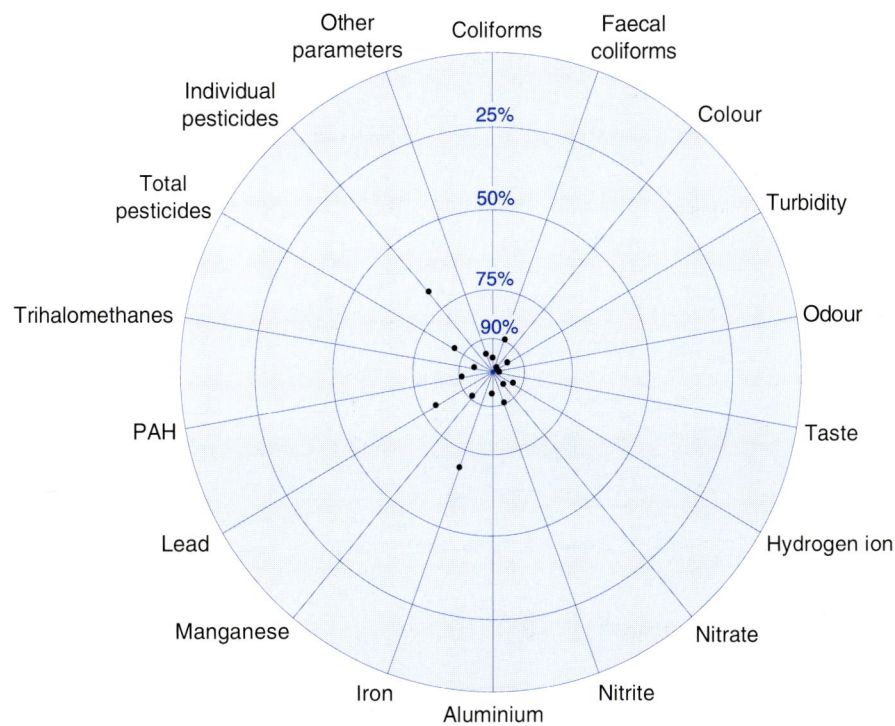

Chapter 5 Improvement Programmes and Enforcement Action

Improvement programmes

5.1 Programmes of remedial action by water companies are in progress to improve drinking water quality where necessary. Many programmes are associated with undertakings given under section 20 of the Water Act 1989 Act (since consolidated into section 19 of the Water Industry Act 1991) to carry out improvements to deal with breaches of the water quality standards by a specified date. Other programmes are associated with the relaxation of standards authorised by the Secretary of State under regulation 4(1)(c).

5.2 Many undertakings were given shortly after the commencement of the new regulatory framework in 1989. Others have been given since then by the majority of companies as a result of consideration of enforcement action arising from technical audit or assessment of drinking water quality incidents by the Inspectorate. Illustration of this process is given in the paragraphs below.

5.3 During the inspection of companies and periodically throughout the year the Inspectorate has made an assessment of the progress with each scheme to check that it is on target to meet the dates specified in the undertaking or the conditions of relaxations. A summary for each company of general progress with all its improvement programmes extant in 1995 is given in the individual company sections in Chapter 3. A total of 209 individual schemes was due either for full completion or completion of intermediate steps during 1995. Three schemes were associated with relaxations authorised under regulation 4 and the rest with undertakings. Of these schemes, 174 (83%) were completed on or ahead of time. Of the 35 schemes delayed two were associated with relaxations. These two were completed behind schedule for reasons associated with the drought. Assurances were accepted from the Company concerned that the schemes would be completed early in 1996 and this has been done.

5.4 The remaining 33 delayed schemes were associated with undertakings. Delays in completing 15 schemes were for reasons beyond the control of the companies concerned.

5.5 For 13 schemes the Inspectorate considered the issue of Notices of Intention to make a Final Enforcement Order but the Companies concerned subsequently completed the necessary works and it was not necessary to issue the Notices.

5.6 For five schemes the Inspectorate issued Notices of Intention to make a Final Enforcement Order. In four cases the Companies concerned took appropriate action to complete the remedial works within the period of the Notices and Orders were not required. In the fifth case an Order is to be issued after the expiry of the necessary period for representations or objections to be made. (Additional investigations had to be made by the Inspectorate before issuing the Notice of Intention to make a Final Enforcement Order in this case.)

Distribution system undertakings

5.7 The Inspectorate has accepted or is in the process of accepting new undertakings from 25 companies to take further steps to improve their distribution systems for water quality driven requirements, including securing and facilitating compliance with the standards for iron, manganese, PAH and other relevant parameters. These undertakings deal with the next tranche of priority distribution work up to 31 March 2000.

5.8 To facilitate this process the Inspectorate advised water companies in DWI Information Letter 5/95 of the procedures for the monitoring of these undertakings, the requirements for the provision of information to the Inspectorate and the reporting timetable. Following discussions individually with all the companies offering distribution system undertakings and with the industry collectively, through the Water Services Association and Water Companies' Association, further details and clarification of requirements were set out in DWI Information Letter 4/96. The three main areas covered by this letter were the programme for monitoring and reporting, the methods for pre- and post-renovation assessment, and the information to be recorded and reported to the Inspectorate.

5.9 To assist with distribution system issues, the Inspectorate let two consultancies. Warren Associates (Pipelines) Limited reported on procedures which could be adopted to determine the on-going appropriateness of distribution system undertakings, and assessment of progress and benefits to consumers arising from the steps taken to discharge the obligations in the undertaking. Mr Colin Evins, Consultant, was appointed to provide the Inspectorate with expert advice and assistance on distribution system matters, and, in particular, on issues relating to water company proposals for pre- and post-renovation assessment.

Enforcement action - its significance

5.10 As explained in greater detail in Chapter 1 of this Report, the duty of water undertakers to supply wholesome water and the provisions of Parts IV to VII of the Regulations are enforceable under section 18 of the Water Industry Act 1991 by the Secretary of State, who is required to take enforcement action in respect of contraventions unless he is satisfied that a contravention is trivial, is unlikely to recur, or that the company has already given an undertaking to take steps to secure or facilitate compliance with the requirements.

5.11 Consideration of enforcement action against a water company is thus the first step in a legal process which could potentially reach a court of law unless the company either demonstrates that the contravention is unlikely to recur - usually by reference to remedial work - or submits a legally enforceable undertaking which is acceptable to the Secretary of State. In many cases, the notification that enforcement action is under consideration can be withdrawn following demonstration by the company that remedial action has been taken. In other cases, undertakings to carry out improvements are promptly submitted to the Secretary of State. Where a Company does not fulfil its obligations under an undertaking, or an undertaking is no longer appropriate, the duty to take enforcement action arises again. In such circumstances it may be necessary to move to a provisional or final enforcement order.

Enforcement action in 1994 - an update

5.12 Chapter 5 of "Drinking Water 1994" contained tables summarising the enforcement action under consideration by the Inspectorate as a result of the 1994 technical audit of companies. The following paragraphs and tables show the outcome of those considerations.

5.13 Table 5.1 summarises the position, as at May 1996, of enforcement action considered as a result of the 1994 technical audit in respect of contraventions of water quality standards in water supply zones. Of the 17 key parameters which have been considered in Chapters 3 and 4 of this Report, enforcement was considered for 1994 in respect of 11 - no enforcement action was necessary in respect of the parameters for colour, odour (quantitative), aluminium, iron, lead and total pesticides. The table shows, for each parameter, the number of zones for which companies either completed satisfactory remedial action or gave assurances acceptable to the Secretary of State that breaches would not recur, so that it became unnecessary for the Inspectorate to progress the enforcement action under consideration for the zones concerned. Where satisfactory remedial action or assurances were not immediately forthcoming for some or all of the zones in respect of which enforcement action was considered, companies have submitted undertakings for consideration by the Secretary of State.

5.14 Table 5.2 gives a corresponding summary in respect of breaches in 1994 of regulation 3(7). Table 5.3 summarises the position in respect of the breaches of other enforceable regulations.

Table 5.1 ENFORCEMENT ACTION 1994 IN RESPECT OF BREACHES OF REGULATION 3(3)
relating to water quality in water supply zones

Zones with:

column II: enforcement action considered;

column III: satisfactory remedial action or assurances;

column IV: undertakings submitted.

Parameter	II	III	IV
Coliforms	[a]4	4	0
Faecal coliforms	[a]3	3	0
Turbidity	[a]3	0	3
Taste	6	6	0
Hydrogen ion	22	2	20
Nitrate	1	0	1
Nitrite	[a]8	1	7
Manganese	1	0	1
PAH	41	0	41
Trihalomethanes	5	1	4
Individual pesticides	5	0	5
Benzo-3,4-Pyrene	1	0	1
Phosphorus	1	1	0

[a] Corrected from "Drinking Water 1994"

Table 5.2 ENFORCEMENT ACTION 1994 IN RESPECT OF BREACHES OF REGULATION 3(7)
relating to water quality in service reservoirs and of water leaving treatment works

Number of treatment works/service reservoirs with:

column II: enforcement action considered;

column III: satisfactory remedial action or assurances;

column IV: undertakings submitted.

Parameter	II	III	IV
Water treatment works			
Coliforms	15	5	10
Faecal coliforms	4	1	3
Service reservoirs			
Coliforms	(a)9	4	5
Faecal coliforms	12	4	8

(a) Corrected from "Drinking Water 1994"

Table 5.3 ENFORCEMENT ACTION 1994 IN RESPECT OF BREACHES OF OTHER ENFORCEABLE REGULATIONS

Columns II to IV show the number of companies in the following categories:

column II: companies for which enforcement action was under consideration;

column III: companies which completed satisfactory remedial action or which have given assurances that the breach will not recur;

column IV: companies which have submitted undertakings.

Regulation	II	III	IV
10 - general provisions for monitoring	1	1	0
11 - sampling points	1	1	0
13 - sampling - zones	3	3	0
17 - sampling works	1	1	0
18 - sampling - service reservoirs	2	2	0
21(2)(a)- representative sample	1	1	0
21(2)(c) - sample integrity	2	2	0
21(2)(d) - analysis "as soon as maybe"	1	1	0
21(2)(d)(i) - analytical supervision	1	1	0
21(2)(d)(ii) - analytical equipment	1	1	0
21(2)(d)(iii) - analytical systems	5	5	0
29 - Public Record	2	2	0
30 - provision of information	2	2	0

Enforcement action in 1995

5.15 Tables 5.4, 5.5 and 5.6 show the enforcement actions considered as a result of the 1995 technical audit of water companies or as a result of the completion in 1995 of the assessments of water quality incidents. More details of any enforcement action under consideration for a particular company, and a tabulated summary of the separate instances of breaches of regulations giving cause for the enforcement, can be found in the relevant section of Chapter 3.

Table 5.4 ENFORCEMENT ACTION, 1991 - 1995, IN RESPECT OF BREACHES OF REGULATION 3(3)
relating to water quality in water supply zones

Parameter	Zones with enforcement action considered in:				
	1995	1994	1993	1992	1991
Coliforms	10	[a]4	11	28	48
Faecal coliforms	3	[a]3	10	11	17
Colour	1	0	1	0	0
Turbidity	5	[a]3	1	0	1
Odour	0	0	1	1	9
Taste	1	6	3	6	5
Hydrogen ion	2	22	26	27	35
Nitrate	0	1	0	2	3
Nitrite	55	[a]8	7	7	7
Aluminium	0	0	11	3	5
Iron	4	0	3	6	1
Manganese	3	1	1	2	1
Lead	3	0	3	3	0
PAH	2	41	69	65	47
Trihalomethanes	0	5	24	45	18
Total pesticides	0	0	3	7	0
Individual pesticides	7	5	35	7	19
Ammonium	0	0	1	0	4
Phosphorus	0	1	1	0	0
Barium	0	0	0	1	0
Benzo 3,4 pyrene	0	1	0	1	3
Tetrachloromethane	0	0	0	1	0
Total items	**96**	**[a]101**	**[a]211**	**[a]223**	**223**

[a] Corrected from "Drinking Water 1994".
Colour enforcement action arose through assessment of an incident from 1994 - not compliance assessment in 1995.
Enforcement action for lead arose through reassessment of lead results from 1994 and 1993.

Table 5.5 ENFORCEMENT ACTION 1991 - 1995 IN RESPECT OF BREACHES OF REGULATION 3(7)
relating to quality of water leaving treatment works and in service reservoirs

Parameter	Enforcement considered in:				
	1995	1994	1993	1992	1991
<u>Water treatment works</u>					
Coliforms	10	15	43	98	63
Faecal coliforms	1	4	16	34	25
<u>Service reservoirs</u>					
Coliforms	17	[a]9	18	26	51
Faecal coliforms	11	12	24	42	45

[a] Corrected from "Drinking Water 1994".

Table 5.6 ENFORCEMENT ACTION 1991 - 1995 IN RESPECT OF BREACHES OF OTHER ENFORCEABLE REGULATIONS

Regulation	Number of companies for which enforcement considered in:				
	1995	1994	1993	1992	1991
10 - general provisions for monitoring	1	1	0	0	0
11 - sampling points	0	1	0	0	1
13 - sampling - zones	1	3	5	9	3
17 - sampling - works	1	1	0	1	4
18 - sampling - service reservoirs	0	2	1	2	4
21(2)(a) - representative sample	1	1	0	0	4
21(2)(c) - sample integrity	0	2	0	2	0
21(2)(d) - analysis 'as soon as may be'	1	1	0	0	0
21(2)(d)(i) - analytical supervision	0	1	1	0	0
21(2)(d)(ii) - analytical equipment	0	1	0	1	0
21(2)(d)(iii) - analytical systems	2	5	1	17	8
23 - treatment processes	0	0	0	4	2
29 - Public Record	0	2	2	9	(a)
30 - provision of information	2	2	5	4	(a)
Water Undertakers (Information) Direction 1992. Paragraph 5 'failure to notify'	2	-	-	-	-

Note (a): This regulation became enforceable only from September 1991.

Comparison of enforcement action, 1991-1995

5.16 The circumstances in which enforcement action has to be considered are described above in paragraph 5.10. For the most part, those circumstances, and the means whereby the Inspectorate identifies them, have not changed since the commencement of the current regulatory arrangements with the coming into force of the major part of the Regulations in September 1989. It is instructive to compare the extent of enforcement action considered for companies in each of the previous five years. A full discussion of the scope and limitations of such comparison was given in Chapter 6 of "Drinking Water 1992".

5.17 There was a drop in 1995 in the number of items of enforcement in respect of breaches of regulation 3(3). This reflects the continuing improvement in the already high compliance of zones with the water quality standards which is shown overall in Chapter 4. The number of items of enforcement in respect of breaches of regulation 3(7) has remained about the same. However, contraventions of other regulations has generated fewer items of enforcement action in 1995 than in previous years.

Chapter 6   Drinking Water Quality Incidents

> **KEY POINTS:**
>
> - **guidance on notification of incidents;**
>
> - **83 incidents, potentially affecting approximately 2.3 million consumers, notified in 1995;**
>
> - **enforcement action considered for 3 companies as a result of completion of assessments of incidents occurring in 1995;**
>
> - **only a very few incidents in which water unfit for human consumption may have been supplied;**
>
> - **in most of these, there were no grounds for prosecution; and**
>
> - **prosecution proceedings instigated against one company.**

Introduction

6.1 The Water Undertakers (Information) Direction 1992 (the "Information Direction" hereafter) requires companies to notify the Secretary of State of:

- the occurrence of any event which, by reason of its effect or likely effect on the quality or sufficiency of water supplied by it gives rise or is likely to give rise to a significant risk to the health of persons to whom the water is supplied.

The Information Direction also requires companies to notify the Secretary of State of any other matter relating to the supply of water which:

- in the opinion of the company, is of national significance; or

- which has attracted or, in the opinion of the company, is likely to attract significant local or national publicity; or

- which has caused or is likely to cause significant concern to consumers.

6.2 The Information Direction requires the company to notify the Inspectorate as soon as possible by telephone or other appropriate means. Within 72 hours, the company must provide an initial report in writing which gives details of the incident and the action the company has taken or proposes to take. A full report must be submitted within one month, a period which can be extended if the company's investigations are not complete.

Action by water companies

6.3 Advice to companies is given in "Guidance on Safeguarding the Quality of Public Water Supplies" on the action to be taken if a drinking water quality standard is infringed. If a significant water quality failure occurs, companies should presume that there is a potential risk to public health and immediately obtain expert advice. Companies should also:

(a) take all reasonable steps to rectify the situation and get supplies back to normal as soon as possible;

(b) take appropriate action to protect consumers, which may include switching to alternative temporary supplies, providing water by tanker, issuing advice to consumers to boil water for drinking and cooking and providing information to the local media;

(c)   notify relevant officers of the local authorities and district health authorities, as required by regulation 30(5), and consult them with regard to the steps to be taken;

(d)   carry out increased operational monitoring of the water supplied; and

(e)   consider whether an application should be made for an emergency relaxation under regulation 4(1)(a).

Rôle of Inspectorate

6.4 When notified of an event under the terms of the Information Direction, the Inspectorate checks that the company has taken appropriate action to minimise any risk to public health. It assesses the company's final report and advises the Secretary of State on the following matters as relevant:

(a)   the thoroughness of the investigation carried out by the company, the promptness and adequacy of the steps taken to inform and protect consumers, the adequacy of the liaison with local authorities and health authorities and compliance with the Direction;

(b)   whether a contravention of a standard or other requirement of the Regulations occurred and, if so, whether it should be regarded as trivial or unlikely to recur;

(c)   if such a contravention was not trivial or is likely to recur, whether enforcement action should be considered under Section 18 of the Act or whether a relaxation of a standard should be authorised under regulation 4;

(d)   exceptionally, whether the circumstances of the use of a substance or product not approved for use under the provisions of regulation 25, or the use of a process prohibited by the Secretary of State under the provisions of regulation 26, were such that the Secretary of State needs to consider whether a prosecution under regulation 28 should be initiated; and

(e)   whether water unfit for human consumption was supplied and, if so, about the circumstances so that the Secretary of State can consider whether a prosecution under Section 70 of the Act should be initiated.

Guidance on notification

6.5 DWI Information Letter 2/94, issued on 9 May 1994, provides further guidance on implementation of paragraph 5(1) of the Information Direction. Information Letter 3/94, also issued on 9 May 1994, sets out, in the form of check lists, the information which is likely to be required by the Inspectorate when receiving initial notifications and final reports. As reported last year many companies re-evaluated their interpretation of the reporting requirements and now assiduously follow this guidance. The Inspectorate commended these companies even though it has resulted in an increased number of notifications. A number of Companies do not appear to have amended their interpretation of the reporting requirements and the Inspectorate will be examining more closely their reporting procedures.

Terminology

6.6 DWI Information Letter 2/94 pointed out that whereas notifications to the Inspectorate under the Information Direction had been collectively referred to by the Inspectorate as "Incidents" it had become apparent that the word "incident" popularly had overtones of real emergencies in which water supplies were significantly affected. Not all events or matters which are required to be notified are actually of that nature. Therefore, and without prejudice to the fundamental requirements of notification, the Inspectorate has reserved the term "incident" for an event or sequence of events as a result of which the quality of water entering or in public supply has demonstrably deteriorated or in which - regardless of actual effect on water quality - the disinfection of water supplies was compromised. Other events which threatened - but did not have - such results are referred to simply as events. This Report describes and discusses incidents in the light of this terminology.

Incidents in 1995

6.7 Eighty-three incidents affecting the quality of water supplied to approximately 2.3 million consumers were notified to the Inspectorate in 1995. The period during which water quality was actually or potentially compromised, ranged from a few hours to several days. The main categories of these incidents were:

- disinfection failures (12 incidents);

- microbiological contamination of water discovered in, or traced to, service reservoirs (8 incidents);

- microbiological contamination of water in distribution systems, probably not implicating service reservoirs (13 incidents);

- contamination occurring after mains bursts or during repairs or other associated work on mains including rezoning (21 incidents);

- detection of *Cryptosporidium* in water supplies (3 incidents);

- backflow into water mains (3 incidents);

- advisory concentration for pesticide exceeded (2 incidents);

- chemical contamination associated with treatment works (11 incidents) or water sources (4 incidents); and

- others (6 incidents).

In addition to these 83 incidents, a further 74 events were notified.

6.8 Fifty-six of the incidents involved potential or actual microbiological contamination of water supplies. In most of these cases, the companies involved, usually after consultation with local authorities and district health authorities, issued advice to consumers to boil water for drinking and food preparation while action was being taken to remedy the problem.

6.9 A short description of each of these incidents is given in the relevant individual company sections in Chapter 3 of this Report.

Assessment of incidents

6.10 The Inspectorate carries out a full assessment of each incident, often involving protracted consultations with other organisations and advisors. Each incident then requires careful and consistent reporting. The Inspectorate has a target for completion of the assessment of incidents of three months from the receipt of the final report from the company. Progress has continued to be made in addressing the backlog. At 1 May 1996, assessment had been completed of all of the 88 incidents notified in 1990, of all of the 61 incidents notified in 1991, of 66 of the 67 incidents notified in 1992, of all of the 52 incidents notified in 1993, and of 72 of the 78 incidents notified in 1994. Assessment of 48 of the 83 incidents notified in 1995 had also been completed by 1 May 1996.

6.11 The Inspectorate's purpose in assessing incidents is to secure as far as possible that incidents are avoided in future, but also that any which do occur are handled effectively by the company to minimise and as swiftly as possible eliminate any risk to consumers. Accordingly, in nearly every case, the Inspectorate's assessment of incidents has resulted in suggestions or recommendations being addressed to the company. It must be recognized however that in not all cases was the cause of the event or incident necessarily within the control of the company.

The assessment includes a view on the way in which the company handled what may have been a totally unpredictable occurrence. In most cases, companies have been able to take appropriate steps immediately to prevent recurrence so consideration of enforcement action is not necessary.

6.12 Where assessment shows that an enforceable regulation has been breached, the Inspectorate considers whether the breach was trivial or unlikely to recur. If a need for enforcement action is found, the company is informed that enforcement action is under consideration. This is a first step in a legal process which secures remedial action in a timescale acceptable to the Secretary of State. As a result of 58 incident assessments completed in 1995, enforcement action is, or has been, under consideration for three companies in respect of breaches of regulations which occurred in three incidents.

6.13 All assessments consider whether water was supplied which was unfit for human consumption. In this consideration, the Inspectorate takes into account data on the quality of water supplied during the incident and information on whether any illness or discomfort arose amongst consumers as a result of ingestion of or contact with the water. Because water quality standards are generally set with a wide margin of safety, contravention of standards - and these do not occur in all incidents - does not necessarily mean that the water was unfit for human consumption. The Inspectorate takes expert advice as necessary in order to come to a conclusion on whether the extent of a contravention was such that the water was not fit to drink. In the majority of assessments so far completed, the conclusion has been easily reached that the incident's effect upon water quality was not such as to render the water unfit for human consumption.

6.14 In a very small number of incidents, the water may have been unfit for human consumption, either because its taste, odour or appearance was so bad that consumers would not drink it, or because it may have been detrimental to health. The Inspectorate, aided by its legal advisers, then considers whether there are grounds for recommending a prosecution under section 70 of the Act. This consideration takes into account the sufficiency of the evidence and also the availability of the defence for the company to show that it had no reasonable grounds for suspecting that the water would be used for human consumption, or that it took all reasonable steps and exercised all due diligence for securing that the water was fit for human consumption on leaving its pipes or was not used for human consumption. In one case, which occurred in 1994, the assessment was that water unfit had been supplied. A prosecution was brought in 1995 and the company pleaded guilty to the offence of supplying water unfit for human consumption. A report on this incident including the lessons to be learnt from it has been delayed but it is expected to be published by the Inspectorate later this year.

6.15 The outcome of the Inspectorate's assessment of incidents has generally been communicated in the form of a letter addressed to the company and copied to the relevant Customer Services Committee (CSC) of the Office of Water Services. Copies also go to the local authority or authorities for the area affected by the incident and to the relevant district health authority or authorities. For those incidents where the Inspectorate considers that there are general lessons to learnt a report is prepared for distribution to all water companies.

6.16 Mrs S Quennell, Consultant, was appointed to undertake a review of incidents from 1990 to February 1995. The objectives were to:

- categorise the type of incidents, causes and frequency of occurrence;

- carry out a critical appraisal of water companies' responses to incidents, including actions taken to protect and inform consumers, to communicate with health and local authorities and to prevent recurrence of incidents;

- assess the effectiveness of water companies' arrangements for responding to incidents and the actions taken to rectify and faults in the treatment/distribution system, identifying areas of weakness;

- identify those incidents which were outside the control of the company and those incidents which were avoidable;

- identify those regulations which are commonly breached;

- make recommendations appropriate to the findings from the above on any issues which warrant wider consideration;

- visit certain companies and assess the response to any recommendations arising from the Inspectorate's assessment of the incident; and

- produce a report to the Chief Inspector.

The Inspectorate will communicate the results of the review to water companies later this year.

Chapter 7 **Private Water Supplies**

Introduction

7.1 Private water supplies are defined in section 93 of the Water Industry Act 1991 as any supplies of water provided otherwise than by a statutorily appointed water undertaker. The regulatory framework covering private water supplies is described in Chapter 1 of this Report.

7.2 Data collected by the Department of the Environment and Welsh Office from local authorities in England and Wales show that there are about 50,000 private water supplies in England and Wales supplying about a third of a million people with water for domestic purposes. Approximately 30,000 of these supplies serve people in a single dwelling. However, many more people will consume private supplies used for food production purposes such as brewing or for supplying places such as hospitals, hotels, schools or campsites.

7.3 Although there are some private supplies in urban areas, particularly those used for industrial purposes, most private supplies are situated in the more remote rural parts of the country. The source of the supply may be a well, a borehole, a spring or a stream. The supply may serve just one property or several properties through a network of pipes. The circumstances of private water supplies are highly variable.

7.4 The Water Industry Act 1991 continues the long standing duty of local authorities to keep themselves informed of the sufficiency and wholesomeness of both public and private water supplies in their areas. The Private Water Supplies Regulations 1991 (PWS Regulations) made under the Act, which came into force on 1 January 1992, require local authorities to take samples and cause them to be analysed, in order to protect public health. The legislation is designed to enable local authorities to tailor their actions to the particular circumstances of individual supplies.

7.5 There is advice and guidance to local authorities and owners and users of private water supplies in the following documents: Circular 24/91 (Welsh Office 68/91) on the Private Water Supplies Regulations 1991; a Department of the Environment and Welsh Office leaflet - A guide to the laws controlling private water supplies; and the DWI Manual on the Treatment of Private Water Supplies (HMSO).

Regulation 19(2)(e)

7.6 The Private Water Supplies Regulations include a provision for checking the quality of analysis of samples taken from private water supplies. Regulation 19(2)(e) requires that any laboratory at which samples are analysed has a system of analytical quality control (AQC) that is subject from time to time to checking by a person who is:

(i)   not under the control of either the laboratory or local authority; and

(ii)   approved by the Secretary of State for that purpose.

In respect of this regulation, paragraph 22 of Appendix 7 in Circular 24/91 advises that, at present, the Drinking Water Inspectorate will be responsible for checking, or arranging to check, the AQC procedures in laboratories.

7.7 Since the PWS Regulations came into force the Inspectorate, or consultants acting on its behalf, have carried out inspections of 34 local authorities selected at random to obtain information on how the Regulations are being implemented. These inspections have included checks on the laboratories used by these local authorities except where the laboratories belong to water companies and are already subject to inspection under the Inspectorate's duties in respect of public water supplies. The conclusions from the inspection of a laboratory enable the Inspectorate to assess the extent to which local authorities using the laboratory are meeting the requirements of regulations 19(2)(c) and (d).

Questionnaire

7.8 In 1995 the Inspectorate decided that it should obtain wider information on the laboratories used by local authorities to enable it to consider how many further inspections of laboratories were necessary in respect of its duties under regulation 19(2)(e). To this end, a short questionnaire was sent to all 406 local authorities in England and Wales in May 1995. The questionnaire requested local authorities to give the names of laboratories used for the analysis of samples from private water supplies, an estimate of the approximate number of samples taken annually and information on regulation 21 which allows local authorities to enter into arrangements with a relevant person for the taking and analysis of samples or any other person for the analysis of samples.

7.9 331 local authorities responded to the questionnaire. The Inspectorate is grateful for their co-operation. 44 local authorities replied that they had not identified any private water supplies covered by the PWS Regulations within their area. 287 local authorities reported that they used 57 laboratories for non-microbiological analysis, including 19 water company laboratories, and 93 laboratories for microbiological analysis including 51 Public Health Laboratory Service (PHLS) laboratories and 17 water company laboratories. 33 laboratories undertook both types of analysis. The local authorities estimated that they submitted to these laboratories approximately 18,000 non-microbiological and 29,000 microbiological samples from private water supplies annually. 46 local authorities reported that they had one or more formal arrangements under regulation 21.

Laboratories selected for inspection

7.10 Out of the total of 117 laboratories, 46 had already been inspected by DWI. This included all the water company laboratories and 27 other laboratories during previous inspections of local authorities. Of the remaining 71 laboratories, many analysed only a very small number of samples from private water supplies. 18 laboratories were selected for inspection based either on the number of local authorities submitting samples or the total number of samples analysed. These laboratories carried out work in 1995 for 108 local authorities. The laboratories inspected were:

(1) Bangor PHLS laboratory

(2) Geoffrey Schofield Laboratory, Cumbria

(3) Lancashire County Analyst's Laboratory

(4) Leicester PHLS laboratory

(5) Lincoln PHLS Laboratory

(6) National Rivers Authority Laboratory, Nottingham

(7) Newcastle upon Tyne PHLS laboratory

(8) Pattinson Scientific Services, Newcastle upon Tyne

(9) Preston PHLS laboratory

(10) Associated Laboratory Services, Braintree

(11) Avon County Scientific Services

(12) Cardiff PHLS Laboratory

(13) Carmarthen PHLS Laboratory

(14) Herbert J Evans & Partners, Carmarthen

(15) Ipswich PHLS Laboratory

(16) Luton PHLS Laboratory

(17) Mid Glamorgan County Scientific Laboratory

(18) National Rivers Authority Laboratory, Llanelli.

It should be noted that the analysis of private water supplies represents only a small proportion of the work undertaken by each of these laboratories.

Inspections

7.11 The inspections were carried out between November 1995 and January 1996 by consultants acting on behalf of the Inspectorate under the direction of David Drury, Principal Inspector. Water Quality Management Limited inspected laboratories 1-9 and R M Walls, Consulting Scientist, inspected laboratories 10-18. The Inspectorate is grateful for the co-operation received from all the laboratories.

7.12 The inspection process included checks on the following:

(i) the arrangements for analysis and, where applicable, sub-contracting analysis;

(ii) the supervision and competence of laboratory staff;

(iii) the arrangements for sample storage;

(iv) the arrangements for determining the performance characteristics of analytical methods;

(v) the arrangements and detail for internal and external analytical quality control;

(vi) the arrangements for reporting results;

(vii) where relevant, the documented arrangements with local authorities and relevant persons; and

(viii) a detailed audit of the analytical systems for selected parameters.

A general overview of the results of the inspections is given in the following paragraphs. The identified deficiencies should not be allowed to detract from the good performance of most of the laboratories inspected but do highlight the need for independent audit of laboratories undertaking regulatory analysis.

Overview of the results of the inspections

7.13 With very few exceptions, the inspectors were able to conclude that the laboratories were carrying out analysis of samples from private water supplies competently and the majority of the laboratories met most of the very strict criteria necessary for the local authorities using them to meet the requirements of regulation 19(2)(d). However, in many cases local authorities would not be able to demonstrate this compliance because of a lack of contractual obligations and deficiencies in the laboratories' arrangements for reporting analytical results.

7.14 Nine of the laboratories had UKAS accreditation for the analytical systems used for private water supplies and a further four were in the process of applying for this accreditation. No laboratory had UKAS DWTS accreditation.

7.15 The Inspectors concluded that there was generally satisfactory liaison between the laboratories and local authorities. However, the arrangements were usually informal; few laboratories had written contracts with local authorities for the analysis of samples from private water supplies. Therefore, there was no written obligation in respect of carrying out analysis to a standard that would enable the local authorities to meet the requirements of regulation 19(2)(d) or on turn around time for analysis or the reporting of results. This does not mean that the analysis was unsatisfactory in such cases and some laboratories did have general policy documentation available but the Inspectors concluded that it is as an area of weakness in the arrangements. The Inspectorate's Information Sheet for local authorities, 1/1995, strongly recommended that local authorities should have written contracts with all laboratories carrying out analysis on their behalf.

7.16 The Inspectors were generally able to conclude that samples were analysed by, or under the supervision of, persons who were competent to perform the task although in one case Inspectors concluded that the laboratory lacked experience in the analysis of potable water samples. Most laboratories had training schemes for analytical staff and these were usually well documented. Where appropriate, most laboratories had adequate or good arrangements for non-microbiological sample storage and preparation although these procedures were not always well documented.

7.17 Policy on determining the performance characteristics of analytical systems varied widely. The best practices were generally found in laboratories handling large numbers of water samples. Not all performance testing followed the procedures recommended in Guidance on Safeguarding the Quality of Public Water Supplies (the Guidance). A small number of laboratories analysing a few samples considered the use of a documented standard method to be sufficient demonstration of performance. Inspectors found isolated instances of laboratories using methods from "Analysis of Raw, Potable and Waste Water (1972)" and the 1969 edition of Report 71, both of which have been out of date for many years.

7.18 All laboratories operated a system of internal AQC although one had suspended recording AQC results for non-microbiological parameters because of pressure of workload! Most laboratories used procedures similar to those recommended in the Guidance although not all compiled control charts or recorded any action taken when deviations occurred. All but two laboratories participated in independent external AQC schemes which are an essential check of a laboratory's analytical systems. Performance in these schemes was generally good although some laboratories lacked documented procedures to follow in the event of a flagged poor AQC result or failed to keep records of any investigations and there were isolated incidents of no action being taken in respect of analytical systems flagged as performing poorly.

7.19 Inspectors generally selected lead and nitrate for the detailed audit of non-microbiological parameters. Most laboratories were using methods from the Standing Committee of Analysts Blue Book series, usually atomic absorption spectrophotometry or ICP-MS for lead and ion chromatography, colorimetric spectrophotometry or direct absorbance in ultra-violet for nitrate. A number of systems had not been calibrated close to the PCV as recommended in the Guidance and two laboratories were not acidifying samples for lead before sub-division of samples which could affect the accuracy of the result. All analyses were accompanied by some AQC although not all to the level recommended in the Guidance.

7.20 Few problems were identified with microbiological analysis. All but three laboratories used the membrane filtration method for coliform analysis. One had changed from multiple tube to membrane filtration just prior to the inspection.

Methods generally followed those recommended in Report 71 although many laboratories had slight variations which had not been performance tested. All the PHLS laboratories and most other laboratories were aware of the new recommendations for coliform analysis in Report 71 (1994). However, two (non-PHLS) laboratories were still using gas production from lactose as a criterion for coliform identification and not all laboratories commenced coliform incubation within two hours of filtration. One point noted during the inspections was that only three laboratories undertaking analysis for faecal coliforms had incubation equipment capable of meeting the recommendation in Report 71 (1994) that incubation temperature should be 44°C± 0.25°C. Two of these laboratories used waterbaths. One laboratory had carried out tests to demonstrate that there was no difference in results when temperature tolerance was ±0.5°C. Not all laboratories met the recommended temperature tolerance for coliform incubation of 37°C±0.5°C. All these laboratories performed well in external AQC schemes.

7.21 There was wide variation in the quality of analytical reports provided for local authorities by the laboratories. In general, the advice in Information Sheet for local authorities, 1/1995, had not yet been taken on board. Only five laboratories included information on the method used for analysis, a few others stated that information was available on request. Information on the AQC accompanying analysis was absent from all reports although one referred to meeting the requirements of regulation 19 and one other that it was available on request. Few reports made reference to the PWS regulations. Not all flagged contraventions of PCVs, some referred to maximum admissible concentrations. Some reports of microbiological results did not differentiate between presumptive and confirmed coliforms. Almost every report scrutinised by the Inspectors had been signed by a senior designated member of laboratory staff. The average reporting times were three and nine days respectively for microbiological and non-microbiological parameters. However, there were several examples of over fifty days in respect of organic analysis which did not appear to have been queried by local authorities. Most laboratories would inform a local authority as soon as they were aware of a sample result that contravened a PCV but such arrangements were often informal and not recorded. Not all local authorities requested this service.

7.22 The Inspectorate has sent a copy of the inspection report to each laboratory and to each local authority using that laboratory, together with a letter highlighting areas of full compliance with regulatory requirements and drawing attention to any points that could be improved. However, the Inspectors reported that many laboratories had taken action already, either during the inspection or on receipt of the initial draft report.

7.23 The Inspectorate receives many enquiries from local authorities on technical aspects of the PWS Regulations and is always willing to discuss and advise on any technical points local authorities raise.

Chapter 8   **Drinking Water Research**

Introduction

8.1.1 The Department of the Environment's water quality and health research programme is managed by the Drinking Water Inspectorate, which provides the chairman of the Research Programme Committee and the Nominated Officer responsible for managing water quality and health research contracts. The objectives of the programme are:

(a)   investigation of issues which relate to drinking water quality and health;

(b)   development of new or improved analytical techniques; and

(c)   investigation of changes in quality brought about by the treatment, distribution and storage of water.

8.1.2 This research assists the Department of the Environment (DoE) and the Welsh Office to formulate policy relating to the quality of water supplies and to make an input to European and International debate on drinking water issues. Approximately £800,000 were allocated to drinking water research in 1995.

8.1.3 Details of the Department's research can be found in the DoE Research Report. Current and future research requirements are publicised in "DoE Research Market" and "Environmental Protection Group Research Newsletter". Copies of these publications may be obtained from Miss B Kong, Room A320, Romney House, 43 Marsham Street, London SW1P 3PY.

8.1.4 During 1995 a contract was awarded to Science Connections Ltd, following a competitive tendering exercise, to carry out an assessment of the water quality and health research programme during the period 1987 to 1995. The assessment is intended to establish whether the research programme has adequately addressed policy objectives, the technical quality of research work and the extent to which objectives were met, and whether value for money has been achieved. A report on the assessment will be available during 1996.

Research completed during 1995

8.2.1 Copies of all research reports are placed in the DoE library. Unless there is a prior commitment to publish a report, a publication is made only if the anticipated sales are expected to cover the cost of publication. If a report has not been published, it is usually possible to obtain a copy on loan. Specific enquiries about the water quality and health research programme, including requests for loans, should be directed to Mr M S Smith, Room B153, Romney House, 43 Marsham Street, London SW1P 3PY.

Disinfection By-Products

8.2.2 WRc published a report entitled "Occurrence and formation of halo-acetic acids" (reference DWI 3286). This includes a review of possible modelling techniques for concentrations of halo-acetic acids in treated water and a study of concentration changes within distribution systems.

8.2.3 The mutagenicity of bromodichloromethane, chlorodibromomethane and bromoform was investigated under a research contract awarded to Huntingdon Research Ltd. These studies showed that the compounds were not mutagenic at concentrations encountered in drinking water. The contractor has submitted a paper for publication in a peer reviewed journal and copies of the report are available on loan.

Cryptosporidium

8.2.4 The second report of the Expert Group on Cryptosporidium in Water Supplies was published by HMSO in 1995. This report included a review of all work carried out under the national collaborative research programme.

8.2.5 The Proceedings of a Workshop on Treatment Optimisation for Cryptosporidium Removal from Water Supplies were also published by HMSO in 1995. This publication included a report of work funded by DoE on possible surrogate measurements for Cryptosporidium. Further details of this research were included in the publication "Removal of Cryptosporidium during Water Treatment" which has been published by UK Water Industry Research Ltd (UKWIRL).

8.2.6 An interlaboratory trial of analytical procedures for Cryptosporidium was completed in 1995. The procedures included an immuno-magnetic separation technique developed with DoE funding at the Scottish Parasitic Diagnostic Laboratory (SPDL), the Standing Committee of Analysts "Blue Book" method, and flow cytometry. This results showed that immuno-magnetic separation gave better recoveries in certain circumstances and that flow cytometry can underestimate oocyst concentrations in low turbidity water. The report is being considered by the Standing Committee of Analysts (SCA) Panel 2.8 of Working Group 2, which is responsible for updating the Blue Book on detection methods for protozoan parasites.

8.2.7 An investigation of the concentrations of oocysts in sewage effluents and sewage sludge applied to land was completed by SPDL in 1995. This research showed that sewage works can constitute a significant source of oocysts.

8.2.8 WRc has published a report entitled "Removal of oocysts of Cryptosporidium from private water supplies - assessment of point-of-use filters" (reference DWI 3932). This report provides an assessment of manufacturers' claims for oocyst removal in three filtration systems which are suitable for use in treatment of private water supplies.

Chemical Incidents

8.2.9 WRc published a report entitled "Health and other effects of short term exposure to chemicals affecting taste and odour of drinking water" (DWI 4049). This report included a review of possible health affects from chemicals most commonly implicated in taste and odour incidents.

8.2.10 A second report has been published by WRc entitled "Assessing the value of epidemiological studies of acute chemical contamination incidents affecting drinking water" (reference DWI 4080). This report reviewed eleven epidemiological studies undertaken following chemical contamination incidents and included recommendations on the design of studies to be undertaken following chemical contamination incidents.

Drinking Water Consumption Survey

8.2.11 MEL Research has published a report entitled "1994 Drinking Water Consumption Survey". This study, which included consumption of bottled water and tap water based beverages, indicated an average consumption of 1.1 litres of unboiled tap water per person per day.

Microbiological Modelling

8.2.12 A study carried out by WRc considered modelling techniques and their applicability to the modelling of microbiological contamination of drinking water. A follow up study on modelling of Cryptosporidium in water supplies will be completed in 1996.

Current Research

8.3.1 Nineteen new contracts were let during 1995. All contracts were awarded following competitive tendering unless stated otherwise.

Cryptosporidium

8.3.2 The Foundation for Water Research was appointed by selective tendering to provide the secretariat to the DoE Cryptosporidium Research Steering. The Committee provides a forum for discussion of research needs and membership includes representatives of organisations with interests in Cryptosporidium research.

8.3.3 An investigation of a possible correlation between drinking water consumption and incidence of cryptosporidiosis in West Cumbria is being funded jointly by the Department of the Environment and the Department of Health. The study is being carried out by the North Cumbria Health Authority and the Communicable Disease Surveillance Centre.

Emerging Pathogens

8.3.4 A contract was placed with the Public Health Laboratory Service to review the incidence of those waterborne pathogens in humans which have increased in prevalence in the past two decades or which threaten to increase in the near future.

Disinfection by-products

8.3.5 DoE has funded a long-running programme of research with WRc into the risks to health from certain disinfection by-products. A new contract for a three year programme of work was placed with WRc in 1995 after selective tendering. During 1995, work on the modelling of changes in trihalomethane concentrations during distribution and investigation of by-product formation during UV disinfection was commenced. The output from the study will include production of information dossiers on disinfection by-products. The dossiers will include information on occurrence, control measures and toxicity of all by-products considered by the World Health Organisation in its 1993 review of guideline values for drinking water quality.

European standardisation

8.3.6 The Department of the Environment funds a significant programme of research which assists in development of policy on European standardisation and also seeks to ensure that the traditions and practices of the United Kingdom water industry and its suppliers are taken into account in the development of European standards.

8.3.7 Research into European procedures for testing materials used in contact with drinking water has been undertaken by The Water Quality Centre. During

1995 specific areas of work included representation of the Inspectorate's interests within CEN (The European Standards Organisation) working groups and participation in a European interlaboratory investigation into methods of analysis for toxic metals in lime products.

8.3.8 A contract was placed with Mr L Young to represent the Inspectorate's interests on CEN Working Groups engaged in development of water supply product standards. A contract to investigate the feasibility of streamlining the approval of polyethylene water pipes by adapting the Dutch approval system was awarded to WRc. Reports of all studies will be available in 1996.

Water Byelaws

8.3.9 The Inspectorate is responsible for providing technical advice to DoE policy Divisions on the Water Byelaws. The Water Byelaws are due to be replaced by regulations when they expire in 1997. Current research includes investigations into the reliability of seals used in water closets and deterioration in microbiological quality of water in expansion vessels. These studies are being carried out by WRc Evaluation and Testing Centre and the Building Research Establishment respectively. Reports on these studies will be available in 1996.

Microbiological Quality of Bottled Water

8.3.10 An objective of the water quality and health research programme is to investigate whether consumption of drinking water might be responsible for an as yet unattributed fraction of gastro-intestinal symptoms. Extensive data is available on the quality of public water supplies but relatively little data is available on the quality of bottled waters. An investigation is being carried out by Leeds University into the microbiological quality of still bottled waters and still natural mineral waters. The results of this investigation will be published in 1996.

Microbiological Quality of Private Water Supplies

8.3.11 A research contract is being undertaken by Leeds University to establish whether the sampling frequencies for microbiological parameters prescribed by the Private Water Supply Regulations 1991 provide adequate protection for the health of consumers. The study is investigating a selection of private supplies and will compare the results of local authority sampling with results obtained in a more intensive sampling programme. The results of the study will be published in 1996.

Actinomycetes in Water Distribution Systems

8.3.12 Actinomycetes are known to cause odour problems in water supplies but suitable detection methods are not available. Some species are known to generate toxins which might, in certain circumstances, be of significance for health. A research contract evaluating new methods for the isolation and detection of actinomycetes in water was awarded to the International Mycological Institute. The results of this evaluation are expected during the Autumn of 1996.

Animals in Water Distribution Systems

8.3.13 A pilot study conducted by WRc reviewed the literature relating to animals in water distribution systems. Recommendations for further research will be considered in 1996.

Development of analytical methods

8.3.14 The performance of a method for the detection of polychlorinated biphenyls in sludges and biota is being evaluated by Mountainheath Ltd. A similar contract involving detection of polychlorinated biphenyls in biota was placed with the Water Quality Centre. Mountainheath Ltd was also awarded a contract to evaluate a method for the analysis of acid hydrolysable herbicides. The results of all three studies will be considered for publication as Blue Books by Panel 6.3 of SCA Working Group 6.

8.3.15 An interlaboratory evaluation of methods for the analysis of chemical oxygen demand was undertaken by Yorkshire Environmental. The results will be considered for publication as a Blue Book by SCA Working Group 3.

8.3.16 A method for the detection of microcystin isomers using the protein phosphatase inhibition assay has been evaluated by the University of Dundee. WRc has supervised an interlaboratory trial of an high performance liquid chromatography method for analysis of microcystin isomers. The results of both studies will be considered for publication as Blue Books by SCA Panel 6.11 of SCA Working Group 6.

Definitions and Glossary of Terms

After-growth the growth of micro-organisms within distribution systems.

Bulk supply water supplied in bulk, usually in treated form, from one water company to another.

Coliforms a group of bacteria which may be faecal or environmental in origin.

Compliance assessment a comparison made by the Inspectorate of data gathered by water companies against standards and other regulatory requirements.

Contravention a breach of a regulatory requirement.

Cryptosporidium a protozoan parasite.

Determination an analysis for a specific parameter.

Distribution systems a water company's network of mains, pipes, pumping stations and service reservoirs through which treated water is conveyed to consumers.

EC Drinking Water Directive Council Directive 80/778/EEC relating to the quality of water intended for human consumption.

Enforcement action the means, as set out in the Water Act 1989 and consolidated into the Water Industry Act 1991, by which the Secretary of State requires a water company to comply with certain regulatory requirements.

Epoxy resin relining a rehabilitation process in which a cleaned section of iron water main is sprayed with a mixture of epoxy resin and hardener to produce a thin but strong coating of material on the inside of the main.

Faecal coliforms a sub-group of coliforms, almost exclusively faecal in origin.

Giardia a protozoan parasite.

Groundwater water from aquifers or other underground sources.

Guidance Document "Guidance on Safeguarding the Quality of Public Water Supplies". HMSO 1989 (ISBN 0 11 752262 7).

ICA	instrumentation, control and automation.
Improvement programmes	improvement works, associated with undertakings or conditions of regulation 4 relaxations.
Incident	an event affecting or threatening to affect drinking water quality.
Indicator organism	an organism which indicates the presence of contamination and hence the possible presence of pathogens.
Inspectorate	the Drinking Water Inspectorate.
Key parameters	17 parameters chosen for these Reports to indicate quality of water in supply zones.
Legal requirements	the requirements as specified in the Water Act 1989, now consolidated into the Water Industry Act 1991, and the Regulations made under the Acts.
m³/d	cubic metre per day.
mg/l	milligram per litre.
Ml/d	megalitre per day (One Ml/d is equivalent to 1,000 m³/d, or to 220,000 gallon/d).
µg/l	microgram per litre.
ng/l	nanogram per litre.
Notice of Intention to make a Final Order	A necessary precursor to the issue of a Final Enforcement Order which must be advertised with a minimum of 28 days being allowed for representations or objections to the proposed Order.
Operational guidelines	"Operational guidelines for the protection of drinking water supplies". Water Authorities Association, September 1988 (ISBN 0 947886 18 4). A booklet on safeguards in the operation and management of public water supplies in England and Wales.
Operational Guidelines and Code of Practice (OGCP)	"*In situ* Epoxy Resin Lining - Operational Guidelines and Code of Practice. A source document for the Water Mains Rehabilitation Manual." I C Warren. WRc 1989.
PAH	a group of organic compounds known as polycyclic aromatic hydrocarbons, comprising for the purposes of the Regulations six substances: fluoranthene, benzo 3,4 fluoranthene, benzo 11,12 fluoranthene, benzo 3,4 pyrene, benzo 1,12 perylene and indeno (1,2,3-cd) pyrene.

Parameters
the substances, organisms and properties listed in Schedule 2 and regulation 3 of the Regulations.

Pathogen
an organism which causes disease.

PCV
see 'Prescribed concentration or value'

Pesticides
any fungicide, herbicide or insecticide or related product (excluding medicines) used for the control of pests or diseases.

pH value
a measure of the acidity or basicity related to the concentration of the hydrogen ion.

Plumbosolvency
the tendency for lead to dissolve in water.

Polycyclic aromatic hydrocarbons
see 'PAH'

Prescribed concentration or value (PCV)
the numerical value assigned to water quality standards defining the maximal or minimal legal concentration or value of a parameter. In certain circumstances, the PCV may be authorised by the Secretary of State under regulation 4 to be relaxed to a specified extent - see 'Relaxation'.

Private supplies
water taken from private sources or supplied by non-licensed suppliers: supplies of water provided otherwise than by a statutorily appointed water undertaker.

Public record
the information made available to the public as required by regulations 29 and 30.

Public supplies
water supplied by a company licensed for that purpose.

Regulations
the Water Supply (Water Quality) Regulations 1989, as amended, made under the Act or, in the case of private water supplies, the Private Water Supplies Regulations 1991.

Regulatory requirements
see 'Legal requirements'.

Relaxation
a relaxation of the standards according to regulations 4 and 5 – subject in most cases to the completion of improvement works – in emergencies or as a result of exceptional meteorological conditions or by reason of the nature and structure of the ground from which the supply emanates.

SCADA
systems control and data acquisition.

Secretary of State	the Secretary of State for the Environment or the Secretary of State for Wales, as the context may require.
Service reservoir	a water tower, tank or other reservoir used for the storage of treated water within the distribution system.
Springs	groundwater appearing at the surface at the outcrop of the junction of a permeable with an impermeable stratum.
Standards	the prescribed concentrations or values listed in Schedule 2, Tables A to E and regulation 3 of the Regulations.
Surface water	water from rivers, impounding reservoirs or other surface water source.
Technical audit	the means of checking that water companies are complying with their statutory obligations.
THM	a group of organic substances known as trihalomethanes, comprising for the purposes of the Regulations four substances: trichloromethane (also known as chloroform), dichlorobromomethane, dibromochloromethane and tribromomethane.
Time of supply	the moment when water passes from the water company's pipework into a consumer's pipework.
Treated water	water treated for use for domestic purposes as defined in the Regulations.
Trihalomethanes	see 'THM'.
Undertaking	an undertaking given by a water company to the Secretary of State for the purposes of section 20(5)(b) of the Water Act 1989, now section 19(1)(b) of the Water Industry Act 1991.
Water supply zone	the basic unit of supply for establishing sampling frequencies, compliance with standards and information to be made publicly available.
Wholesome/ Wholesomeness	a concept of water quality which is defined by reference to standards and other requirements set out in the Regulations.
WRc	Water Research Centre (1989) plc and/or, as the context may require, its predecessor body.

Erratum

A small number of significant errors have been detected in Drinking Water 1992 and 1993 and the corrected information is given below:

DRINKING WATER 1992

Page 237 Table 5.3

Column headed ZONES CBU -

For individual pesticides delete 2082, insert 908.

DRINKING WATER 1993

Page 209 Table 4.3

Column headed ZONES CBU -

For	Colour	delete	399	insert	678
	Turbidity	delete	1,337	insert	1,616
	Hydrogen ion	delete	50	insert	333
	Aluminium	delete	505	insert	695
	Iron	delete	1,593	insert	2,344
	Manganese	delete	869	insert	1,123

Learning Resources
Centre

Printed in the United Kingdom for HMSO
Dd 0302466   C12   6/96   3400   355076   24/35649